A CONCISE HISTORY OF IRELAND

Situated on one of Europe's busiest sea-roads, Ireland has always been connected to other cultures. This accessible and engaging history explores these connections across 1,600 years, from the arrival of Christianity in the fifth century to the present day. While the Norman invasion in 1169 brought the English crown into Irish politics, the impulse to preserve the Irish language and early Irish history united many of the Gaelic-Irish and Anglo-Normans from the fourteenth century. The Irish nationhood that emerged later was based more on Catholicism, as Ireland became a minor theatre of bitter European conflicts of the early modern period. Political (and religious) loyalties which solidified at this point determined Irish politics for the next three centuries. Alongside these major political events, Caitriona Clear examines the living and working conditions of ordinary men and women – what they traded and farmed, how they lived and loved, and how they were often affected, but not always overwhelmed, by the politics of their time.

Caitriona Clear lectured in history at the University of Galway until her retirement. Her publications include *Nuns in 19th-Century Ireland* (1987), *Women of the House in Ireland 1926–1961* (2000), *Social Change and Everyday Life in Ireland 1850–1922* (2007) and *Women's Voices: Women's Magazines in Ireland in the 1950s and 60s* (2016).

CAMBRIDGE CONCISE HISTORIES
A full list of titles in the series can be found at:
www.cambridge.org/concisehistories

Cambridge Concise Histories offer general introductions to a wide range of subjects. A series of authoritative overviews written by expert authors, these books make the histories of countries, events and topics accessible to both students and general readers.

A CONCISE HISTORY OF IRELAND

CAITRIONA CLEAR

CAMBRIDGE
UNIVERSITY PRESS

CAMBRIDGE UNIVERSITY PRESS

Shaftesbury Road, Cambridge CB2 8EA, United Kingdom

One Liberty Plaza, 20th Floor, New York, NY 10006, USA

477 Williamstown Road, Port Melbourne, VIC 3207, Australia

314–321, 3rd Floor, Plot 3, Splendor Forum, Jasola District Centre,
New Delhi – 110025, India

Cambridge University Press is part of Cambridge University Press & Assessment,
a department of the University of Cambridge.

We share the University's mission to contribute to society through the pursuit of
education, learning and research at the highest international levels of excellence.

www.cambridge.org
Information on this title: www.cambridge.org/9781009493970

DOI: 10.1017/9781009493987

© Caitriona Clear 2026

This publication is in copyright. Subject to statutory exception and to the provisions of
relevant collective licensing agreements, no reproduction of any part may take place
without the written permission of Cambridge University Press & Assessment.

When citing this work, please include a reference to the DOI 10.1017/
9781009493987

First published 2026

Cover Image: James Brenan, *Letter from America*, 1875, (oil on canvas), Crawford
Art Gallery Collection

A catalogue record for this publication is available from the British Library

*A Cataloging-in-Publication data record for this book is available from the
Library of Congress*

ISBN 978-1-009-49397-0 Hardback
ISBN 978-1-009-49400-7 Paperback

Cambridge University Press & Assessment has no responsibility for the persistence
or accuracy of URLs for external or third-party internet websites referred to in this
publication and does not guarantee that any content on such websites is, or will remain,
accurate or appropriate.

For EU product safety concerns, contact us at Calle de José Abascal, 56, 1°, 28003
Madrid, Spain, or email eugpsr@cambridge.org

CONTENTS

List of Figures	*page* viii
List of Maps	x
Acknowledgements	xi

Introduction — 1

1 Transformation: Early Medieval Ireland c. 430–1169 — 7
   1.1 Introduction — 7
   1.2 Circa 430–795 — 8
   1.3 Circa 795–1169 — 27
   1.4 Conclusion — 33

2 Invasions: Late Medieval Ireland, 1169–1520 — 35
   2.1 Introduction — 35
   2.2 Politics — 36
   2.3 Law and Administration — 44
   2.4 Religion — 46
   2.5 Economy and Society — 53
   2.6 Conclusion — 59

3 Wars: From Silken Thomas's Rebellion to the Penal Laws, 1534–1704 — 62
   3.1 Introduction — 62
   3.2 Political Developments, 1534–1704 — 63
   3.3 Religion, 1534–1704 — 77
   3.4 Conclusion — 87

Contents

4 Peace? Ireland's Short Eighteenth Century, 1704–1791 ... 89
   4.1 Introduction ... 89
   4.2 The Penal Laws ... 89
   4.3 Politics ... 94
   4.4 Economy and Society ... 99
   4.5 Language and Culture ... 105
   4.6 Women ... 110
   4.7 Conclusion ... 113

5 Construction and Destruction: War, Peace and Famine, 1791–1851 ... 118
   5.1 Introduction ... 118
   5.2 The 1798 Rebellion and the Act of Union ... 118
   5.3 Catholic Emancipation and Repeal ... 126
   5.4 Administrative, Legal and Welfare Reforms ... 130
   5.5 Economy and Society ... 135
   5.6 The Great Famine ... 140
   5.7 Conclusion ... 144

6 Modernization: From the Famine to the Farmers' Victory, 1850–1903 ... 146
   6.1 Population, Emigration and Marriage ... 146
   6.2 Work and Education ... 150
   6.3 Non-agricultural Work ... 152
   6.4 Politics: The Fenians, the Land Struggle and the Home Rule Party ... 157
   6.5 Religion ... 169
   6.6 Conclusion ... 172

7 Revolution: Twenty Decisive Years, 1903–1923 ... 175
   7.1 How the People Lived, 1903–1923 ... 175
   7.2 Unionism, Nationalism and Trade Unionism, 1903–12 ... 183

7.3	Politics, 1913–1923	188
7.4	Conclusion	202

8 Stability, 1922–1969 — 204
- 8.1 Introduction — 204
- 8.2 Ireland, 1922–1969 — 204
- 8.3 Northern Ireland, 1922–1969 — 223
- 8.4 Conclusion — 230

9 The Thirty Year 'Troubles', 1969–1998 — 233
- 9.1 Introduction — 233
- 9.2 Northern Ireland, 1969–1998 — 233
- 9.3 Ireland, 1969–1998 — 245
- 9.4 Conclusion — 260

10 Prosperity/Austerity/Prosperity? 1998–c. 2016 — 264
- 10.1 Ireland — 264
- 10.2 Northern Ireland — 282
- 10.3 Conclusion — 286

Conclusion — 292
- C.1 Places and Names — 293
- C.2 The Changing Landscape — 299
- C.3 *Ar Scáth A Chéile A Mhaireann Na Daoine:* Irish People, Good People, People — 303

Appendix: Irish Population, 1821–2016 — 309
- A.1 From 1821 to 1911 — 309
- A.2 From 1926 to 2016 — 309

Further Reading — 311

Index — 338

FIGURES

0.1	Postcard: 'Top of the Morning'.	page 5
1.1	Ring fort.	13
1.2	The Rock of Cashel, Co. Tipperary.	19
1.3	St Brigid's Cross.	22
1.4	Kilmacduagh, Co Galway.	23
2.1	King John's Castle, Limerick.	37
2.2	Pallas, Tynagh, Co. Galway.	58
3.1	Hugh O'Neill (c. 1550–1616).	67
3.2	Rothe House, Kilkenny.	73
4.1	Nano Nagle (1718–1784).	93
4.2	Damer House, Roscrea, Co. Tipperary.	102
4.3	Oliver Goldsmith (1728–1774).	109
4.4	The Rotunda Lying-in Hospital, Dublin.	114
5.1	Theobald Wolfe Tone (1763–1798).	120
5.2	Daniel O'Connell (1775–1847).	127
5.3	Cork District Mental Asylum.	134
5.4	Bridget O'Donnel and her children.	141
6.1	Millworkers, Belfast, c.1890/1900.	152
6.2	Michael Davitt (1846-1906).	158
6.3	The 'Manchester Martyrs'.	160
6.4	Charles Stewart Parnell (1846–1891).	163
7.1	Mother and child, Tyrone c.1902.	176
7.2	Dublin tenements.	177
7.3	Edward Carson (1854–1935).	184

List of Figures

7.4	Arthur Griffith (1871–1922) and Eamon de Valera (1882–1975) at the Peace conference in Dublin, 1921.	194
7.5	Mary MacSwiney (1872–1942).	201
8.1	Ardnacrusha Hydro-electric power station, Co. Clare.	212
8.2	Edel Quinn (1907–44).	221
8.3	Stormont Buildings Belfast.	224
8.4	Maura Laverty (1907–1966).	232
9.1	Bernadette Devlin.	236
9.2	Gable-end, Sandy Row, Belfast.	241
9.3	David Trimble and John Hume with the joint Nobel Peace Prize 1998.	242
9.4	Action for the Homeless meeting, Dublin 1986.	252
9.5	President Mary Robinson setting out for her inauguration, December 1990.	259
10.1	St Patrick's Day Parade, O'Connell Bridge, Dublin, 2022.	273
10.2	Ballinasloe Horse Fair October 2015.	280
10.3	Great Western Greenway, viaduct at Newport, Co. Mayo.	288
10.4	Wind turbines in Inis Mór, Oileáin Árainn, Co. Galway.	289

MAPS

1.1	Ireland in the eighth century.	*page* 9
2.1	The dioceses of Ireland in the fourteenth century.	47
3.1	The pattern of English-Scottish settlement in Ulster, 1609–1641.	71
4.1	Irish counties after the shirings of the thirteenth and seventeenth centuries.	100
7.1	Irish Railways 1906.	181
8.1	Partitioned Ireland, 1922.	205

ACKNOWLEDGEMENTS

Thanks to Cambridge University Press for inviting me to write this concise history, and to Liz Friend-Smith for her help and support throughout the process. Thanks also to the four anonymous readers of my proposal, to the encouraging reader of the completed manuscript, and to Jodie Mardell-lines, Rupasree Murali, Adam Bell and others who worked patiently and kindly with me on the final production

Special thanks to Dáibhí Ó Cróinín and Steven Ellis who generously read the early chapters for me and gave me some very useful advice on them. After such meticulous guidance, any mistakes, misreadings and misinterpretations are most definitely my own.

Not every historian is lucky enough to have an in-house mapmaker, illustration consultant and encyclopaedia on all aspects of early modern history. In my house this resource is Pádraig Lenihan, who was a great help in those areas, and willing, moreover, to talk endlessly about history at all times. I cannot thank him enough.

I am very grateful to Dr Michael Waldron of the Crawford Gallery in Cork for allowing me to use James Brenan's painting for the cover illustration. Dr Michelle Comber of University of Galway's ever-helpful archaeology department gave me the choice of several images of ring-forts, and plenty of information, too, for Chapter 1.

The Brigidine Sisters at Solas Bhríde Centre and Hermitages, Kildare, supplied the St Brigid's Cross. The Presentation Sisters' Union, Monasterevin, Co. Kildare, gave permission to use the image of Nano Nagle in Chapter 4. The Ulster Folk and Transport Museum gave permission to use the photograph of the Tyrone mother and baby. Dublin City Libraries provided the photograph of Dublin's tenements, and the Legion of Mary permitted me to use the photograph of Edel Quinn. Sincere thanks to all for their goodwill and interest in the book.

Thanks to the James Hardiman Library, University of Galway, for allowing me to borrow books even though I was retired. This was a great help.

Bhain mé an-buntáiste, chomh maith as an dualgas a bhí orainn i Roinn na Staire, in Ollscoil Náisiúnta na Gaillimhe, gach cúrsa a theagasc tré Ghaeilge chomh maith le Béarla. Nuair a bhí orm Gaeilge úr agus cruinn a chur ar théarmaí léannta a bhain ní hamháin le stair na hÉireann ach le stair na hEorpa agus leis an stair ar leibhéil domhanda i gcomhthéacsanna polaitiúla, soisialta, agus eacnamúila, scaoil mé le mórchuid sean-nathanna cainte de chuid na staire, agus thosaigh mé ag scrúdú gach focal, fiú, a bhí á rá agam, ní hamháin as Gaeilge, ach as Béarla chomh maith. Ach ghlac mé i gconaí le chomhairle ó na saineolaithe, agus don Gaeilge a úasáidim sa leabhar seo, gabhaim buíochas ó chroí don Dr Síle de Cléir, Ollscoil Luimnigh.

(I also derived great advantage from the fact that in the History department in Galway, we taught every historical course through Irish as well as English. When I had to put fresh, accurate Irish on historical terminology that had to do not only with Irish history but with European and global history, political, social and economic, I began to scrutinize not only every phrase, but every word I was using, not only in Irish but in English too, and I got rid of a lot of historical clichés and hackneyed phrases. But I depended greatly throughout those years on advice from the experts, and for guidance on the Irish I use in this book, I thank from the bottom of my heart Dr Síle de Cléir, University of Limerick.)

There is no learning process as thorough as teaching, and no feedback as effective and incisive as examination scripts, essays, projects and theses, so I thank successive generations of undergraduate and postgraduate history students in the institute of higher education sequentially known as University College Galway/National University of Galway/University of Galway. I also learned a lot from the numerous undergraduate and postgraduate students whose work I examined in other universities, notably Queen's University Belfast, Trinity College Dublin, Carlow College, Mary Immaculate College, Limerick and Galway-Mayo Institute of Technology.

Maura Cronin of Mary Immaculate has said that we are all, regardless of training, historians of our own life and times. I have really benefitted from knowing independent-minded people whose memories of what still seems like the 'recent past', the last seventy years or so, are full of unusual insights. These people are Eileen Clear, Larry de Cléir, Máire Flannery, Síle de Cléir, Mary Coll, Maura Cronin, Niall Ó Ciosáin and Gearóid Ó Tuathaigh. For changes over the last three decades (which have passed me by at warp speed) I've depended on Donncha, Manus, Cora and Síle Lenihan and Megan Howell and Deirdre

Duggan. Manus also provided lots of insights on the medieval period, one of his many historical passions.

Special thanks to my aunt, Sr Carmel Synnott LSA, and my honorary aunt Peigí Hayes, for books and conversations about history recent and distant, personal and national. And lifelong thanks to Paddy and Kathleen Clear (nee Synnott), both now *ar shlí na fírinne*, for the love of history and the sense of wonder they transmitted to us all.

Thanks, finally, to Pádraig for a lot more than history:

'Life is the ocean, love is the boat.'
'The Voyage', Johnny Duhan (1950–2024)

Introduction

∽

'Songs of our land, ye are with us forever', sang Donegal's 'blind poetess' Frances Brown in the 1840s, but she was wrong. Although feted and garlanded in her time, and awarded a pension by Prime Minister Robert Peel (not a noted lover of Ireland, as we shall see), she and her stirring anthems are virtually forgotten now. Histories, like songs and poems, belong to the time in which they are written, and inevitably reflect their writers' interests, preoccupations and experiences. This concise history is written by an Irish female born in 1960 and reared in an urban, lower-middle-class Catholic extended family in which there was as strong a devotion to history in all its forms (political, social, archaeological, local, national, international and, of course, familial) as there was to religion. Nearly forty-five years of 'doing history' – learning, researching, writing, teaching, reading, lecturing and talking to people – has reinforced the early childhood conviction that study of the past is both a worthwhile pursuit and a pleasant use of one's time. The late Raphael Samuel was right when he declared that history was a pastime as well as a passion, 'a social form of knowledge; the work, in any given instance, of a thousand different hands'. The bibliography at the end of this book gives a list of the many secondary works consulted in the writing of this history, but the sense of the past which drives this narrative comes from numberless influences, sights, memories, sounds and stories absorbed over a lifetime, which would take another lifetime to list and to catalogue, assuming they could all be remembered.

This history follows the conventional timeline of nationalist Irish history, because events like the coming of Christianity, the Scandinavian and Norman invasions and the wars of the bloody sixteenth and seventeenth centuries really did change the lives of people in Ireland, and added new cultural and ethnic elements into the population. Headlining invasions, wars and changes in political leadership, however, can give the impression of a people lurching from crisis to crisis, always losing, always lamenting. 'It would never be spring, always autumn | After a harvest always lost', Patrick Kavanagh wrote in 1944, in 'Memory of Brother Michael', about the one of the seventeenth-century Four Masters who wrote a history of Ireland which (unsurprisingly for the time) emphasized defeats and losses. Kavanagh's two lines have stayed in the back of my mind for almost half a century, as a warning against exaggeration of the victim narrative in writing about any oppressed or 'marginal' people. Ireland's history, while it had its traumatic moments, was a lot less 'distressful' than that of many other small islands in the world, and there were, in Ireland as elsewhere, long periods of peace and normality throughout these sixteen centuries. The hidden history of Ireland, like that of any country, is the story of the vast majority of people of all classes and conditions who got on (when they were able to do so) with living, working and caring for each other as best they could, who, in George Eliot's resonant words, 'lived faithfully a hidden life, and rest in unvisited tombs'.

This concise history is aimed at anybody newly interested in Ireland, or in history, or anyone who wants a convenient 'starter' reference book. It is the history of Ireland from the coming of Christianity in or around AD 432 (and the beginning of written records), to the centenary of the 1916 Rising in Ireland and Brexit (the United Kingdom's vote to leave the European Union) in Northern Ireland, in 2016. The emphasis is on telling a story, and every attempt has been made to present a fair and balanced picture of Ireland over 1,600 or so years. Discerning readers are invited to make up their own minds on controversial topics by reading further into the subject, in the books and articles listed at the end. More space is given in this history to Irish history after 1541 than to early and late medieval history. This would be true of any survey history of any country, firstly because there are far more sources for the later centuries, but secondly because comparatively recent events which shaped the modern political and social sphere seem to require more explanation. This might give the impression that the millennium from the fifth to the sixteenth century was somehow static or unchanging. It was not. Apart from the invasions from the eighth to the twelfth centuries, agriculture and trade developed, religion went through several cycles of corruption and reform (even before the Reformation), fortunes were made and lost, urban settlements grew and others declined, dwellings were built and eventually toppled or absorbed back into the landscape, and new methods of communications, commerce and defence developed to cope with changing circumstances. It is hoped that the two chapters which cover these 1,100 years will spur the interested reader to a closer examination of an Ireland whose traces – in the form of grassed-over ring forts, ruined monasteries, round towers and old castles – are everywhere.

Irish people have been described by outsiders for so much of their history (since at least the eleventh century) that it is impossible to disentangle their sense of who they were or are from their reactions to outsiders' descriptions of them. Questions of 'identity' have been discussed at great length by historians, literary scholars, political scientists, sociologists, anthropologists, and many others. This history considers all people, regardless of origin, who made their permanent homes anywhere on the island from the fifth to the twenty-first centuries as 'Irish', whether they would have accepted or rejected such a designation. Of course, their origins (Anglo-Norman, New English, Scottish/English) often have to be specified, so as to explain their allegiances and loyalties. But it is not only confusing but downright inaccurate to refer to politically privileged landowning Protestants from the eighteenth century onwards as the 'Anglo-Irish'. Ireland from the late seventeenth century had some powerful Protestant O'Briens, O'Haras, Conollys, O'Neills, and others whose origins went back before the Norman invasion. Also, many who were of settler stock came to describe themselves as Irish too, developing a distinctive identity within the greater British polity. Even the descendants of the northern Protestant settlers of the seventeenth century spoke with Irish accents, used Irish idioms and place names, understood some Irish and became attached to their native soil. 'My country is Kiltartan Cross | My countrymen Kiltartan's poor', wrote W. B. Yeats during the Great War in the voice of Major Robert Gregory of Co. Galway, in 'An Irish Airman Foresees His Death'. Gregory, whose mother was the famous Augusta (Lady)

Gregory, belonged to the landlord class; should his love of place (even at one remove through the mouth of Yeats) be reckoned less sincere than that of a thousand poems and songs written in Irish eulogizing the country in part or in whole?

A very popular 'recitation', written by John Locke, which many Irish people born between the 1890s and the 1920s knew off by heart, begins with the words: 'Glory be to God but there it is | The dawn on the hills of Ireland!' (Figure 0.1) It goes on:

> O Ireland isn't it grand you look,
> Like a bride in her rich adorning.
> With all the pent-up love of my heart
> I bid you the top of the morning.

FIGURE 0.1 Postcard: 'Top of the Morning'. From author's personal collection. This postcard, incorporating Locke's famous verse, was sent by a man from east Clare to his son in Boston, USA, around 1910 or 1912. (The stamp and postmark are missing.) A later generation of Irish people would reject such images as 'stage-Irish', but they were very popular in the early twentieth century.

Geological time being what it is, the dawn on the hills of Ireland is not that different today from what the young Patrick, chained in his slave ship, saw in the fifth century, although in his case, the love would come later. Our story begins with him and with the coming of Christianity, which brought modern writing and the beginning of written records, and forged new bonds with Britain and much of the European continent.

I
Transformation

~

Early Medieval Ireland c. 430–1169

1.1 Introduction

People have been living in Ireland since about 7500 BC. The early settlers lived near rivers and lakes and ate deer and wild boar, fish, and nuts and berries of various kinds. Cattle and sheep were domesticated around 3000 BC and the sowing of wheat, oats, barley and rye gradually developed from about 2500 BC. Pottery was made in Ireland from about 2000 BC, as were axes and other tools. Elaborately worked tools and ornaments were made in Ireland from about 1000 BC – there were copper mines in Cork and Kerry – but also imported from as far away as the Baltics and the Mediterranean. Ireland was on a busy sea-road at a time when the most efficient and capacious transport was by water, so it was never remote. The Celts began to arrive from around 500 BC, bringing their language with them, which became the language of the entire country. They arrived gradually, rather than in one big invasion force, and probably assimilated the original inhabitants rather than wiping them out. Writing was developed in the second or third centuries AD in the form of Ogham, a hieroglyphic form of writing that survives mainly on stones in Ireland and Wales, although written Ogham found its way into the Books of Ballymote and Lecan, produced in the later medieval period.

Up to about AD 700 the Romans called this island Hibernia and everyone else, including the Irish, called it Scotia; Scotland was so-called because of the Irish settlers there. The name Éire started to emerge around the eighth century and the Scandinavians used a version of it. The full title of the famous ninth-century Irish scholar Johannes Scotus Eriugena combines both names – *eriugena* means born in Éire. By the tenth century this island was Éire, anglicized as Ierland, or Ireland.

History is based on written records, and in Ireland, writing began with the coming of Christianity in the fifth century, so this is the starting point for this history.

1.2 Circa 430–795

1.2.1 *The Land and the People*

By the fifth century, Ireland was divided politically into '*cúigí*' (fifths): *Ulaidh*, which grew to correspond more or less to modern Ulster and contained *Emain Macha*, later Armagh and Airgialla, anglicized as Oriel; *Míde* or Meath, which took in a good chunk of what is now north Leinster and south Ulster, stretching from the Irish Sea to the Shannon – modern-day Louth, Meath, Longford, Westmeath, part of Offaly; *Mumu* or *Mumha* (modern-day Munster), comprising Clare, Limerick, Tipperary, Cork, Kerry and most of Waterford; *Laigin* was most of modern Leinster – Wicklow, Wexford, Carlow, Kildare, modern Laois and some of Offaly; and Connacht, which was all territory west of the Shannon (see Map 1.1). The population of Ireland was between half and three-quarters of a million.

IRELAND
Political Units c.800
Religious Centres

MAP 1.1 Ireland in the eighth century. By Pádraig Lenihan. On or around the time of the Scandinavian invasion and before the growth of the major cities, this is how Ireland divided up politically, into *cúigí* (fifths) – *Ulaidh;Mídhe*, the eastern midlands, *Connacht*, more or less west of the Shannon, *Mumha*, the entire south-west extending into the eastern midlands, and *Laigin*, the eastern part of the country. Settlements mentioned in the text are marked.

The west and south of Ireland always had trade links with France and Spain, while northern and eastern Ireland traded more with Britain and northern Europe. Within Ireland, waterways were vital connectors. In the south-east are the 'three sisters', the rivers Barrow, Nore and Suir, which connected the south coast with the eastern midlands, while the Slaney connected Wexford to Wicklow. In the west, the Shannon stretches from the Atlantic Ocean to Cavan, in the east the broad sweep of the Liffey from Kildare to the Irish Sea made the coast an irresistible site for a settlement, and the Boyne opened up Meath and Louth. The Blackwater in Cork was also important. In the north were the Bann, the Foyle and the Lagan. The most important political and ecclesiastical sites in early medieval Ireland, *Teamhrach/*Tara, *Emain Macha/*Armagh, *Caisil Mumhan/*Cashel and *Cill Dara/*Kildare, were situated on or near key waterways. Not all of these rivers were navigable all the way, but boats could be pulled across land for short distances (as at Limerick and Clare on the Shannon). River fords were focal points for settlement and marked territorial boundaries going back to Neolithic times, indicated by the prefix or suffix *áth* or, less commonly, *fearsad*, in place names – Athlone (*Áth Luain*), the ford of Luan; Athboy (*Áth Buí*), the yellow ford; Belfast (*Béal Feirste*), the mouth of the ford.

Five important roads or *slighte* radiated from *Teamhrach/*Tara: one to *Emain Macha*, the most important settlement in the north of the country; one to *Cualu*, now south Co. Dublin/north Wicklow; one to the north-west as far as it could go; one to *Osraighe* (Ossory) or modern Kilkenny; and one to the River Shannon. Throughout the country local kings and leaders maintained tracks and trails to enable them to travel through the areas they ruled over, on horseback, with their goods and chattels in carts drawn by horses or oxen.

Visitors to Ireland, mainly bishops, priests and scholars from about the sixth century, marvelled at the mild climate which enabled grass to grow and livestock to be left outdoors all year round. Cattle were vital for meat and milk and its by-products, and for hides, tallow (for lighting) and draft. The basic unit of currency was a heifer. Long-legged pigs were common, horses were reared by those who could afford them, and sheep were reared mainly for wool. Tillage farming was most successful in the drier and sunnier eastern counties, though traces of it have been discovered even in the fields which intersperse the barren landscape of the Burren of north Clare. Then as always, people used whatever land they could, however they could. Oats were the basic carbohydrate in the diet, wheat was for special occasions and the better-off, rye was grown as far west as Galway (*Ceapach a' tSeagail*, anglicized as Cappataggle, translates as the field of rye) and barley was for fast days, although it was also used to thicken soups and, of course, for ale. Grinding of grains was either by stones, by hand or, towards the seventh century, in mills for those who had access to them. Demographic shifts brought changes in consumption patterns and a surge in tillage farming after 800 went to feed and clothe the non-farming populations in the growing monastic centres and the nuclei of the ports later developed by the Scandinavian invaders.

Diet depended, as it always does, upon income and what could be grown or reared or kept back from sale. Wild animals, including Ireland's native deer, ducks and many other species, were trapped for food. Animal hides were highly prized for everything from furniture-covering to apparel to drinking or storage vessels. There were varying grades of butter and milk, depending on income; the milk of cows, sheep and goats was mixed in some butters found buried in bogs. (A number of reasons, from ritual to refrigeration, have been suggested for this practice, which lasted for about a thousand years, up to the twelfth century.) Hens were an easily movable livestock and their eggs were prized. Fish and puffins and cormorants were consumed by those who lived near coasts and rivers. Hazelnuts had long been a rich source of protein and fat, and wild hedgerow fruits including bilberries were relished for flavouring and medicinal purposes. Wild honey had been used as a sweetener from time immemorial, but apiculture, probably introduced by the British/Roman influence, became so common that an entire legal tract (the *Bechbretha*) was devoted to it in the seventh century, and its prevalence is indicated in some Irish place names, for example, Clonmel, *Cluain Meala*, the meadow of honey. (The surname Behan comes from Ó *Beacháin*, beekeeper.) Beeswax was used for liturgical candles and for monks' writing tablets. The less well-off lit their homes with tallow or rushlight, or used the light of the ever-burning fire. People drank mainly spring water and various kinds of milk (buttermilk, whey, new milk), and beef broth was common. Mead, a wine made from honey, was for the wealthy and reserved for special occasions, and there was also an ale made from honey.

Most people lived in circular settlements called cashels or ring forts (Figure 1.1) These enclosures varied in diameter, but the smallest would have been about twenty metres wide. The stone walls were about six feet high and nine feet deep, and probably as much for protection against the elements and wild animals (boars and wolves roamed the forests which covered much of Ireland) as raiders. Within the walls were several dwellings made out of wood or wattle, outhouses for storage, drainage

FIGURE 1.1 Ring fort. By kind permission of Dr Michelle Comber, Department of Archaeology, University of Galway. This ring fort (*rath* or *lios*), from Rathgurreen, Co. Galway, dates from the fifth or sixth century. Up to about the eleventh century everyone lived in this kind of enclosure, which included dwellings, forges, limekilns, granaries and animal shelters – and, in the case of religious foundations, cells and chapels.

ditches, vegetable gardens, kilns for drying hides and grains, forges and sometimes burial places. The art of making pottery, so important in prehistoric times, had died out; vessels for drinking, cooking, eating and storage were made of wood or metal (also used for needles, knives and other utensils) or leather. Some ring forts were man-made elevations in the middle of small lakes, called *crannóga*. Dwellings were usually one-room, and people probably worked, ate and, if the weather was good, cooked in the open air, using their dwellings only for sleeping and for shelter from bad weather. The stone huts in west Kerry called 'beehive huts' – so-called because of their shape – were built mainly for monks; ingeniously constructed with flat stones so as to be watertight, they were probably originally plastered on the outside and lined with mud on the inside, for warmth. Other stone dwellings dating from the period have been uncovered throughout the country in or around monastic foundations. But most dwellings within and outside ring forts were probably made of wood and have left no trace.

The homes of the rich were not very different from those of less well-off farmers, craftsmen and labourers. The rich had better food and more of it, more space for storage, more fuel for fires, more hides and blankets to keep the cold out and prettier ornaments, jewellery and toys. The comfortably off farmer should have, according to one prescription, several cooking-pots, a vat for brewing ale, troughs for washing, tools for cutting and working, a kiln and a mill, and he and his wife should have four changes of clothes. The king or local lord had all of this and additional decorative items of bronze, silver and gold, and dedicated sleeping spaces instead of shakedowns in the communal area. The homes of political leaders had to have space for multiple hangers-on and animals for leisure too – hunting dogs for the menfolk and lapdogs for the ladies. Silk and amber and other luxuries were imported from areas stretching from the Baltics to Baghdad. Frescoes in the chapel built by Cormac MacCárthaigh on the Rock of Cashel, in the twelfth century, were coloured with lapis lazuli imported at great expense from what is now called the Middle East, via Venice. Wine, mainly imported for liturgical reasons after the fifth century, was also enjoyed by some wealthy people.

Flax was widely cultivated for linen, and people's clothes were made of linen and wool. Hides kept out the worst of the cold in winter and no doubt covered sleepers at night too, and the ordinary working man wore trousers. The *brat* or cloak covered rich and poor, varying in quality and accessories according to the wealth of the wearer. Ornamental metal fasteners were highly prized and used for ceremonial display.

Human settlements had grown over the centuries around trading posts at the mouths or confluences of rivers. The forts of kings – *cathracha* – were surrounded by clusters of traders, craftsmen and workers. Major ecclesiastical settlements like Clonmacnoise in modern Co. Offaly, Glendalough (Co. Wicklow) and Clonard (Co. Meath) also had satellite populations of farmers and tradespeople, serving their seminaries and schools, of up to 5,000. Smithing, metalwork and woodworking were busy trades, while textile and garment manufacturing and food processing and preparation were continuous. These settlements, particularly secular ones, were also sites of entertainment and every king had a *file* (poet/storyteller) and a few musicians on the payroll to cheer people up on the dark winter evenings.

Mention of song and story leads naturally to language. Surviving manuscripts from all over the country show that the same language –now known as Old Irish – was written by the learned classes, poets, lawyers and clerics. Irish must also have been the common spoken language among the people, particularly as kings and other elites, while they certainly exercised power, were not culturally aloof from those over whom they ruled, sitting down to eat with their working men and enjoying the hospitality of their chief landholders for extended periods.

Ireland was abundant in food, but just as there were plagues in the sixth, seventh and ninth centuries, there were crop failures too. There were free and bonded farmers and tradesmen, and people without land or trade. And there was the brutal reality of slavery. If the basic unit of currency was a heifer, the next most basic was an enslaved girl or *cumhal*. (A female was more highly prized than a male because of her breeding potential.) People did not have to own enslaved girls to engage in trading, but the fact that these humans were benchmarks of value shows how commonplace slavery was. People were bought and sold, not only within Ireland but internationally, long before the Scandinavians brought a new vigour to this trade in the ninth and tenth centuries. Slavery was an economic fact of life and also a weapon or reward of war; non-combatants in raids and battles were carried off as slaves, and either ransomed or sold. Slavery was finally abolished in the twelfth century.

1.2.2 Kingship and Kinship

If the enslaved girl was at the bottom of the human hierarchy, the king (*rí*) was at the top. Politics was for men, kin was defined by men, and among powerful people the *derbfine* comprised several generations of males (in the male line) who took their name from their great-grandfather. The prefix *Ua* or *Uí*, later anglicized as 'O', means grandson or great-grandson. '*Mac*' means son. (*Ní* means daughter.) The *Uí Néill* kin group, political leaders in Ulster until the early seventeenth century, were the lineage of Niall of the Nine Hostages, a powerful leader in the fifth century. In these kin groups every male of suitable age and vigour was a potential king or lord, elected by kinsmen. Eldest sons had no greater advantages than any other males, though the sons of primary wives were given precedence. The practice of polygyny – a man having several wives – was common among the very wealthy, but no woman could have more than one husband.

Kingship was determined by wealth, based on ownership of land and cattle. Those whose riches disappeared simply fell out of the leading elite; an impoverished king was a contradiction in terms. However, kings could lose their positions if they behaved dishonourably or lost face – if they harboured malefactors, killed their kin, did not uphold the law, refused hospitality, neglected their obligations or tolerated criticism or satire without challenging it. Royal personages had obligations; the Irish word for generous, *flaithiúil*, has its roots in *flaith*, a king or prince. There were at least three tiers of kings – overkings who commanded the allegiance of major kings, who in turn reigned over minor kings. A kingdom was a *tuath* and the non-enslaved men who lived in the *tuatha* owned their own land and leased cattle from the king or were otherwise bound to him by complex ties of obligation. If farmers, they supplied a certain amount of food to the king; if tradesmen, they were expected to do a certain amount of work for him, or to contract others to do it. Hospitality was also expected from the major clients during the party season which extended from January 1 to Shrove Tuesday. The king and his entourage would travel from host to host, and as every king had a retinue of at least seven men, one can imagine that it was not only clerics who took a keen interest in the dating of Easter. Kings were always surrounded by kinsmen and clients and followers, for prestige as well as for security, and they exercised power through these networks. Their bureaucrats were the lawyers, who advised the king on legal matters, and the *filidhe*/bards or poets, who gave scholarly and poetic proof of kings' lineages and right to rule.

Provinces had their dominant dynasties, but there was talk of a *Rex Scottorum/Hiberniae* in the seventh century, showing the aspiration towards a high kingship. The *Uí Néill* dominated the north and northern midlands – *Ulaid* and *Mide* – and they had several kings under them. *Emain Macha* was their most important site, and they also laid claim to the ancient royal site of *Teamhrach*/Tara. A loose confederation of related groups known as the *Eogánacht* dominated Munster or *Mumha* from the seventh century, and their meeting place for periodic *oénaigh* (gatherings where might and status were displayed, arbitrations and meetings were held, and fun was had) was at Cashel, in modern Tipperary (Figure 1.2) The earlier *Múscraighe* confederation used to meet at *Imleach*/Emly, also in Tipperary, which became an important ecclesiastical site. *Laigin* or south Leinster had no such headquarters; its key families in these centuries were the *Uí Dunchadha* in the north and the *Uí Cennsalaig* in the south. Connacht was dominated by the *Uí Brúin* until the eighth century, and after this by the *Ua Conchobhair*. In north-east Ulster, the kingdom of the *Dal Riata* extended over into Scotland, spreading the speaking of Scottish-Gaelic to those lands.

Despite (or perhaps because of) the large number of political rulers – some estimates are as high as 150 at any given time – wars were not constant or continuous. In the seventh and eighth centuries different branches of the *Uí Néill* tried to take territory from each other and to extend their power south and east, but in some parts of the country

FIGURE 1.2 The Rock of Cashel, Co. Tipperary. DEA/W. BUSS/De Agostini/Getty images. From pre-Christian times the headquarters for the periodic gatherings (*óenaigh*) of kings of Munster, this striking natural feature was later the site for a cathedral, a church built by the McCarthy family, a round tower and several other dwellings added over the centuries. The sizeable town of Cashel which grew up around the Rock is hidden from view in this photograph.

a hundred years could pass without any conflict at all. When invasions and raids happened they could be bloody and unsparing of women and children, although the fact such savagery is remarked on in the annals with shock might mean that it was unusual. Mostly, the men were killed and the women and children taken as slaves (which was bad enough). But all these centres of authority, while they bred restlessness in the most powerful and uneasiness in the least powerful, could have balanced each other out, leading to a relatively stable society overall.

Small kingdoms alongside each other reinforced friendship through marriage alliances and fosterage. It was common to send boys and girls from the ages of seven to fourteen from one wealthy family to live with another, unrelated family. And although kinship was officially determined through the male line, females used informal strategies to strengthen ties of obligation and affection. Women could not exercise political power or inherit property (though they could be gifted it), but they could encourage attachments between their brothers and their own sons, or advance their husbands' and sons' interests. They could exert influence over their daughters and sisters in the same way.

The only invasion of Ireland in these years was the unsuccessful attempt of the Northumbrians under Ecgfrith to invade Brega (mainly north Dublin and Louth) in 684, to bolster Ecgfrith's power by eliminating a potential rival.

Early medieval Ireland was also early Christian Ireland, and religious alliances were extremely important politically and socially.

1.2.3 *Christianity*

Ireland's patron saint, whose feast-day on 17 March is celebrated with such enthusiasm around the globe, could also be the patron saint of trafficked people. Patrick, a third-generation Christian, the teenage son of a British civil servant in the Roman administration, was kidnapped by Irish raiders along with many others from somewhere in the north of England, and sold as a slave in Ireland. He tells the dramatic story of how he escaped, trained as a priest and was drawn back to the land of his captivity in or around 432 to convert the Irish to Christianity in his own blunt, vivid words in his *Confession*. Although he was the most high-profile evangelist, Patrick was not the first Irish Christian. In 431 Pope Celestine appointed Palladius as bishop to the

Irish Christians, which suggests that there were Christians in Ireland already. Declan of Ardmore (Waterford), Ibar of Wexford, Ailbe of north Munster and Ciarán of Ossory (not to be confused with the later Ciarán of Clonmacnoise) were Christian preachers before Patrick. Patrick's operations were nearly all north and west of a line from Wicklow to Galway, and his most important foundation, *Ard Macha/* Armagh, was very near *Emain Macha*, in *Ulaidh*.

Irish political leaders and people took to Christianity almost immediately, and religious foundations and seminaries sprang up all over the country. Brigid, an early follower of Patrick (she was born in or around 450) established several houses of women who took religious vows, the most famous being at *Cill Dara* (Kildare) with a monastery for men alongside it, under her authority (see Figure 1.3). Columcille, also known as Columba, founded monasteries at Durrow, Kells and Derry, before setting off for Iona in 561. He was a student of Finnian (who died in 549), whose seminary at Clonard, in the rich pasturelands of Meath, saw about 3,000 students pass through in the sixth century. Ciarán, who founded Clonmacnoise in the mid 540s, was another Clonard alumnus, as was Brendan who was active in Kerry and Clonfert (Galway) in the second half of the sixth century. To the west, Enda/*Éanna* had a seminary on Inis Mór, the biggest of the Aran Islands, from about the year 500. Islands and wild places were revered – *Inis Cathaig* or Scattery Island, on the Shannon estuary, settled by Senan (who died 544), *Sceilg Mhichíl* (Skellig island 'of St Michael') off Co. Kerry, settled in the sixth century, and craggy *Sliabh Liag* (Donegal), where Asicus, a disciple of Patrick himself, preached – but they were atypical. The more common religious settlements of these early centuries were near

FIGURE 1.3 St Brigid's Cross. By kind permission of the Brigidine Sisters, Solas Bhríde Centre & Hermitages, Kildare. This particular kind of cross made of rushes has been woven to mark St Brigid's Day, 1 February, from time immemorial. It is still displayed in many houses to remember Ireland's female patron, whose feast coincides with the coming of spring.

busy waterways or on established *slighte*, and surrounded by supporting trades. Accessibility was important: the seventh-century Cronan of Roscrea moved his monastery so as to be nearer a road, and the sixth-century Atracta of Sligo deliberately established her religious foundation where several roads converged. Religious, male and female, lived, like everyone else, in cashels and ring forts, where smaller dwellings and trades clustered around a church inside a large enclosure. (Figure 1.4) There were no religious orders; early medieval religious communities in Ireland as elsewhere were 'micro-Christendoms', semi-autonomous entities, with an undefined relationship to episcopal authority, which was not very strong at that time.

FIGURE 1.4 Kilmacduagh, Co Galway. Andrea Pistolesi/Photodisc/ Getty images. Founded by the gentle Colman (who died in 625), its name – *Cill Mac Duagh*, the church of the son of Duagh (a local nobleman) – illustrates how important local lineage was for early medieval religious foundations. The round tower, the tallest in Ireland, was added in the tenth or eleventh century.

The Irish were quick to learn the international language of Latin, enabling them to hold their own at the Synod of Whitby in 664, which settled the date of Easter, among other controversial topics. The links between the two islands were very strong; Finnian, founder of Clonard, had studied under David in Wales. Knowing Latin also facilitated continental travel. Columbanus (not to be confused with Columba/Columcille), from the eastern midlands, founded several monasteries on the continent including Luxeuil in Burgundy before ending up in Bobbio, northern Italy, where he died in 615. (Colm or Colum, from the Latin word Columba (dove), was a popular name for those aspiring to sanctity.) Among other Irishmen who went to the continent were Killian, who was martyred in Wurzburg, Fiacra, who went to Gaul, and Donatus who went to Fiesole (in Italy, just outside Florence) in the seventh century. Dympna, the sixth-century daughter of a minor Ulster king, is said to have fled her mad father and gone to Gheel, in modern-day Belgium; the community she founded there became a place of pilgrimage for those suffering from mental affliction. Nearer home, Aidan founded Lindisfarne off England's north-eastern coast in 634, and in the early seventh century Fursey from Galway went to East Anglia before going on to Peronne, in France.

Some of Patrick's most enthusiastic early converts were women from the kingly class, although Patrick expressed strong sympathy for enslaved women too. Part of Brigid's legendary power might have stemmed from the fact that, as the daughter of an enslaved woman and a king, she exemplified both the 'highest' and the 'lowest'. Íte set up a monastery in *Cell Íte* (Killeedy) in west Limerick (Munster) in the sixth century which was still important enough to be raided by Scandinavians 300 years later. Gobnait, having travelled from the Aran islands to *Corca Dhuibhne* (the Dingle peninsula) is still commemorated in *Baile Bhúirne* (Ballyvourney) in Cork, where she ended up. Samthann founded Clonbroney in Longford in the late seventh century, and a cult of her was promoted by Virgilius (another Irishman) in Salzburg in the eighth century. Female satellite communities also grew up around male foundations, at Clonmacnoise and Glendalough. Brothers and sisters in blood could also be brothers and sisters in Christ, and staying single to serve God allowed women to remain affiliated to their families of origin instead of going into a new family. These early female foundations took many forms, but they did not evolve into nunneries as such until the later medieval period.

Religious houses needed support not only for their construction but also for their ongoing maintenance, and links with the wealthy were crucial. Brigid used her noble connections to great advantage. Columcille/Columba was from the Conaill dynasty, after whom *Tír Chonaill* (roughly, modern Donegal) was named. Columbanus came from a landed family around Carlow-Wexford. However, Finbar of Cork (who died in 610) was the son of a metalworker and an enslaved woman, and Ciarán of Clonmacnoise was the son of a tradesman – Ciarán *Mac an tSaoir* (son of the freeman, i.e., tradesman). Intelligent and enthusiastic aspirants often found ready sponsors among the rich.

Because of liturgical requirements, monastic settlements also developed the skills of masonry and metalwork (Kildare was famous for its metallurgy), but the skill which wrought the greatest and most long-term change of all was writing. Christianity, by introducing the reading and writing of Latin, introduced a writing culture to Ireland, and a Latin grammar in Irish was produced at the end of the sixth century. Latin was written in the Romanized British way – script going left to right, words separated, punctuation. Writing Latin led to Old Irish being written in this way from the late sixth century, on vellum and other materials, and Irish has a strong claim to be the first European written vernacular. Several manuscripts produced by Irish monasteries survive, the most important of which was the Book of Kells, produced in Iona and brought to Ireland by Columcille's successors in the early ninth century. By the ninth century, Irish monastic seats of learning were teaching Greek and Latin literature as well as the Church fathers, and producing scholars like Johannes Scotus and Sedulius Scotus, who made names for themselves on continental Europe and Britain.

Not all learned people were in monasteries. *Filidhe*, or poets/bards, have already been mentioned, and there were lawyers in abundance too, who left comprehensive legal texts behind them.

1.2.4 *Law*

Often called brehon law, this code of conduct governed every aspect of life, economic, social, personal and political. Because of this, surviving legal texts from this period are historians' main source of information about early medieval Irish life. Covering everything from battles to beekeeping and from marriage to murder, these laws were administered by the lawyer or *breithim*/brehon class. There was no concept of criminal law; punishment was by payment of compensation (*éiric*) to the damaged individual, which is now sometimes called restorative law. This compensation could, however, take the form of a death penalty, and it was illegal for anyone to harbour a homicide. Men could have as many wives as they could afford, while women were limited to one husband. Only primary wives had property rights in marriage, and even these rights were attenuated. Furthermore, the status of offspring depended upon whether their mothers were primary or secondary wives or concubines. Women could divorce husbands, but husbands had a greater range of grounds for divorcing wives.

Brehon law prevailed among the Gaelic-Irish until the sixteenth century, but it was increasingly challenged by

English common law after the coming of the Normans in 1169. The earlier Scandinavian invaders did not interfere with Irish law at all.

1.3 Circa 795–1169

1.3.1 *The Scandinavians/Vikings*

From the 790s onwards, fierce raiders in well-equipped ships from Norway and Denmark made sporadic and eventually, more regular raids on Britain and Ireland. They turned their attention to these two western islands because of disruption to their usual trading activities in northern and eastern Europe. From the beginning they were traders as well as raiders; there would have been little point in seizing cattle in Brega (modern Louth) in the late eighth century if they could not have been sold locally, because Viking ships were not equipped for livestock. Although they are remembered chiefly for raiding monasteries and carrying off the precious items they found there, they took everything of value that they could lay their hands on. Mostly hit-and-grab up to about 830, they rarely ventured more than twenty miles inland, and they were successfully driven off in the north-east in 811 and in Kerry and Mayo in 812. Despite their two-headed axes and reputation for ferocity, they were not effective land fighters, and the Irish (like the British in their own land) had the advantage of knowing the territory better. By 841 fleets of Norse ships were appearing on the Liffey and the Boyne. Over the following century the Scandinavians founded the cities of Dublin, Limerick, Waterford and Cork. Viking involvement in Ireland went on for almost 300 years. Some of the invaders settled down and assimilated to Ireland while others came and went, and eventually stopped coming, probably from lack of encouragement from those who had already settled. They were never a united force and they even fought each other occasionally.

What the Scandinavians contributed to Ireland were rudimentary coinage, a particular type of long house, certain new skills in carpentry and boatbuilding, open-air markets, assembly halls, some place names, buttons (the Irish word for which, *cnaipí*, is of Nordic origin), and (maybe) fair skin and red hair. For their part, the Irish exported the term 'blak' or *bláthach* for buttermilk to the Faroe Islands. Did the Norsemen develop the Irish town? Probably not: towns were as new to the Scandinavians as they were to the Irish, and might have evolved here in any case, without their input. But the invaders certainly influenced the design of urban space.

At the Battle of Clontarf in 1014, there were Munster Vikings fighting with Brian Boru, the Irish leader, and his opponent King Sitric (who, although of Scandinavian origin, was Christian, and had a daughter a nun) had the support of the Leinster families. Brian Boru died at this battle, which was more about establishing *Uí Briain/*O'Brien supremacy than about driving the Scandinavians out entirely. When the Normans invaded in 1169, Vikings were still a distinctive enough group to help the Irish to resist them, but they were not often identified as a separate entity after that.

All through the years of Scandinavian incursions and settlements, Irish political life continued to evolve, with emerging competition for a high kingship.

1.3.2 *The Changing Political Scene*

Struggles for supremacy were not new among Irish kings. *Teamhrach*/Tara, which had ancient resonances, became the preferred seat for this high kingship and the main contenders in early ninth-century Ireland were the *Uí Néill* and the Munster dynasties. *Feilimid macCrimthainn*, king of Munster, assumed his high-king seat at Tara in 840. *Mael Seachnaill* of the *Uí Néill* regained it the following century, establishing himself as high king in 980. However, from the 930s onwards the *Dal gCais*, a dynasty centred around north Munster, specifically Clare, were gaining in power and because the leading character in this was Brian, these became known as the *Uí Briain*/O'Briens. Brian Boru became high king of Ireland in 1002. After Brian's death at the Battle of Clontarf the *Uí Néill* regained the upper hand for a while, then it swung around to the *Uí Briain* again, until the *Ui Chonchobair*/O'Conors of Connacht assumed dominance in 1122. Meanwhile, there were smaller dynasties equally powerful in their own regions – the *Uí Ruairc*/O'Rourke of Breifne (north-west Connacht), the *MacCarthaig*/McCarthy in south Munster, the *MacLochlainns* in north-west Ulster and the *MacMurchadas*/MacMorroghs in south Leinster. No dynasty from Leinster ever assumed the high kingship, but smaller dynasties, like smaller countries, can sometimes exercise influence out of all proportion to their size, and this is what happened in twelfth-century Ireland. A conflict between Diarmait MacMurrough, king of Leinster, and Tiernan O'Rourke of Breifne came to boiling point in 1166, because MacMurrough kidnapped O'Rourke's wife Dervorgilla. We know nothing of Dervorgilla's feelings in the matter, but when it came to using sexual violence as a weapon of war, MacMurrough had form. In 1160, as part of a conflict with the *Ua Conchubhair*/O'Conor, he burned the ancient and venerated nunnery in Kildare, Brigid's sixth-century foundation, with the loss of about 150 lives, and abducted and raped the abbess.

Ruairí O'Conor, the newly elected high king, sided with O'Rourke on the abduction, so MacMorrough appealed to King Henry II of England to recruit Normans settled in Wales, to help him to get his lands back. For the next few years Anglo-Normans were trickling into Ireland, but the decisive invasion date was 1169, when Richard de Clare, or Strongbow, landed his force in Wexford.

This invasion had the approval of Pope Adrian IV, the Englishman Nicholas Breakspear, who had been hearing worrying stories about the church in Ireland from the Archbishop of Canterbury. All over Europe since the tenth century there had been sweeping ecclesiastical reforms to correct laxity and corruption in an organization coming up to its first millennium. Ireland was part of this reform, and the church there underwent many changes from the ninth to the twelfth centuries.

1.3.3 Religion

Although the Irish church was mainly organized among monastic lines from the fifth to the eleventh centuries, bishops were increasing in power from the eighth century onwards, trying to exert Rome's authority. The monastic life attracted some powerfully spiritual men and women and intensified the power of the wealthy families who supplied both money and membership. Because much of our information about monastic worldliness and corruption (in this period and later), comes from those who had their own reasons for criticizing these institutions (not to mention coveting their property), it must be treated with caution. Nonetheless, money and gifts of precious liturgical objects must have compromised an abbey's independence, and furthermore, many abbacies passed not only from uncle to nephew, but from father to son. (Celibacy was not compulsory for the ordained in the universal Church until the thirteenth century.) The emergence of a cult like the ascetic and unworldly *Céli Dé* – inaugurated by *Mael Ruain* in Tallaght, near Dublin in 774 and spreading rapidly – shows how far the mainstream church was seen to have strayed. Not long after, the Scandinavians knew what they were looking for (in both Britain and Ireland) when they targeted religious foundations as well as forts and castles, for gold and silver and jewelled objects. Clonmacnoise was raided eight times by them between 837 and 953, and it was raided twice as many times by Irish kings and chiefs. Its survival is a testament not only to the faith of successive generations of monks and religious women but also, it must be said, to the limitless resources at the monks' disposal, who always managed to pick themselves up and carry on, after all these depredations.

It was at the time of the Scandinavians that the very distinctive round tower which survives in Clonmacnoise, Glendalough, Kilmacduagh and other places, was developed at monastic sites. (Figure 1.4) These structures, which range in height from 60 m to 130 m, were called *cloighthigh* (belfries) and their doors are about 10 m above the ground (accessible by ladders). They were used to summon worshippers, but also as storage for precious objects and refuges for a select few of the monastic and wider community in the face of raids.

The twelfth century saw two major changes in the Irish church. Early in this century, Malachy, bishop of Armagh (later canonized), stopped off with Bernard of Clairvaux on his way to Rome, and was so impressed with the Cistercian order that he invited them to make a foundation in Ireland, which they did in Mellifont in Louth in 1152. A much-travelled man, he was also so impressed with the Augustinian canons in Flanders that he invited them too. Within twenty years Mellifont had established twenty daughter houses. The Cistercian model, discussed in the next chapter, changed the face of Irish monasticism entirely over the succeeding centuries. Meanwhile, from 1111 onwards, parishes and dioceses were laid out. The Synod of Kells of 1152 carved Ireland into the diocesan boundaries which still survive (more or less). (See Map 2.1.) Parish boundaries, many of which still survive in rural areas, were also set. There were four archbishoprics or provinces – Armagh, Cashel, Tuam and Dublin. Armagh and Cashel were ancient sites of political power, Tuam was the major political site in Connacht since the eighth century and also had a monastic foundation, and the pre-eminence of Dublin reflects the growing importance of this port, and of ecclesiastical relationships with the neighbouring island, a short sea-journey away. Diocesan divisions often reflected those of the kingdoms or *tuatha*, and this explains their often geographically inexplicable boundaries. Ossory was *Osraighe* (mostly Kilkenny), Kilfenora (north Clare) was the kingdom of *Corcomru*. Meath is in Armagh, not Dublin, province, because in the twelfth century it was part of *Uí*

Néill territory, and the far-flung diocese of Killaloe stretches from western Laois to west Clare, because this was all territory controlled by, or allied with the *Uí Briain*/ O'Briens. (See Map 2.1.) Every diocese, moreover, had to have riverine or coastal access, to enable transport to (and more importantly from the point of view of central authority, from) Rome. These diocesan divisions of Ireland predated the county boundaries.

1.4 Conclusion

A story was still being told in *Corca Dhuibhne*, the Dingle peninsula, in the 1930s, about the region's patron saint, Brendan, who died around AD 580. In the story, Brendan climbs to the top of the mountain which is now called after him, *Cnoc Bhreanáinn* or Mount Brandon, to his little chapel at the summit, to say Mass. A large crowd assembles to hear him. But when he gets to the top, he discovers that he has left his Mass-book after him in his cell at the foot of the mountain. Word is sent down through the crowd, and the Mass-book is fetched from the cell and passed up to Brendan by human chain, without anyone having to move from their positions. The point of this story is the sheer number of devotees Brendan could attract – a crowd that stretched all the way from his hermitage to the summit of Ireland's second-highest mountain would indeed be vast. But the story also illustrates how important the book was for sixth-century Christians; Brendan, like most seasoned celebrants, probably knew the words of the liturgy off by heart, still, he had not only to read it but to be *seen* to read it, for the sacrament to be celebrated correctly.

Although it would be another millennium and a half before all pilgrims to Mount Brandon would be able to read and write, by the sixth century, the written word had rooted itself firmly in Ireland. If writing intensified and consolidated the power of kings and lawyers and poets and priests, it also offered a powerful tool with which to moderate and question some of those authorities. Knowing Latin integrated Irish people with the British and European world, but the use of Latinised script to write the language spoken all over the island also strengthened a sense of Irish cultural identity and led to secular learning. This identity was so strong it eventually absorbed the Scandinavian settlers, and it would go on to absorb the Norman invaders, though never completely, as we shall see.

Seven hundred years is a long time to compress into one chapter, which is what has been attempted here. Over these many generations, political leaders and religious movements grew and flourished and decayed and grew again in different forms. In the National Museum there is a fourteenth-century wooden statue of St Molua of Sligo, a seventh-century monastic founder, who was still commemorated and venerated in his home place seven centuries later. The days of Patrick, Brigid, Finian, Columcille and Íte were as far away in time from the fourteenth century as the fourteenth century is from us, today.

2

Invasions

~

Late Medieval Ireland, 1169–1520

2.1 Introduction

The '700 years of oppression' which early twentieth-century Irish nationalists often mentioned began in 1169, because the coming of the Anglo-Normans brought a new player onto the field, the English Crown. Yet the Norman conquest, begun with great force and energy, was poorly resourced and never completed. Many Irish landowners retained their lands and even took back some power from the invaders over the succeeding centuries. The English crown, continuously challenged from outside and inside England, forgot about Ireland for half-centuries at a time between 1169 and 1494, and even the newcomers themselves sometimes forgot that they were supposed to be conquerors.

The Norman invasion was not the only change wrought in Ireland over this period. Changes in the structure of the Church and in monastic life, outlined in the previous chapter, were already under way by Strongbow's arrival, and Irish political life was also changing.

2.2 Politics

In 1169–1170, Richard de Clare, or Strongbow, and Raymond le Gros among others, with well-equipped forces, landed in Wexford and took Waterford and Dublin, defeating a large force of Gaelic-Irish resisters led by the high king Rory O'Conor, allied with Norse and Manx forces. De Clare married Aoife, the daughter of Diarmuid MacMurrough. The leaders of the invasion were mainly Norman settlers in Wales of Flemish origin, but as far as the Irish were concerned they were the 'English' and were often called that, and they called themselves that. However, to avoid confusion with the English Crown's immediate representatives in Dublin then and later, and because many of the invaders were assimilated into Irish political and social life, the late twelfth-century incomers will be called Anglo-Normans in this chapter, while the adjective 'Norman' will be used to describe the changes they introduced. The original inhabitants of Ireland (including those of Scandinavian origin who had been absorbed) will be called the Gaelic-Irish.

In its early stages, the conquest appeared so successful that an alarmed King Henry II travelled to Ireland in 1172 to prevent Strongbow from getting any ideas above his station. The Irish bishops acknowledged Henry and pledged loyalty to him in the same year, and the high king, Ruairi O'Conor, accepted a fait accompli and did the same in 1175. By 1185 the rudiments of an administration were put in place, including a king's representative, the justiciar. In 1210 King John visited, in a further show of strength. (Figure 2.1) By 1264 there was a parliament made up of prominent lords and churchmen, which met

FIGURE 2.1 King John's Castle, Limerick. Robin Bush/Photodisc/Getty images. One of the bigger fortress-type castles built by the Anglo-Normans, this was completed in 1210, the year King John visited Ireland, and is strategically situated on one of Ireland's most important waterways, the Shannon.

periodically in various Norman towns mostly in Leinster – Dublin, Drogheda, Naas, Trim, Kilkenny, Castledermot – though it ventured into Munster occasionally, to Waterford, Clonmel, Cork, Cashel and Limerick.

In the thirteenth century plenty of money poured in from England to help the conquest, but Ireland was giving back far more than it took, and was very lucrative for the Crown in agricultural produce and other natural resources. The early invaders seized land reachable by river and sea; it was not so much that they left the 'bad land' to the Gaelic-Irish, as that they did not know the passes through bogs and mountainous areas and settled wherever was easier for them, and wherever Gaelic-Irish opposition was feeble, divided or disputed. The de Courcys took part of east

Ulster, the de Lacys, Meath, the de Burgos (later Burkes) ventured west of the Shannon into Connacht. In the early successful years, the FitzStephens and de Clares went into north Munster, the Fitzgeralds into south Munster and mid-Leinster, and the Butlers into Kilkenny and east Munster. The Irish geographical descriptors Thomond (*tuath-Mumhan*, north Munster), Desmond (*deis-Mumhan*, south Munster) and Ormond (*iar-Mumhan*, east Munster) were given to these Norman lordships. Farmers and tradesmen (with names like Roche, Fleming, Power) mainly settled in Leinster and east Munster. Some lords brought tenants with them; a dialect, Yola, a mixture of Middle English, Welsh and Flemish (and probably Irish too), was widely spoken in Wexford up to modern times. The fact that Walsh (Gaelicized as *Breathnach*, which means British) is one of the four most common surnames in Ireland today suggests that there was a strong settlement of people from that part of Britain, either as landowners or their tenants.

Many Gaelic-Irish chiefs and kings were not just undefeated, they were never tackled at all. Nearly a century after the conquest, in 1258, Tadhg O'Brien of Munster and Felim O'Conor of Connacht felt reasonably confident in nominating Brian O'Neill (Ulster) as high king, and appealed to King Haakon of Norway to lead them against the Anglo-Normans. This did not come to pass, but half a century later, when Edward Bruce, king of Scotland, landed a force in north-east Ulster, in 1315, it took three years for him to be defeated after campaigning vigorously in the east coast and midlands. The Scottish and Irish spoke more or less the same language, the kingdom of *Dal Riata* had straddled the Northern Channel in the first millennium, and in the thirteenth century, Irish chiefs began to employ Scottish mercenaries, gallowglasses (*gall-óglaigh* – foreign volunteers). Bruce's invasion was not supported by all the Gaelic-Irish chiefs, and it did not succeed in driving the Anglo-Normans out. Still, unsuccessful though it was, the campaign heralded a fourteenth-century revival of Gaelic-Irish confidence throughout the island. In 1318 the O'Briens drove the de Clares from Thomond, taking over their stronghold at Bunratty, the McCarthys encroached on the Fitzgeralds/Desmonds in south Munster, the O'Byrnes, O'Tooles and MacMorroghs in the mountainous regions of Leinster expanded their territories and in Connacht the de Burgos/Burkes – now split into two families, the Clanrickards and the McWilliams which controlled, respectively parts of Galway and parts of Mayo – had the MacDonaghs, the O'Conors, the MacDermotts, the O'Kellys, the O'Maddens and O'Haras to contend with, not to mention the O'Flahertys to the west. They held on, as did the Butlers of Ormond. The O'Rourkes reigned supreme in north-east Connacht. Vast areas of Ulster remained under the control of three big Gaelic-Irish families – the O'Donnells in west Ulster, the O'Neills in mid-Ulster and the McDonnells in the east. The MacMahons and Maguires in south and east Ulster were so preoccupied with heading off the O'Neills and O'Donnells that the Anglo-Normans were barely on their radar. A further blow was dealt to the Anglo-Norman interest, when the plague or Black Death of 1348–1349, and its brief reprise in the 1360s and 1370s, spread most rapidly and most destructively in the more populated areas. The English Crown, distracted and impoverished by the Hundred Years' War with France (1338–1453) did not have time or money for beleaguered

Anglo-Normans, although in 1361 Edward III sent over a massive force under his son, Lionel, to lead a campaign against the Leinster Gaelic-Irish. This was the context for the Statutes of Kilkenny in 1366, so-called because Kilkenny was where the parliament met that year.

These new laws attempted to separate the Anglo-Norman communities from the Gaelic-Irish ones for once and for all. Thirty-five in number, they forbade intermarriage between the two groups, trade between them, use of the Irish language, music or dress by Anglo-Normans, and the admission of Gaelic-Irishmen to Anglo-Norman religious houses or cathedral chapters. These statutes only ever applied in Dublin and its immediate hinterland, and sometimes, not even there. Norman towns would have failed had they not traded with the Gaelic-Irish living beyond their gates and, more often than not, within their walls too. Any Anglo-Norman lord who could not understand Irish would have found himself fooled in commercial dealings and betrayed in political ones. Although Norman and Gaelic-Irish territories were separate from each other, there were no borders or frontiers, and people from both backgrounds, especially tradesmen, farmers and workers of all kinds, mixed freely and spoke the same language. At elite level, the housing, food and furniture of the wealthy O'Neills, O'Donnells and McCarthys was not that different from that of the Kildares, Desmonds and Ormonds; the Gaelic-Irish wore what they liked and could afford. Intermarriage was part of the colonization process from the very beginning, when Strongbow married Aoife MacMorrogh. Anglo-Norman–Gaelic-Irish hostility flared up even among 'men of God', but the two communities were drawing nearer each other in these centuries and further away from the Crown. When King Richard II visited twice, in 1394 and 1399, to try to bring the Leinster Gaelic-Irish under control, he had trouble keeping all the Anglo-Normans on side. England made the occasional show of support for its interests but it was not prepared to put its money into Ireland except in short, sharp shocks that had no lasting effect. Over the following century the power in Ireland shifted away from the Crown's representative in Dublin to the big Norman lordships and the Gaelic-Irish chiefs.

This was because, far from being hold-outs from an earlier dispensation, the Gaelic-Irish were developing politically as well. The term *'tuath'* was obsolete, and from 1300 the area ruled over by a chief was an *oireacht* (anglicized as 'iraght'), and its ruler a *taoiseach* or a *tighearna* (lord). From the fourteenth century, Gaelic chiefs stopped calling themselves kings and used instead their surnames, or the names of the territories they ruled over, emulating Anglo-Norman earls or barons, and to an extent, recognizing an external Crown. The old brehon rules of elective leadership prevailed and some Anglo-Norman lords adopted them. Another Gaelic custom which many Anglo-Normans adopted with great gusto was that of kings and lords demanding extensive seasonal hospitality for themselves and their large retinues from their chief clients. The English administration deplored this custom, which they called 'coyne and livery', as a regrettable example of degeneracy and the spending of money which could be better spent on economic development, or handed over to the Crown. But some native customs were just too attractive to resist.

By the English Wars of the Roses, which spluttered sporadically from 1455 to 1487, the biggest political forces in Ireland were the Anglo-Norman lords of Kildare who controlled much of north Leinster (Fitzgeralds), the Ormonds in Tipperary and Kilkenny (Butlers), the Desmonds of south Munster (also Fitzgeralds, with some Fitzmaurices) and the Gaelic-Irish O'Neills and O'Donnells who ruled much of Ulster. The Anglo-Normans never established a strong foothold in the north. Lesser Anglo-Norman lords like the Clanrickard Burkes in Connacht and lesser Gaelic-Irish chiefs like the McMorrogh-Kavanaghs in south Leinster exerted power successfully on a smaller scale. The O'Briens, who had driven off the de Clares in the early fourteenth century, were still formidable in Thomond (north Limerick, modern Clare) and the McCarthys ruled over large areas of west Cork and Kerry.

England's pragmatic acceptance of the limits of its power in Ireland is illustrated by the existence of 'the English Pale', a term coined in 1495 by Edward Poynings, the king's representative who had previously governed the 'English Pale' at Calais. The Pale encompassed the area known hitherto as the 'four obedient shires', the medieval shires of Dublin, Louth, Meath and Kildare, which incorporated parts of modern Wicklow and Westmeath. Here, the English language was in the ascendant among the politically powerful classes, although the 'sworn English' farmers and labourers who worked the land in Kildare and Meath were all Irish speakers down to the late eighteenth century. Dykes were dug around it to prevent cattle drives out of it, but the Pale was in no other way barricaded or cut off from the rest of the country, and neither were Palesmen and women prevented from venturing outside of it.

Richard, Duke of York, Irish Lord Lieutenant from the 1440s, came to terms with a good selection of lords and chiefs from both sides, and in 1460 a parliament he summoned in Drogheda came very close to declaring legislative independence for Ireland. The most powerful leaders in Ireland (except for Ormond) were mainly Yorkist for the following decades, even after the Lancastrian victory at Bosworth in 1485. The Yorkist 'pretender' Lambert Simnel was crowned King Edward VI in Christchurch in Dublin in 1487 and Anglo-Norman and Gaelic-Irish alike teamed up with English supporters of the Yorkists to invade England with a force of 4,000 in the same year. Although they were eventually defeated at Stoke, they were a serious challenge to the king. King Henry VII (the Lancastrian victor, a Tudor) appointed Edward Poynings as deputy lieutenant in Ireland in 1494, and thus was promulgated Poynings' Law, which limited the legislative powers of the Irish parliament.

To drive home his authority, the king summoned the Great Earl of Kildare, *Gearóid Mór* (Great Gerald), to London on suspicion of sedition in 1496, at which point all hell broke loose in Ireland with a combination of Anglo-Norman and Gaelic-Irish potentates – Desmond, O'Neill, O'Donnell, Clanrickard, and several others – supporting another Yorkist 'pretender', Perkin Warbeck. *Gearóid Mór*/Kildare agreed to be the king's man and returned to Ireland to restore order and to consolidate support for the Tudors. Kildare was the man to do it because if he had had three feet, he would have had one in England, one in Anglo-Norman Ireland and one in Gaelic-Ireland. The names by which he was known – Lord Kildare and *Gearóid Mór* – testify to his combination of both ethnicities on the island. He was Anglo-Norman, his second wife, Elizabeth St John, was a relative of Henry VII, his sister was married to Conn O'Neill, head of the O'Neills, and three of his daughters were married into prominent Gaelic-Irish families.

On his return, Kildare faced opposition in his pledge to support the Tudors. He fought the O'Briens (who were allied with the Anglo-Norman Clanrickard Burkes), in one of the bloodiest Irish battles ever, at Knockdoe, Co. Galway, in 1504. In 1510 there was another battle against the O'Briens and the McCarthys at O'Brien's Bridge, Co. Clare, on the Shannon. In 1513 the Great Earl died and was succeeded by his son *Gearóid Óg* (Young Gerald), as the king's deputy. Now there was a new king on the throne, Henry VIII, whose future actions were to be so decisive for Ireland. Henry was well disposed towards *Gearóid Óg* – they had met as boys – and, at first, glad to have him in charge. Henry's pronouncement in the early 1520s that he wanted to deal with the Gaelic-Irish through 'sober ways, politic drifts and amiable persuasions' boded well. Henry also hoped to establish an amalgam of brehon law and English common law in the border areas in Ireland. This never came to pass, but the fact that an English king even harboured this ambition shows how resilient and respectable Irish law was, just before it disappeared forever.

2.3 Law and Administration

When King John came to Ireland in 1210 he tried to establish English common law (still evolving in England) in Ireland. Courts and coroners and keepers of the peace were established in the Anglo-Norman areas in the thirteenth century. By the early fourteenth century Ireland was shired into the counties Dublin, Louth, Meath (incorporating modern Westmeath and parts of Longford), Kildare, Carlow, Waterford, Roscommon, Cork, Limerick, Tipperary, Kerry, Wexford and Kilkenny. The fact that Ulster and Connacht, properly speaking large provinces, were also shires in themselves, shows how weak Norman influence was west of the Shannon and in the entire north. English law was never extended to Gaelic-Irish areas, which still operated brehon law, although Gaelic-Irish people could use the Norman courts if they wanted to. Inheritance was still partible and men could still have several wives, although polygyny (only ever practised by the wealthy in any case) was already dying out. Brehon law was influenced more by Roman law from the twelfth century onwards, and Anglo-Normans who lived in 'marcher' (border) areas often adopted brehon inheritance laws. Brehon arguments and precedents were often accepted as arbitration in Anglo-Norman law courts. The 4th Earl of Ormond, James Butler, had a brehon lawyer in his retinue in the fifteenth century. Brehon law survived as long as it did because of the non-penetration of the Anglo-Normans into many areas of the country, but also because of the compromises and negotiations it made with more modern legal culture. It was gradually eroded after 1541, but its last recorded use was during the reign of James I, in the early seventeenth century.

Religion was another area of contention between the Anglo-Normans and Gaelic-Irish, though more from the standpoint of power and personnel than doctrine and practice.

2.4 Religion

All over the Christianized world, political leaders not only took an interest but had an interest (financial, patronal, territorial or personal) in the religious chain of command in countries under their authority. Christians expected their monarchs to exercise power in the appointment of bishops and abbots. The Pope in Rome was the ultimate authority but, for most rulers, Rome was far away and the schism of the fourteenth century weakened papal authority even more.

Religion was an everyday cultural frame of reference, in Ireland as everywhere else. Christian feasts were superimposed on the Celtic turning of the year – *Imbolc* became St Brigid's Day (February 1) and *Samhain* became All Hallows' Eve (October 31), while Midsummer became St John's Eve (23 June). The political ceremonies of both Gaelic-Irish and Anglo-Norman chiefs used religious liturgies to give them added authority. After the twelfth century, as in England, legal, financial and university terms followed a religious calendar (Lady Day, March 25, and Michaelmas, September 29, for example), civic life observed feast days and fast days, and the newly forming guilds of tradesmen in towns adopted saints as patrons.

Although papal approval for the Norman invasion was granted so as to bring the 'ill-disciplined' Irish Church under the authority of Canterbury, the Church in Ireland was already changing. The twelfth-century reforms of Malachy, as described in the previous chapter, inaugurated a countrywide network of dioceses and parishes. (Map 2.1) Monastic life became more standardized when

MAP 2.1 The dioceses of Ireland in the fourteenth century. By Pádraig Lenihan. Diocesan divisions were drawn in the mid twelfth century (1142) before the Norman invasion, and reflected areas of political influence rather than natural geographical boundaries. All had coastal or riverine access, for ease of communication with each other, with the four archbishoprics and with Rome.

the Cistercians arrived in 1152. These modern stone-built monasteries were constructed along plans that would be adopted by all houses of male religious, Cistercian or not – chapels, individual cells, staircases, cloisters for ambulant prayer, refectories for communal eating, sophisticated sanitation systems based on piped water from nearby springs or rivers, efficient drainage, and vast farms or granges, not just for the monks' own use, but for commerce. Mellifont, by 1300, had three lay brothers to every monk. Lay brothers, although they took religious vows and prayed, did not say Mass or hold positions of authority or vote in or attend chapters (regular administrative meetings) and they worked at the manual tasks not only of monastery maintenance but of farming and craftmanship. Tintern Abbey in Wexford (founded in the twelfth century from the abbey of the same name in Wales, later immortalized by Wordsworth) sent out gangs of lay brothers every Monday to Saturday to camp while working their outlying farms.

The next big development in monastic life was the arrival of the mendicant friars originally from the continent, but via England, in the thirteenth century. As their name suggests, the mendicants relied chiefly upon alms rather than commerce for their support and represented a reforming movement in the church. The Dominicans came to Dublin and Drogheda in 1224, the Franciscans to Youghal in 1230, the Carmelites to Carlow in 1271 and the mendicant Augustinians (as distinct from the Augustinian canons introduced by Malachy a century earlier) to Dublin in 1282. By 1341 there were ninety-six mendicant houses in Ireland. They spread rapidly, firstly in Anglo-Norman areas and, after 1400, into areas controlled by the Gaelic-Irish. The fifteenth century brought reforms to the mendicant friars, with even greater emphasis than before on poverty and on pastoral care of the faithful. Mendicant or not, all monasteries depended on the powerful for security and protection as well as for money. Elizabeth de Clare (Anglo-Norman) founded an Augustinian friary in Ballinrobe, Co. Mayo, in 1312, and the Macnamara family (Gaelic-Irish) in Clare founded Quin Franciscan Abbey in 1433. Meelick Franciscan friary in east Galway (at the time of writing the oldest Catholic church still in use in Ireland) was founded by the O'Maddens (Gaelic-Irish) in 1477. The Anglo-Norman Fitzgeralds (Desmonds) of Munster were responsible for many Franciscan foundations and the Butlers of Ormond founded Carmelite houses in Kilkenny and east Tipperary.

In both the older orders and the mendicant friars there were tensions between Anglo-Norman and Gaelic-Irish monks, and these flared up particularly at the time of the Bruce invasion (1315–1318) when one Anglo-Norman Franciscan in Drogheda reputedly declared that it would be no sin to kill an 'Irishman'. The appointment of the Gaelic-Irish William O'Reilly as head of the Irish province of the Franciscans in 1445 was noted with concern not only by many of his confreres but by King Henry IV. Kings had little power over religious orders, but they had a veto on the appointment of bishops. Bishops in Ireland were either Gaelic-Irish or Anglo-Norman, or, occasionally, English, Spanish or Greek. Some bishops, such as William O'Farrel of Ardagh and Richard Bennet of Killala in the late fifteenth and early sixteenth-century, doubled up as political chiefs.

Celibacy for priests was introduced throughout the universal church in the thirteenth century but in Ireland it was practised more among the Anglo-Normans than the Gaelic-Irish. Many popular Irish surnames in Ireland today indicate direct descent from clergy and ecclesiastics; Cleary – *Ó Cléirigh* – means grandson or great-grandson of the priest; MacAnespie is *Mac an Easpaig* – son of the bishop; and McInerney – *Mac an Aircinnigh* – son of a cleric in minor orders. Bishop Murtough O'Kelly of Clonfert (who died in 1423) had four sons, three of whom went on to be ordained. Cormac MacDavid, abbot of Boyle Cistercian monastery in 1414, was the son of a previous abbot. And lest it be thought that clerics who were fathers in every sense were far removed from the mainstream of continental Christianity where celibacy was imposed since the thirteenth century, the bishop of Clogher in the late fourteenth century, Johannes Ó Corcráin, who received his doctorate at Wurzburg, had a son, Tomás, who also went to the German lands for his education. However, not all ordained men married. Most rank-and-file monks did not, many secular priests in humbler situations could not afford to, and the most dynamic monastic movement, the mendicant friars, insisted upon celibacy.

Sexual relationships, a convenience and comfort for men, are a complication for women, carrying as they do the risk of childbearing. Therefore, while there were occasional highly publicized female breaches of the rule of chastity, the vast majority of women religious had good reason to observe it. There were about sixty-five nunneries in Ireland over this period, most of them founded in the twelfth and thirteenth centuries. Murchadha Ó Méalseachlainn, king of Meath, founded Clonard nunnery in 1144, and Kilcreevanty convent, in Galway, founded by the O'Conors in 1200, followed a Benedictine rule. The Anglo-Normans also endowed religious houses for women. Relatives of founding families more often than not occupied positions of authority, as in male foundations. Nunneries were less elaborate in structure than monasteries, lacking chapter houses and, often, cloisters. They were supposed to be strictly enclosed for reasons of discipline (Rome was then, and would remain, nervous of women under religious vows) but abbesses or superiors had to conduct ecclesiastical business and property transactions on behalf of the convents, and this sometimes took them outside, or brought outsiders in. Nunneries did not normally have commercial enterprises on the same scale as monasteries, though Lismullen in Co. Meath had two mills and the convent at Kilculiheen in Co. Waterford had salmon weirs, rabbit warrens and brewhouses. The Augustinian nuns in Peter's Cell, founded in the late twelfth century, educated the daughters of Limerick city's merchants; the fostering of children carried out by female religious foundations in the early medieval period evolved into schooling later. Wherever they put down roots, women religious ran their businesses and projects, tended the sick and fed the hungry. Nuns' existence is recorded in place-names – Ballynacally (*Baile na Callaigh*) in Clare, Ballycally (similar) in Mayo, Calliaghstown (a hybrid of Irish and English) in Co. Dublin. A *cailleach* is a veiled woman, a nun, an old grandmother, a witch, or any woman of authority. The formal ecclesiastical Irish term for nuns is '*mná rialta*', women regulars.

Irish Christians in the late medieval period maintained strong links with Britain and the continent and were acutely aware of developments in the wider Church. Irish seminarians attended Oxford, Cambridge, Glasgow, Paris and Bologna universities. (Attempts to set up universities in Ireland in Dublin, Youghal and Drogheda in the thirteenth and fourteenth centuries, all failed.) In Donegal, St Patrick's

Purgatory, believed to be a portal into the next world, attracted pilgrims from as far away as Spain, Greece and Hungary. Irish monks in leadership roles regularly travelled to their orders' chapters in Paris, Rome and Lombardy, among other places. In the Great Schism of 1378–1417, most Irish bishops and priests followed England in supporting the Roman pope, Urban VI, but some French-influenced priests, both Gaelic-Irish and Anglo-Norman, in Tuam and Armagh, supported Clement VII in Avignon, and there were two contending bishops of Killaloe in the first half of the fifteenth century. This period also saw heightened lay involvement in religion. The Third Order of St Francis, a very popular confraternity, spread among the laity all over the country. One of its most enthusiastic promoters, and the founder of a Third Order Friary in Donegal, was Manus Ó Domhnaill, the powerful Gaelic-Irish nobleman, who completed a biography of St Columcille – *Betha Colaim Cille* – in 1532. French and Italian devotional books were translated into Irish, and some Irish people who could afford it went on pilgrimages; Tomás Óg Maguire of Fermanagh and Margaret O'Carroll from the midlands, went to Rome in 1450. The Dominicans promoted the devotion of the Rosary all over the country, which would become a very important religious practice in Cromwellian and Penal times when Mass attendance was sometimes impossible.

Ireland in the later medieval period was no more devout than any other country. Belief and practice were woven into everyday life, and it was sometimes difficult to distinguish ecclesiastical power from political power. This was true everywhere, as the reverberations of the Protestant Reformation would demonstrate in the sixteenth century.

2.5 Economy and Society

There was enough money in the country over these centuries to support thriving towns and multiple religious houses and to wage intermittent war; both Gaelic-Irish and Anglo-Norman for the earlier part of this period lived in a state of sporadic attack and defence. Despite serious setbacks such as the great European famine of 1315–1318 and the outbursts of plague in that century, the Irish economy flourished in these years.

Tillage farming was not new to Ireland but the Anglo-Norman manor, or estate system, commercialized it more than ever before, as did the Cistercian order wherever it settled. Cereal production became far more widespread. Rabbits and game birds like pheasants were introduced, and there were forty deer parks in Ireland by the thirteenth century, with a new breed of deer introduced from Britain. Monasteries also developed institutional and inland fisheries, for their own fast days and for sale, bringing bream, carp, perch and other fish from Britain.

Not all trade was from monasteries; they were just part-players in a thriving economy. Animal hides were exported to Flanders and Italy, wool to Bristol and Lisbon, linen and timber were also sent long distances and there was great demand in England not only for Irish horses but for Irish hawks for falconry, a popular sport among the gentry. Trade with Spain and France was particularly important for Galway, Dingle, Cork, Waterford and other ports on the south and west coasts, and Gascony was a popular destination for Irish wool and hides in particular.

Out in the country, as in the town, people lived mainly in wooden houses. The ring fort died out by the eleventh century. People's relationship to the land and their overlords depended on whether they were Gaelic-Irish or Anglo-Norman. Bondage to the land was introduced by the invaders but it did not survive the labour shortages of the fourteenth century, although there were still serfs on the lands of the Archbishop of Dublin in the early sixteenth century. A *biatach* or middling tenant could live fairly comfortably and independently, with a few beasts, a few acres and a surplus for sale.

One great stimulus to agricultural production was the growth and development of towns, and it was after the Norman invasion that the major urban development happened away from the major ports. Town charters and town governance gave a solid administrative basis to these developments. Nearly all of the new Norman towns were south and east of an imaginary line from Inishowen to Galway (the exceptions were Sligo, Ballinrobe and Galway city itself), and south of an imaginary line from Carlingford (one of the Norman-founded towns) to Galway. There were very few Norman towns in Ulster, except for Carrickfergus in Co. Antrim and Newry, on the borders of Down and Armagh. Older settlements like Waterford, Limerick, Cork and, of course, Dublin, were developed by the newcomers and Kilkenny, one of the foremost Norman towns, was built on the site of the church of Canice, whose life had spanned the sixth and seventh centuries (*Cill Chainnigh*). Defence against the Gaelic-Irish was the reason for large fortified castles built in the early thirteenth century in key settlements like Trim, Limerick and Carrickfergus, but the walls in smaller towns like Kilmallock and Athenry which developed over the following centuries were more of a signal of these towns' ambitions to be places of consequence that traders had to pay to enter. Fairs and markets soon evolved and tradesmen's guilds set standards for work and forming rules of entry. Small towns had the food-processing trades of baker, miller and brewer, and there were also tailors, shoemakers, carpenters and masons and smiths. Luxury trades like goldsmith were in the bigger towns.

Anglo-Saxon and Scandinavian coins had been in very limited circulation up to now, but the Anglo-Normans established a royal mint in Dublin not long after their arrival, and soon coins were in common circulation, although exchanging eggs and butter and other agricultural produce for shop goods would be a common practice for many small farming people right down to the twentieth century. Under the reign of Edward IV in 1461, coins were issued with St Patrick on them. The Statutes of Kilkenny (1366) forbade Anglo-Normans from trading with the Gaelic-Irish, but this was largely ignored. Many towns developed an 'Irishtown', sometimes outside the walls, sometimes within them, as in Limerick city and Athlone, and the houses there were not notably smaller or meaner than those in the 'English town', though they were a bit more crowded together. Houses in towns were two or three stories high, built on 'burgages' – plots of land held from the local authority – mainly of wood, though stone began to be used in the fifteenth century. Some towns developed specializations. Waterford had a shipbuilding industry up to the fifteenth century. Sligo throve on the fortunes of the herring fisheries, which made fortunes for many north-western merchants, and ensured good livelihoods for others, until the shoals deserted these shores for Newfoundland around 1500.

Standards of living improved for all classes, with greater use of linen clothing; when mendicant monks wore scratchy woollen underwear next to the skin, it was for penitential reasons. House furnishings depended upon income and situation, but inventories or wills from the period show that even ordinary tradesmen like cobblers could possess some precious metals and fabrics. Richer landowners and merchants had linen, silver and jewellery, brocade from Byzantium, silks from the Middle East. Wine had been a key import since the coming of Christianity and wine importers in towns on the Atlantic route (especially Waterford) grew very prosperous as wine became popular for non-liturgical consumption. Home-brewed ale, or broth or fruit juices were the comfort drinks for those who could not afford wine. It was around this time that 'sowens', a drink from soaked or fermented oats or barley or other grain chaff, originated, and it would remain popular as a refreshing drink for workers on farm and bog until the late twentieth century. Milk and butter remained cornerstones of the diet, although cheese was produced mainly by monasteries, as a portable protein for monks going on working parties to outlying farms. (Cheese was rendered suitable for fast days by rennet developed from nettles.) Among the populace at large there were several different kinds of breads, flat and risen, and many porridges and broths made from different grains and legumes which provided much-needed bulk.

The fourteenth century brought devastation to Ireland, as well as to Europe, with the famine of 1315–1318 (aggravated in Ireland by the disruption of the Bruce invasion) and the Black Death of 1348–1349, which broke out again in the 1360s and 1370s. Dublin's population shrank to about 8,000 (from 12,000 in the twelfth century). The labour shortage was grievous but there was quicker recovery in Ireland than elsewhere because of the comparatively low level of urbanization and the ready adoption of nomadic pastoralism, or the 'creaght' system, of driving herds from place to place. People accustomed to making a living on bad or indifferent land cope better with adversity than those who take good land for granted.

Fortification was important from the very beginning, and before they could build their castles (which took time), the early Anglo-Normans dug themselves into temporary motte and bailey structures. These were artificial elevations topped by wooden watchtowers, surrounded by walled settlements. The Leinster landscape, in particular, is dotted with the traces of these settlements, and there is one at the old monastic site of Clonard, in Meath. The castles of the early settlement (thirteenth century) were large, elaborate constructions – King John's Castle in Limerick is a perfect example of this, (Figure 2.1) Trim in Co. Meath another. Slightly smaller castles were built in the thirteenth and fourteenth centuries, and the most common kind of castle, however, was the so-called tower house built from the early fourteenth century. This was given a boost in the fifteenth century after King Henry VI in 1429, in one of his periodic bouts of nervousness about Ireland, made grants of £10 available to Anglo-Norman families for this very purpose. Though some Gaelic-Irish magnates built similar castles, tower houses were most common in the Norman-settled areas of the country, and few and far between in the Gaelic-controlled Ulster. The ruins of these castles dot the rural landscape of Munster, Leinster and Connacht. In their own time they were surrounded on at least one side by large 'bawns' or enclosed areas, sometimes with gatehouses. The ground floors might have been used for storage and livestock. The walls were plastered and painted and often lined with wooden panelling, the upper floors were where fires were lit, probably in summer and winter, there would have had to be plenty of woollen blankets, and hides to sit and sleep on. No doubt, as in the dwellings of the poor, everyone clustered together for warmth in one room on winter evenings, bedding down on straw and hides before the fire rather than retreating to chilly chambers. (Figure 2.2).

FIGURE 2.2 Pallas, Tynagh, Co. Galway. Built by the Burkes in the fifteenth century and taken over by the Cromwellian Nugents in the seventeenth century, this is a strikingly well-preserved example of a tower house built by minor nobles in the late medieval period.

2.6 Conclusion

The Anglo-Normans and the Gaelic-Irish remained two distinct groups throughout these centuries. They married each other, certainly, but intermarriage does not neutralize political tensions, as the experience of many royal European dynasties shows. When they banded together against a common foe, as they frequently did in the fifteenth century, that foe was usually an amalgam of other Anglo-Norman and Gaelic-Irish interests, or one English royal faction in opposition to another. They believed in the same God and held to the same articles of faith, but they did not always worship in the same churches or serve alongside each other in religious communities, parishes or cathedral chapters. Pope John XXII excommunicated all those involved in the Bruce invasion; papal authority usually weighed in on the side of the Anglo-Normans.

Yet it would be a mistake to describe them as parallel peoples; rather than two tracks running alongside, the Gaelic-Irish and the Anglo-Normans were a tangle of lines of two different colours intersecting and merging and cutting across each other, but always identifiable. The two groups had developed, despite their differences, a common culture to enable them to do this.

The fourteenth century saw a resurgence not only of Gaelic-Irish political power but of cultural life as well. English was spoken in Dublin and the counties surrounding it, in the towns on the southern coast and it was understood in far western towns like Galway and Dingle by the fifteenth century (as was Spanish, among the merchant classes), but Irish was still the spoken language of the country as a whole, urban and rural, and even the

Crown's representatives in Dublin had to understand it. A new reading public grew up among the elite Gaelic-Irish and Anglo-Norman. Irish had been written down since the sixth century, and now, Marco Polo's travels, Arthurian romances and classical literature, as well as devotional classics like Thomas à Kempis' *The Imitation of Christ* (early fifteenth century) were translated into Irish, as were Bede's history of England and even Gerald of Wales's notoriously negative eleventh century description of Ireland. These books were in the libraries of Anglo-Norman as well as Gaelic-Irish families. Many Anglo-Norman nobles had *filidhe* on their payroll, and supported Irish bardic schools. The Irish-language poet *Gearóid Iarla* (Earl Garrett), the 3rd Earl of Desmond, who died in 1398, had trained under Gofraid Ó Dálaigh, a Master Poet of Munster. The Butlers of Ormond were loyal to the Crown and hostile to the earls of Kildare, but this did not prevent them from supporting brehon lawyers and Irish-language poets – Edmund Butler was involved with the production of a Gaelic-Irish manuscript emanating from Cashel the mid-fifteenth century. Some poems in Irish around the same period are attributed to his relative Richard Butler.

The Anglo-Normans also helped to preserve traces of the Irish past, including the ornate, storytelling high-crosses of the sixth and seventh centuries, of which more survive in areas heavily settled by Anglo-Normans, for example in Monasterboice, Moone, Kells. They also, like the Gaelic-Irish, commissioned replicas of these monuments. Early medieval manuscripts were delicate things, and had to be carefully curated. The powerful of both ethnicities not only did not destroy but actively worked to preserve the early medieval genealogies and law texts, and were directly or indirectly involved in the production of many other manuscripts – the Roches Book of Fermoy, the Book of Lismore, the Lebar Brecc and the Book of Ballymote, for example, produced in the late fourteenth and early fifteenth centuries.

It can be argued, therefore, that a distinctive Irish identity made up of various cultural influences existed by the time Henry VIII proclaimed himself king of Ireland in 1541. *Gearóid Mór*, the Great Earl of Kildare, and his immediate heirs established themselves as quasi-rulers of Ireland by the early sixteenth century because they embodied this fusion of Anglo-Norman and Gaelic-Irish culture. Although they always had the Ormonds (who also fused the two cultures) snapping at their heels, the Kildares did not fall because they were too blinded by greatness to read the writing on the wall, or because they identified too closely with native Irish culture, or because they antagonized important people. They fell because of seismic events in England and on the continent, which will be discussed in the next chapter.

3
Wars

~

From Silken Thomas's Rebellion to the Penal Laws,
1534–1704

3.1 Introduction

At the time of Silken Thomas's rebellion, the lords and chiefs who commanded the allegiance of most Irish people were able to mount formidable opposition to the Crown's nervous representatives who were based mainly in Dublin or the Pale. By 1704, few, if any, of the descendants of those earlier leaders wielded any political power at all, and England had brought the entire island, as far west as the Galway island of Inisbofin, under its control.

The sixteenth and seventeenth centuries also brought changes in how the inhabitants of Ireland saw themselves. The descendants of the twelfth-century conquerors, referred to up to now in this history as Anglo-Normans, became known as the Old English, in contrast to the *New English* who represented the interests of Henry VIII and his successors. With some exceptions, most of the Old English remained Catholic and nearly all the New English were Protestant. Ulster, from the early seventeenth century, was settled by English and Scottish Protestants. The Old English and Gaelic-Irish looked to Rome for guidance, and to France and Spain for practical help, while the New English and all settlers looked mainly to England and Scotland, although European alliances would become much more complicated for both sides in the late seventeenth-century Williamite wars.

3.2 Political Developments, 1534–1704

Henry VII had allowed Lord Kildare, *Gearóid Mór*, to govern Ireland for him. Henry VIII was content for a while to work with *Gearóid Mór*'s son *Gearóid Óg*, (Young Gerald) now Lord Kildare, and declared his intention in 1521 to follow his father's example and deal diplomatically with the Irish. However, when the Pope refused to annul Henry's marriage to Catherine of Aragon to allow him to marry Anne Boleyn in the late 1520s, the king was facing a constitutional crisis and the last thing he needed was political challenge in Ireland. And challenges there were. Many Irish lords and chiefs were alarmed at the king's challenge to the Pope. The earls of Desmond were talking to Francis I of France and Charles V in the late 1520s, who were bitter rivals fighting for supremacy in Italy. The O'Mores, O'Carrolls and O'Connors in Laois and Offaly were challenging the Crown, and *Gearóid Óg*/Lord Kildare, in and out of royal favour throughout this decade, was drawing closer to the Desmonds. Piers Butler, Earl of Ormond, who was deputy (which is what the Crown's representative in Ireland was now called) at intervals throughout the 1520s, could not bring Desmond under control. Henry appointed a number of Englishmen to the Irish deputyship, when he was appointing himself head of the English Church and surrounding himself with loyal supporters. Then he reappointed Kildare as deputy in 1532, but Butler of Ormond, Sir William Skeffington (a previous deputy) and others were sending worrying reports to Henry – Kildare was stockpiling royal weaponry, and there was widespread disquiet in Ireland about Henry's definitive break with Rome, which was announced in 1533. Kildare was called to London in that year, leaving his son Thomas ('Silken Thomas'), Lord Offaly, as Lord Justice. The announcement that Kildare was to be replaced as deputy and the fear that he would be (or had been) executed was the trigger for Silken Thomas's rebellion. For an opening salvo, he denounced the king as a heretic. All of the Kildare Pale supporters joined him, the Desmonds in Munster joined in July, as did the O'Neills, MacMorroughs, O'Mores, O'Connors and O'Byrnes, from Ulster and Leinster, and even though Skeffington arrived with an army in October of that year, the rebels held out until August 1535, until Maynooth castle fell to the Crown. Silken Thomas and five of his uncles were brought to London and executed in 1537. This caused some bitterness in Ireland, but most others who took part in the rebellion were pardoned, because Henry had not completely abandoned his plan to deal reasonably (as he saw it) with the Irish.

But first he had to justify his right to deal with the Irish at all. The initial permission for the English invasion of Ireland in the twelfth century had been granted by Pope Adrian IV, but now that the English Crown had thrown off the Pope's authority, this authority was null. The Irish parliament met in Dublin in 1541 and passed an act recognizing Henry as king of Ireland. But Henry also recognized that Irish lords and chiefs of both ethnicities were a slumbering threat, and so he decided to extend the titles of English aristocracy to all Gaelic-Irish leaders in

Ireland. (The Anglo-Normans, or Old English, already had such titles.) The fact that this scheme existed at all shows how eager the Crown was to placate these leaders. Under 'Surrender and Regrant', as it became known, the O'Neills, the dominant dynasty in Ulster for almost a millennium, became earls of Tyrone, the O'Donnells, earls of Tyrconnel (Donegal), the O'Briens, earls of Thomond, the O'Mores, earls of Leix, the McCarthys, earls of Clancarty, and so on. This put the Gaelic-Irish chiefs on an equal legal footing with the Old English, as the latter could no longer claim to be more favourable to, or favoured by, the Crown.

There had been talk of putting English settlers into Leix/Laois and Offaly, ever since the disturbances of the 1520s by the O'Mores and O'Connors, and the kidnapping of Lord Delvin, the deputy, in 1528. Plantation was mooted again in 1546, so the two families, along with the Desmonds (who were still talking to France, and now, to Scotland as well), rose up against the Crown and, when the rebellion was swiftly put down, the midlanders' lands were forfeit and thus began the first of the Tudor-Stuart plantations. Two fortress towns were built, one at Maryborough (now Portlaoise) in Leix, and one at Philipstown (now Dangan) in Offaly. The territory of Leix was shired into Queen's County and Offaly, King's County. The settlers were to be English, and to maintain armed men. Thus began a pattern that was to become familiar – rumours of plantation provoking rebellion which was savagely put down, rebels punished by the confiscation of the land, and English or Scottish people put in charge and in place.

During the reigns of Mary and Elizabeth (1553–1603) Ireland was described, studied, scrutinized and examined as never before, and an unprecedented number of Crown representatives, military and civil, traversed the country. As well as officials, there were adventurers, many of them second sons of English nobles, eager for territory of their own. One of them was Peter Carew whose assertions of title to lands in Leinster and Munster gave rise to tensions even among those who had conformed to the Protestant faith; a short-lived revolt against his incursions by the Earl of Desmond in 1569 was supported by Ormond, (who had converted to Protestantism) in 1569–1570. Papal and Spanish promises of help encouraged a drawing together of Gaelic-Irish and Old English (though Kildare remained aloof) in the Munster or Desmond Rebellion of 1579–1580. On the Dingle peninsula in Kerry a Spanish force landed at Smerwick in 1579 and was massacred by Crown forces, and although fighting was fierce throughout the three south-western counties, one by one the Desmond castles at Youghal, Askeaton, Kilmallock and other Munster locales surrendered and the Crown forces prevailed. The fighting wrought huge destruction on south Munster in particular, bringing devastation and famine and decimating the native population; the survivors are described by poet Edmund Spenser as ghostlike creatures barely glimpsed in the woodlands and fields. The Munster plantation, begun in the 1580s and complete by 1622, settled 18,000 English people in Munster. Some were farmers and artisans from south-west England, but most were landowners, because there were not enough English immigrants to make up the base of the social pyramid. For the most part, the land continued to be worked by the native inhabitants. The 400-year-old Desmond lordship had already developed farming on the manor system, and many thriving market towns had evolved, so half of the planters' work was done already. The justification for conquest was that the Irish (including the Old English) were all barbarous, and potential Catholic conspirators into the bargain. There was some justification for the latter view. The Pope, and Spain, sent significant military aid to the Munster rebels, and Pope Pius V had issued a bull, *Regnans in Execlsis* condemning Queen Elizabeth in 1570.

Therefore, when Hugh O'Neill, Earl of Tyrone, assumed leadership in the Nine Years' War (1594–1603) against England, he was able to invoke both faith and fatherland. (Figure 3.1) The rebellion broke out initially because of a threatened reorganization of lordship boundaries in Ulster and a fear that the earls' authority would be undermined as had happened in Leinster and Munster.

FIGURE 3.1 Hugh O'Neill (c. 1550–1616). This detail is from a fresco in the Vatican from 1610 by Giovanni Batista Ricci and depicts the fled Earl of Tyrone at a papal ceremony two years earlier. His departure and that of O'Donnell, left the way clear for the Ulster plantation.

O'Neill joined in rebellion with Red Hugh O'Donnell (Earl of Tyrconnell) and Hugh Maguire of south Ulster. The Desmonds rose up in Munster, and the McWilliam Burkes in Connacht, but it was the Gaelic-Irish, not the Old English, who were the leaders in this serious challenge to English power. O'Neill and O'Donnell mustered a modern, efficient army for the gunpowder age. Well provisioned and disciplined, it was not only superior in number to the Crown forces but had the advantage of knowing the terrain. The Crown forces under Lord Bagenal suffered heavy defeat at Ballyshannon in 1597 and, more devastatingly, at the Battle of the Yellow Ford in 1598. The fighting gave the Crown forces excuses to carry out massacres of the non-combatant Ulster Irish, which made subsequent plantation all the easier. The ongoing rising in Munster managed to tie down another English army, under the Earl of Essex. There were also uprisings in south Connacht, and in Carlow and Kilkenny, where Ormond just about managed to keep control for the Crown. Meanwhile a Spanish army of 3,400 under Don Juan del Aguila, sent by Philip III from Spain, landed in Kinsale at Christmas 1601; O'Neill and O'Donnell marched south with their armies to meet it. The battle over the next few days was a decisive victory for the English, although after the battle they lost half of their misfortunate soldiery from hunger, cold and sickness.

It was this close shave, the ongoing expense of the Irish wars, and the prospect of a succession crisis after the death of the queen that made the terms offered to Hugh O'Neill by Lord Mountjoy (by now the deputy) at Mellifont, Co. Louth, in 1603 so generous. Mellifont was chosen because it was on the northern edge of the Pale. Despite having openly rebelled and received aid from a power hostile to England, O'Neill and O'Donnell were allowed to retain their lordships of Tyrone and Tyrconnell respectively. Elizabeth was dead between the time the treaty was drawn up and its being signed, and her successor, the first Stuart monarch, son of Mary Queen of Scots, James VI of Scotland, James I of England, was a more thorough conqueror than any Tudor. He enforced vigorously the Acts of Supremacy and Uniformity, imposing fines and forfeitures on 'recusants' (Catholics who refused to become Protestant), and pouncing on any prominent Catholics suspected of treason. Conor O'Devany, Catholic bishop of Down and Connor, along with one of his priests, was hanged, drawn and quartered in Dublin in 1612 on suspicion of having helped Hugh O'Neill, but really because he was a vocal Catholic ecclesiastic.

Where James really made his mark, however, was with the Ulster plantation. The pretext for this was 'the Flight of the Earls' – the swift departure from Lough Swilly in Donegal of O'Neill/Tyrone and O'Donnell/Tyrconnell, Hugh Maguire and others who had taken part in the Nine Years' War, in 1607. Were the earls fleeing to Spain to organize a force to return in triumph to reclaim Ireland from the English, or were they just fleeing? In the event, bad weather prevented them from landing in Spain and they had to go first to Normandy and then to Flanders (a Spanish possession) and, from there, some went to Rome. Thus ended the millennium-long dominance of the O'Neills over Ulster. Their departure was viewed as treason, their lands were confiscated by the Crown, and some of their relatives imprisoned. A small, rash revolt by Cahir O'Doherty in Donegal in 1608, quickly put down, supplied further justification for more extreme government intervention in the Gaelic-Irish-dominated north, and more lands were confiscated for the coming plantation.

The Ulster plantation began in 1610 and gave four million acres of land in Donegal, Fermanagh, Armagh, Tyrone, Cavan and around the city of Derry, and Coleraine (these county boundaries will be explained later) to some English but mostly Scottish settlers, who numbered 34,000 by 1635. Almost all planters were of the reformed faith. This plantation was the most successful of all, because Crown forces had massacred and evicted so many of the native population during the Nine Years' War. A minority of Irish Catholic natives stayed on as small farmers and labourers, with landholdings on hills and wetlands, and a small minority of large Catholic landowners kept their lands. But from then on, the population of eastern and midlands Ulster was predominantly Protestant. By 1640 Protestants predominated in northeast Donegal, south Antrim, the Ards Peninsula, the Lower Bann and the Clogher valley. Coasts and river valleys were mostly Protestant but much of rural mid-Ulster remained Catholic, especially land distant from a market town. Although the settlers got the better land, this was not always good land. In 1642 acreage in Ulster was rated of lower value than acreage in any other province of Ireland, even Connacht. Nonetheless, Protestant farmers and tradesmen were invariably better-off than the Catholics they displaced. (Map 3.1)

Although it met only rarely – four times between 1543 and 1613, compared to twenty meetings of the English parliament in the same period – there was still, in the early

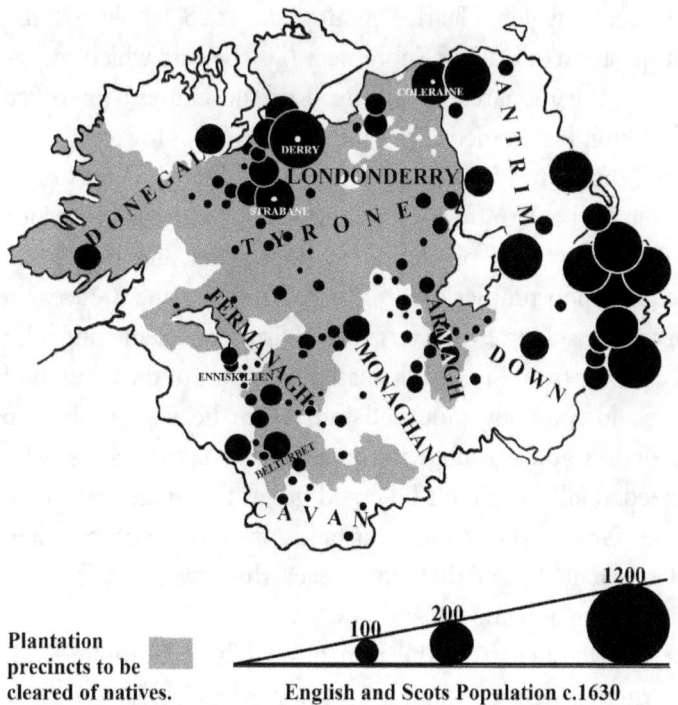

MAP 3.1 The pattern of English-Scottish settlement in Ulster, 1609–1641. By Pádraig Lenihan. The settlers took the better land and the land nearest to ports and long-established towns, for trade and security reasons. The native inhabitants were never completely cleared out.

seventeenth century, a parliament in Dublin, made up of Lords and Commons, and Catholics still made up about half of the total membership. They insisted that they could be loyal to the king without becoming Protestants. The new king, Charles I, from 1625, did not want to antagonize Catholics – his wife, Henrietta Maria of France, was one, and furthermore, he was embroiled in political tangles on the continent in a way that James had not been. The

'Graces', which Charles granted in 1628, abolished the imposition of Oath of Supremacy (i.e. the oath which recognized the monarch as the head of the church) for office holding, legal practice or land inheritance. However, 1633 saw the arrival in Ireland of deputy Thomas Wentworth, later Earl of Strafford. This energetic deputy had plans for everything from plantation to poor relief, but he was an equal-opportunities oppressor, abolishing the Graces in 1536, attacking Presbyterians in Ulster, and removing a lot of power from the Dublin-based members of the Church of Ireland. Nobody mourned him when he was recalled to London and executed for treason in 1641. Charles, who needed all the friends he could get at this stage, regranted the Graces the same year and promised not to plant Connacht, but at that stage, everything was changing, in both England and Ireland.

In October 1641 the remaining Ulster Catholic landowners Phelim O'Neill, Connor Maguire, and others, aided by Rory O'More in Kildare, began a rebellion. Professing loyalty to the king, they had some success in Ulster but their plot to seize Dublin Castle was foiled. In Ulster, the long-simmering resentment and anger of the dispossessed Catholics found expression in a series of brutal massacres and evictions, of around 3,000 Protestant men, women and children. These events became a foundational memory of Protestant Ulster identity. The months which followed saw similar, smaller-scale massacres all over the country, Protestant-on-Catholic in Louth, Meath, Kildare and Tipperary, and Catholic-on- Protestant in Cork, Tipperary and parts of Ulster.

The Civil War in England between King Charles and his republican opponents provided Catholic political leaders in

Ireland with a golden opportunity to portray themselves both as supporters of the king and upholders of the Catholic interest in Ireland. A provisional government of Old English and Gaelic-Irish, known as the Confederate Catholics of Ireland, met for the first time in Kilkenny in 1642. (Figure 3.2) Its disciplined and well-equipped armies were divided according to province between Old English and Gaelic-Irish – Eoghan Rua/Red Hugh O'Neill (nephew of the fled Lord Tyrone) commanded Ulster, Garret Barry (a veteran of the Spanish Netherland wars) was in charge of Munster, Thomas Preston, also Old

FIGURE 3.2 Rothe House, Kilkenny. A typical sixteenth-century urban house (of which very few have survived), this was the headquarters of the Confederate Catholic army of the 1640s.

English, was in charge of Leinster and John Burke, another continental veteran, led Connacht. Charles appointed the ever-loyal Butler of Ormond deputy in 1643, and both looked favourably upon the Confederates. However, Giovanni Battista Rinuccini, the Papal Nuncio who arrived in 1645, urged the rejection of a treaty with the Protestant Ormond and the Crown in 1646, and forced the Confederates further away from any Protestant alliances. Meanwhile, the parliamentarians (who were opposed to the king) made Morrough O'Brien, Lord Inchiquin – Gaelic-Irish but a Protestant – Lord President of Munster and Charles Coote, Lord President of Connacht.

The Catholic Confederation won some important victories especially in 1646 at Benburb, in Tyrone and fought on numerous fronts – against Monro's Scottish army in the north, against Inchiquin in Munster, and against the parliamentary army under Jones, in Leinster. But the English and Scottish were better-resourced with men and ammunition and they just kept coming. The fighting and negotiations continued until 1649, when the Confederates became divided among themselves and demoralized, unsure whether to accept the king's offers of alliance or not. The execution of the king in 1649 shocked everybody. The parliamentarians at this stage believed they had won the English Civil War definitively and decisively, and turned their attention westward.

Oliver Cromwell, leader of the parliamentarians, landed in Dublin in 1649. His forces massacred the garrison and many inhabitants of Drogheda and then made their bloody progress through the towns of Leinster and Munster, leaving their mark on Wexford, Kilkenny and Clonmel in particular. Cromwell departed in May 1650, leaving his son-in-law, Henry Ireton, in charge, and by 1652 the Cromwellian defeat of Irish forces was fully accomplished. Up to 20 per cent of the Irish population was lost between 1649 and 1654, mainly through famine, plague and other epidemic disease, though some were killed by fighting and massacres. Some 34,000 Catholic men fled to Spain to fight in their armies, and 12,000 people, many of them the homeless poor, but some priests also, were transported to Barbados.

While a tiny minority of Catholic lords and gentry who had not taken part in the wars of the 1640s managed to hold onto land, any who had supported the Confederacy, actively or passively, in Munster, Leinster or Ulster – about 44,000 in number – were forced by the Act of Settlement (1652) to surrender their lands and to go to Connacht and Clare. The poet Feardorcha Ó Mealláin compared the Cromwellian transplantation of landowners to Connacht to the banishment of the Israelites to Egypt in '*An Díbirt go Connachta*' (The Exile to Connacht) in the 1650s: '*Má ghoirthear dhaoibhse Páipis | cuiridh fáilte re bhur ngairm*' (If they call you Papishes | Welcome it as your title).

While the people of little or no property – labourers, smallholders, tradespeople – suffered from the food shortages, pestilences and religious oppression, they were not sent across the Shannon, unless they volunteered to accompany their landlords as servants or chief tenants. They were needed in Munster and Leinster to work the land for the new owners, former officers of the Parliamentarian army who could not have expected similar rewards in England.

The monarchy was restored to England in 1660, but few Catholics got their lands back. There were no Catholics in the Irish House of Commons and very few in the Lords. The few powerful Catholics were divided on whether they should recognize the authority of the (Protestant) king. Laws against Catholic practice were relaxed, only to be strengthened again in 1673, but meanwhile, Catholics practised openly, although they still paid tithes to Protestant clergy. The execution of Archbishop of Armagh Oliver Plunkett in Tyburn in 1681 and the death in prison of Dublin archbishop Peter Talbot (who had been once part of Charles II's inner circle) did not happen simply *because* these two men were papist prelates – the usual 'popish plot' was suspected – but their fates illustrate how shaky Catholic power was.

The accession to the English throne of Charles's Catholic brother, James II, in 1685 was a false dawn for the Irish Catholic interest. He appointed Richard Talbot (brother of Peter), Earl of Tyrconnell, as the first Catholic deputy of Ireland for a century, and Talbot/Tyrconnell set about creating a mostly Catholic army in Ireland and disbanding Protestant militias. Some Catholic chapels were reconsecrated, and the Declaration of Indulgence to Catholics in 1687, along with the promise to restore lands, gave great hope. Nor had the Church of Ireland anything to fear, because it was not going to be disestablished. But James was not popular among many of the Protestant English, and in 1688 William of Orange, married to James's Protestant sister Mary, arrived in England and ousted him. James fled first to France, and thence to Ireland, which represented his last chance to take back his throne.

The Williamite wars, as they were called, were the most decisive and bloodiest in Irish history and they lasted as long as they did because they were a sideshow in a wider European war where all sides (including the Papacy) were ranged against France's Louis XIV, who sent material help including generals Lauzun and St Ruth to the Jacobites (followers of King James). The Irish armies were strong, with the advantage of knowing the territory, but William of Orange fielded the largest army which ever fought on Irish soil, made up of British, Dutch, Danish, and a sprinkling of other nationalities. The siege of Derry was a defeat for the Jacobites, as was the Battle of the Boyne in July 1690, after which James II left the country in a panic. However, the following month Jacobite leader Patrick Sarsfield and his forces managed to hold off the Williamites at Limerick having first destroyed much of their ammunition in a daring raid at Ballyneety, south-east of the city. William's superior power won out in the long run, and the Jacobites were decisively defeated at Aughrim, Co. Galway in 1691. The Treaty of Limerick, later that year (1691) offered generous terms to James's Irish supporters and to Catholics generally. The officers and commanders of Jacobite armies, including Sarsfield, were allowed to go abroad. But the promises of religious toleration made by the treaty were broken in 1697 by a Protestant Irish parliament, ushering in over a century of oppression of the majority, Catholics, by the minority, Protestants.

And why were Protestants still a minority? With all the resources the English Crown had at its disposal, why did the Reformation not succeed in Ireland?

3.3 Religion, 1534–1704

3.3.1 *Catholics*

Although opposition to Henry VIII's declaring himself head of the Church was the pretext for Silken Thomas's rebellion, many Irish secular clergy conformed to the Established Church in the years that followed. Under Henry, the Mass was still in Latin, the Consecration was still at the heart of it and the other sacraments, including Confession, remained, and therefore many Catholics might not have noticed a great difference at first. Eight bishops and two archbishops (those of Cashel and Tuam) took the Oath of Supremacy, as did many canons of cathedrals and other prominent churches. This was how St Patrick's and Christchurch in Dublin, St Mary's in Limerick, St Nicholas's in Galway and most of Ireland's oldest places of worship, came under the authority of the Church of Ireland where they remain to this day. Monks and nuns had their communities broken up and their property confiscated in the dissolution of the monasteries in 1536–1541, and Protestants and Catholics alike helped themselves greedily. The O'Neills seized many of the Ulster monasteries and the Old English Barnewall family did well out of Dublin houses. Perhaps many religious communities had, as their critics claimed, become more like businesses than spiritual sanctuaries, but their destruction wiped out centuries of hard-won institutional expertise in everything from animal husbandry to medicine. The mendicant friars, particularly the Franciscans and Dominicans, who had never depended on extensive lands and businesses, managed to survive under the patronage of rich Old English and Gaelic-Irish families, and with the ongoing support of the people. Nuns, more dependent upon patronage because they did not administer the sacraments, found it harder to bounce back. However, the Poor Clares, from an original foundation on Merchants' Quay in Dublin, managed to build an extensive network of convents in the 1630s and 1640s, and the Dominican nuns established their first Irish female community in Galway (where many of the wealthy were still Catholic) in 1644. This was while the Confederate wars were in full swing, and it shows how normal civic life could continue unimpeded during a conflict – for a while, at least.

Meanwhile, going back to the sixteenth century, Elizabeth's reign introduced far-reaching liturgical changes which brought the Established Church closer to the reformed churches on the continent. At the same time the Catholic or Counter-Reformation was getting into its stride. Irish seminaries for secular clergy were established abroad, from about 1560, in Salamanca, Paris, Douai, Bordeaux, Lisbon, Compostella, Louvain, Antwerp, Lille and Rome. Aspirant priests learnt all about the reforms of the Council of Trent (1545–1563) and hurried home to implement them. The Jesuits, founded in Spain earlier in the century, arrived in Ireland in 1542 and by the end of the sixteenth century had Latin schools preparing boys for the seminary in Limerick, Kilkenny, Youghal, Cork, and other towns. The mendicant friars also came under continental influence in their European novitiates. In 1605 James I tried to prevent these newly trained priests from returning to Ireland, with little success. Despite more stringent imposition of fines for 'Catholic practice', 'mass-houses' were still packed every Sunday throughout the country. Catholics were baptized, married and buried with Catholic rites, although they paid fees for these rites to the Church of Ireland (as well as to their Catholic pastors). Despite this double levy, most Catholics remained Catholic. Puzzled Protestants sometimes attributed this loyalty to peer pressure. But one reason was that no serious attempt was ever made to evangelize Irish Catholics.

In the sixteenth century there were no Protestant teaching materials available in Irish, still the language spoken by most people. The invigorated Reformation of the 1590s used many clergy trained in England, not trusting the old ex-Catholic (many of them Irish-speaking) conforming clergy and their successors. After the founding of Ireland's first university, Trinity College in Dublin, in 1592, more Protestant clergy were educated in Ireland, but in English. Irish translations of the *Book of Common Prayer*, and the Old and New Testaments, appeared in the reigns of James I and Charles I, but many Protestant clergy did not know enough Irish to use them. There were exceptions, like the much-loved (by Catholics as well as Protestants) Bishop Bedell of Down and Connor who died in 1641, who translated the New Testament into Irish. But in general, the promotion of the English language and of Protestantism went hand-in-hand.

The most vicious attacks on Catholic personnel and practice came during Cromwell's time. Priests and bishops were hunted down and at least sixty were hanged or murdered on the spot. Gender or geographical remoteness were no protection; two female members of the Dominican Third Order, Honoria Burke and Honoria Magean, were hacked to death by Cromwellians in Burrishoole, Co. Mayo, in 1653. Outraged at female freedom from domesticity, the Cromwellians ordered every nun to marry or leave the kingdom. Some nuns went to Spain, some adopted civilian dress and went underground. This was the era of the hunted priest (£5 reward for every one caught), Mass said in the open air with large rocks as altars and look-outs posted, and the desecration by soldiers of sacred places and images. The haunting song *'An raibh tú ag an gcarraig'* (Were You at the (Mass) Rock), a hymn to the forbidden Eucharist disguised as a love song, dates from this time. The bishops survived, and even managed to hold synods in Tuam and Armagh in the slightly more relaxed atmosphere of 1658–1660, and some monks trickled back in the 1660s and 1670s when the Restoration seemed to promise much. But the fates of Plunkett and Talbot, mentioned earlier, were an ominous sign of greater oppression in the offing.

3.3.2 *Protestants: Church of Ireland, Presbyterians, Baptists and the Society of Friends/Quakers*

The Church of Ireland, also called the Established Church, formed its own identity early on, with the adoption of Twelve Articles of Faith in 1567, as opposed to the Thirty-Nine Articles of the Church of England. In 1570 free diocesan grammar schools (in English) were set up in all the major towns, and in 1592 Trinity College in Dublin was founded as a seminary. In the 1620s the Protestant archbishop of Armagh, James Ussher, traced the origins of the Church of Ireland to St Patrick, whose pure Irish church, he argued, was later corrupted by Rome. Church of Ireland communities were mainly in the larger towns and cities, but there were rural dwellers scattered throughout Leinster and Munster in particular – in Wexford, Kilkenny, Cork, north Tipperary and, of course, in Ulster, although in that province Presbyterianism posed a serious challenge to the Established Church.

In 1672 Presbyterians made up over half of all Irish Protestants. As Dissenters, they were looked upon with suspicion by the Established Church. The first Baptist church in Ireland was set up in Cork in 1640, much smaller than the Presbyterians, this denomination nonetheless added to the rich tapestry of non-conforming Protestant religions. The Society of Friends, also known as the Quakers, were a small but growing group of Dissenters from the 1650s, operating mainly in the midlands and numbering about 3,000 by the end of the seventeenth century.

3.3.3 Administration, Economy and Society, 1534–1704

The process of shiring, begun in the thirteenth century, was completed in this period, when the county boundaries as we know them today were laid out. King's County and Queen's County – modern day Offaly and Laois – were created by Queen Mary, and by 1620 the counties of Longford, Westmeath, Clare, Galway, Sligo, Mayo, Leitrim, Armagh, Monaghan, Tyrone, Donegal, Fermanagh, Cavan and Wicklow were mapped out, as was a county of Coleraine, which would later be absorbed into Londonderry. (Map 4.1) The Highways Act of 1614 enabled the building of new roads, bridges, passes across bogs and through mountains, and causeways. Many forests – barriers to roadways, cover for runaways and political outlaws – were cut down. Urbanization continued and new towns were built by planters especially in Munster and Ulster – Tralee, Killarney, Mallow, Charleville, Bandon, Derry, Belfast, Enniskillen, Dungannon, and many more. The Quakers built Mountmellick in

Queen's County. Hundreds of licences to hold urban markets were granted between 1600 and 1649.

Irish exports remained what they had always been – wool, hides, tallow, wood, fish, and trading was still with the nearest neighbour, but also with other countries on the busy sea-roads, such as France, Spain and the Low Countries. Live cattle were exported to Britain until the Cattle Acts of 1663 and 1667, but even after this ceased, the provisions trade remained lively, especially in meat and dairy produce. Textile weaving took off in the north-east, in Dublin's hinterland and around Waterford. Timber production from all those destroyed forests was buoyant, particularly in the Blackwater valley (mid-to-west Cork). The Lord President of Connacht, Charles Coote set up ironworks in Roscommon and Leitrim at which over 2,000 were employed, in the 1650s.

People still ate mainly grain, along with pulses and dairy products. Oats and rye grew west of the Shannon and in the north, wheat in the Pale, barley in the sunny south-east. The potato, first recorded in Ireland in 1600, spread to Cork and Waterford by the mid seventeenth century as quick-witted smallholders worked out that they could live on it and sell their dairy produce and animal products, but it was still not common fare in Ireland by 1691. French soldiers at the Battle of the Boyne complained bitterly about the mixed-grain bread (barley and rye) they were given to eat, which was probably still the staple carbohydrate throughout most of the island. Had they ventured south-west, their discerning palates would have been beguiled by the quality of the dairy produce. Munster remained the heartland of dairying, more importantly than ever with the growth of towns. The south-east, mid-Leinster and eastern Ulster was the heartland of tillage. Pasture farming (sheep and cattle) was best suited to the uneven terrain and uncertain climate of the western midlands, much of Ulster and west Munster, and 'booleying' – the building of temporary dwellings on summer pastures – was common.

Sometimes observers mistook these primitive booley houses for permanent dwellings and were shocked. But many of the permanent dwellings of farmers and labourers at this time were sturdily built mud cabins with chimneys and windows, which could be as warm, dry and clean as the income and energy of their inhabitants allowed. The growth of towns boosted agricultural production and a new prosperous farmer, the *'scológ'* emerged. Changes brought in by the upper and middle classes often 'filtered down' to all who could afford them – individual plates and bowls instead of communal dishes, wooden trenchers (bases for meals) instead of coarse bread, chairs instead of benches, curtains, canopies and sectioned-off areas in one-roomed or two-roomed dwellings. Women of all classes but the very poor left each other household linen and tableware in their wills. The growth of towns meant that more consumer goods were available. If the potato was slow to take off, that other New World product, tobacco, was not. Brian MacGiolla Pádraig (1580–1652), a poet who became vicar-general of Ossory and would die at the hands of Cromwell's forces, complained in the 1630s (when he had little to worry him) about people walking around with *'a stoc tobac 'na chlab dá lánstéideadh'* (tobacco pipes in their jaws at full blow), in *'Faisean Chláir Éibhear'* (Fashions on Eibhear's Plains). Complaints about fancily dressed working-class or farming people, in every era a reliable indicator of elite unease at improving living standards, also emanated from other parts of the country, in both languages.

Women's earning capacity and control of money probably increased over this period, especially where there was dairying, so much of which (milking, churning, feeding calves) is women's work. Women were also the chief vendors of dairy produce, eggs and vegetables at the ever-growing number of markets. Men sold beasts at fairs. Under English common law women's inheritance rights were greatly improved, when they had anything to inherit, that is. Apart from those measurable changes, we can only pick bits of evidence here and there about women's lives. Some nuns managed to survive living discreetly in small groups with the support of the wider community. Wealthy Catholic women were patrons of Catholic priests and scholars. Protestantism's emphasis on domestic evangelization meant that girls of all classes were taught – as a priority – to read the Bible. Women in the new Society of Friends/Quakers enjoyed at least a nominal equality with men.

Among political personages, *Gráinne Ní Mháille*/Grace O'Malley, whose life span is almost identical to that of Elizabeth I (both died in 1603), leader of a branch of the O'Malleys from west Mayo, stands out. She was exceptional, although her career, like those of the two Tudor queens, shows that leadership could occasionally be exercised by women in extraordinary circumstances. But on both islands throughout this period, nearly all political actors, and certainly all government and office-holders and civil servants, were male.

The widespread famines and diseases that followed the Desmond Rebellion in 1580, the demands made by armies on all sides in the Nine Years' War, the harvest crises 1637–1640, bubonic plague intensifying the end-point of the wars of the 1640s and the Cromwellian invasion, and, in the 1690s, poor harvests all over Europe exacerbated in Ireland by the Williamite wars – all affected the economy, although recovery was quick, especially in the 1690s. Ireland's population doubled, going from one million in 1600 to two million in 1700, and these were not all planters. Dublin grew its population from 5,000 in 1600 to 62,000 a hundred years later, emerging as the second-largest city of the two islands.

The seventeenth-century Irish-language poets who complained about fancy clothes and smoking also complained about the bad English and scorn for the Irish language of those inevitable social intermediaries, shopkeepers and servants. English was the language not only of conquest but of administration, service and, increasingly, commerce in some urban areas. It was also the language in which Ireland was described, sometimes soberly and kindly, sometimes sensationally, by Edmund Spenser, Fynes Morison, Richard Stanihurst and John Davies, among others.

A sense that the language was in danger was one of the reasons for the flowering of Irish scholarship in this century. Bonaventure O'Hussey, a Franciscan, published his *Caibidil Críostaí* (Irish Catechism) in Irish in Louvain in 1608, and an Irish grammar some years later. Geoffrey Keating's *Foras Feasa ar Eirinn* (Encyclopaedia of Ireland) appeared in 1634 as a history of Ireland from the earliest times. The *Annals of the Four Masters*, a compilation of history from various manuscript sources, was completed in the 1630s by four scholars, one of whom was the

Franciscan brother, Micheál Ó Cléirigh, who had trained in Louvain. As well as using (and thereby preserving) older historical sources, the *Foras Feasa* and *Annals* argued that a distinct Irish identity was rooted in generations of scholarship, spirituality and civility. This identity included those of Anglo-Norman/Old English stock; Geoffrey Keating's name was Gaelicized as Céitinn, but it was a Norman one.

There were also popular Irish-language poets, such as Aodh Mac Aingil, Dáibhí Ó Bruadair, Pádraigín Haicéad and Tadhg Rua Ó Conchúir, who wrote not only of politics, but of manners and morals, people and places, love and loss. Their poems were written down, but passed into the oral tradition and were sung or recited around firesides and at social gatherings, by people of all social classes, from the elite to the landless. Irish was still the primary language not only of communication but of enlightenment and entertainment.

3.4 Conclusion

One of the Irish Travellers' origin theories is that they were put on the road during the Tudor and Stuart plantations. Modern Irish Travellers are all Catholic (by ancestry) and their Gaelic-Irish, Anglo-Norman and pre-Reformation English surnames can also be found among Irish non-Travellers (McCarthy, Ward, Sweeney, Joyce, McDonagh, Power, Sheridan, Stokes, Moorhouse, and many more). It is almost certain that some of those thrown off their land by the tens of thousands of English and Scottish settlers over two centuries did not find alternative landholdings. Travellers' antecedents might have been displaced at one remove, by slightly better-off Irish tenants who had been displaced themselves. All Traveller families to this day identify strongly with certain localities, which supports this theory.

They were not the only people on the move in those grim times. '*Bhí mé anuraidh in arm is in éide | Ach tá mé i mbliana ag iarraidh déirce*' (Last year I was armed and in uniform | But this year I am begging), says the *saighdiúir bocht*/poor soldier from '*airm Rí Shéamuis* [King James's army]', in the ballad '*Slán le Pádraig Sairséal*' (Goodbye to Patrick Sarsfield). Tens of thousands of brothers, sons, husbands and sweethearts from these islands and further afield were slain in battle or died of camp disease in summer and cold and hunger in winter, or were demobilized to beg their bread like the *saighdiúir bocht*. The women who accompanied every army as cooks, nurses and cleaners added to the numbers on the move.

From 1534 to 1691, Anglo-Norman/Old English and Gaelic-Irish drew nearer to each other, religious identity trumped 'ethnic' origin, and alliances were forged with Catholic powers in Europe. But although the term 'Irish' was used by O'Neill's forces in the Nine Years' War, the Confederate Catholics in the 1640s and those who fought William's forces in the wars of the early 1690s, no group or individual aspired to political independence. O'Neill and O'Donnell offered the Irish Crown (in the event of success) to Philip II's nephew, the Confederate Catholics of the 1640s half-supported Charles I, and for a long time after 1691 the defeated Irish placed all their hope in the '*rí thar chaladh*' (the king across the water), James II and his descendants.

4
Peace?

~

Ireland's Short Eighteenth Century, 1704–1791

4.1 Introduction

Ireland in this short eighteenth century was ruled over and administered by those elected and selected from 10 per cent of the population. The remaining 90 per cent – mostly Catholic, with some non-Church of Ireland Protestants – were kept out of politics and public life by the Penal Laws, which must be explained before any other aspect of Irish life in this century is understood.

4.2 The Penal Laws

The Williamite–Jacobite wars of 1689–1691 were Protestant–Catholic ones and the Catholics lost. The Catholic political and military leaders and soldiers (about 20,000 of them, romantically known as the Wild Geese) left the country, mainly for France and Spain, after the Treaty of Limerick. However, there were still many potential Catholic leaders in Ireland, landowners who had somehow held on to land, lawyers, bishops and priests. The Penal Laws ensured that no military challenge could be mounted by Catholics against the government by first of all, in the 1690s, forbidding Catholics from bearing arms or from owning a horse (or horses) worth more than £5 (i.e. of cavalry quality). Since 1691, denying the pope's authority and other fundamental tenets of the Catholic faith had been a qualification for sitting in parliament; added to this was the requirement that all who sat in parliament take 'the sacramental test', that is, receive Communion in the Established Church. This excluded not only Catholics, but Dissenting Protestants who did not belong to the Church of Ireland – Presbyterians, Baptists, Quakers and, from 1752 when their first chapel was set up in Dublin, Methodists. The rule applied to all who held public office of any kind – magistrates, members of corporations, grand juries (elected bodies who administered county affairs), coroners, sheriffs, and so on, and to the legal profession. Catholics and Dissenters alike had to pay tithes to the Church of Ireland. In 1728 Catholics were formally deprived of the parliamentary vote. The vote was tied to property-owning and only around 5 per cent of Protestant males qualified for it. Catholics, whose overall share of wealth was substantially less than that of Protestants, made up an even smaller proportion of the electorate, but it was nonetheless deemed important to exclude them formally.

Many eighteenth-century European states insisted that all in positions of authority adhere to the religion of the monarch. In most countries where this conformity was imposed, however, the monarch's religion was that of the majority of the population. In Ireland, 80 per cent of the population were Catholics and about half of the remaining 20 per cent of Protestants were Dissenters. But the Penal Laws did not stop at political representation and public office, and some were aimed at Catholics in particular.

Catholics were not allowed to buy land, and Catholic landowners were obliged to divide their land among all of their heirs instead of passing it on intact to one heir (thus breaking up large estates). This ensured that the share of land in the country owned by Catholics shrank from 14 per cent in 1703 to 5 per cent in the 1770s. (In 1641 Catholics had owned 59 per cent of the land, already a significant drop on their earlier share of ownership.) Catholics were also barred from the learned professions, though some who had qualified earlier continued to practice into the 1730s. As tenants, Catholics could not take leases of more than thirty-one years, while Protestant tenants' leases could endure for three generations.

Parliamentary engagement was for the rich and well connected, the professions were often (though not always) the preserve of the privileged, the laws on ownership of land affected the comfortably-off, and those on leaseholding affected mostly bigger farmers. But rich and poor alike were baptized, confirmed, anointed and buried, which is why the laws against Catholic practice were the most widely experienced – and bitterly remembered – of all penal legislation. In 1697 all Catholic bishops and regular clergy (monks in religious orders) were ordered to leave the country, and in 1704 it was enacted that there could be only one secular priest per parish, and that he must register with the local authority. The ban on continental-trained clergy returning to Ireland was to ensure that these priests would not be replaced when they died (there was no Catholic seminary in Ireland). Catholic schools were prohibited, pilgrimages were outlawed and Catholic places of worship were limited in number. Strident pamphleteers who called for more extreme measures, for example, for all Catholics to be banished from urban areas and all unregistered priests to be castrated (!) were ignored by legislators and deplored by liberal Protestants, but added to the atmosphere of intimidation and persecution. Mechanisms of enforcement were few, but priest-hunters existed and had to be rewarded when they found their quarries, as they sometimes did in the early decades.

Yet, in 1731 Ireland had 1,700 Catholic priests, 892 'Mass-houses' and 549 Catholic schools, nearly every diocese had a bishop, and many regular clergy had returned from the continent. This happened because the laws against practice were not regularly and consistently enforced, but also because Catholic bishops and clergy went very quietly about their business. The threat of prosecution was always there, and anti-clerical laws were applied whenever it suited the authorities to do so. In the 1730s suspicion about a 'Pretender' plot led to the arrest in 1739 of Bishop Michael MacDonagh of Kilmore and the Dominican provincial John Fottrell, and, when they escaped, £200 was offered for their capture. Catholics learned to evade attention in many different ways; one book of Catholic devotions published in Kilkenny in 1762 gave its place of publication as Cologne. 'Mass-houses' were in backstreets and often called by street names rather than those of the saints to whom they were dedicated; the Franciscan Church on Merchant's Quay in Dublin is still known today as 'Adam and Eve's', after the name of the eighteenth-century tavern in which the friars said Mass. Catholics, even rich ones, were nervous. When Nano Nagle, (Figure 4.1) from a landowning Catholic family, set up her free schools for boys and girls in Cork city in 1754, she faced strong opposition from her brother Joseph.

FIGURE 4.1 Nano Nagle (1718–1784). From an unattributed portrait: by kind permission of the Presentation Union, Monasterevan, Co. Kildare. The most influential woman in eighteenth-century Ireland, Nagle defied the Penal Laws by setting up free schools for Catholic boys and girls in Cork city from the 1750s, and the sisterhood she founded in 1775 became, after her death, the Presentation order, one of the most widely distributed Irish teaching congregations in the nineteenth and twentieth centuries.

He had good reason to be nervous because, twenty years earlier, their uncle, also Joseph Nagle, who had qualified as a lawyer before Catholics were banned from doing so, had had his offices raided and his livelihood threatened in the same 'Pretender' panic that led to the arrests of the bishop and priest mentioned previously. Anti-Catholic feeling found vicious expression at times of social and political tension. In 1766, when rural agitation was giving the authorities some headaches, Fr Nicholas Sheehy, an outspoken Tipperary priest, was hanged, drawn and quartered on very little evidence, for the alleged murder of a Whiteboy informer two years earlier.

Catholicism survived because of the money and personnel provided by propertied and landed Catholics, like the aforementioned Nagles, the Mathews, Blakes, Martins, O'Connells, Herberts, Lords Fingal and Kenmare, and others throughout the country. Some wealthy Catholic individuals converted strategically to Protestantism so as to advantage their Catholic kin. But the faith would never have survived without the moral and financial support of Catholics of all classes, and the periodic relaxation of legislation over the two and a half centuries of repression. Monks, and to a much lesser extent, nuns, went quiet but they never went away. The history of one friary gives an idea of how religious foundations survived. The Franciscans came to Multyfarnham, Co. Westmeath, in 1238 as part of the great mendicant friar movement. Their house was dissolved in 1540, but revived in 1555, and survived as a community despite four attacks in the following eighty years. Fully restored in 1641, it was destroyed again by Cromwell's forces. The monks then retreated to ordinary houses in the community but maintained a presence in the community with a small, unobtrusive oratory, returning to the friary site in the early nineteenth century.

Catholics were, however, completely excluded from politics, law and administration until 1791.

4.3 Politics

The heirs of the Williamite/Protestant victory so successfully crushed Jacobites/Catholics that the latter could not even mount a concerted opposition outside parliament.

This should have made for a peaceful parliament where all agreed on the basics, but it did not. Until its abolition in 1800, the Irish parliament was riven by the tension between those who were happy to accept English domination over Irish affairs, and those who were not. As early as 1699, William Molyneux's pamphlet *The Case of Ireland ... Stated* argued strongly for Irish (Protestant) control over what happened in Ireland. So the culture of complaint was well established long before the hotly resented Declaratory Act of 1720 (also called the Sixth of George I) decreed that all laws passed in Ireland had to be referred to the English parliament for approval. Not long after this, there was controversy when the contract for small-denomination Irish coinage was given to a Wolverhampton mint operated by William Wood, rather than to an Irish firm. The 'Wood's Halfpence' furore caused the opinionated Jonathan Swift, Dean of St Patrick's Cathedral, to write *Drapier's Letters* (1724) in the voice of a discontented Irish tradesman; this was only one of many protest publications to appear at this time. Eventually the English government relented and awarded the contract to an Irish mint.

For most of this century, when Irish Protestants referred to the Irish 'nation' they meant the Protestant (i.e. Church of Ireland), politically active nation, and those who opposed England's domination used words like 'slave' and 'helot' to describe the Irish Protestant political position. Although some Protestants in the 1720s and 1730s like Edward Synge, bishop of Elphin and George Berkeley, bishop of Cloyne, and Swift, were uneasy about the Penal Laws, it would take a later generation of Protestants to extend the definition of 'slave' to those who neither voted nor sat in parliament – Catholics and Dissenters.

The House of Lords was made up of Protestant peers and Protestant bishops. The eleven Catholic lords and viscounts who had managed to survive the confiscations were excluded from it. The House of Commons was made up mainly of landowners and higher professionals; merchants and businessmen were in a minority. All belonged to the Church of Ireland.

The parliament sat for six months every two years, from 1732 in the magnificent new houses of parliament in College Green. The king's representative, or viceroy, had his headquarters a five-minute walk away, in Dublin Castle, though no doubt he travelled in a ceremonial carriage for the brief journey. Except for a brief tenure by James Butler, Duke of Ormond, 1710–1714, the eighteenth-century viceroy (or Lord Lieutenant) was always an Englishman who only came to Ireland for the six months when parliament was in session. This clear indication of his purpose in Ireland – to oversee parliamentary business and nothing else – aroused anger among those who insisted on Ireland's right to govern itself. The viceroy sat in neither house of parliament but he had supporters there, derisively known by their opponents as 'undertakers', who would try to ensure that business was transacted to his satisfaction. 'Undertakers' were not Englishmen inserted into Ireland, but Irishmen, like William Conolly, the Speaker of the House of Commons in the early decades (who was of Gaelic-Irish stock), and later in the century, Henry Boyle, Earl of Shannon.

Ireland had a certain amount of fiscal autonomy; its large revenue commission employed hundreds and the parliament had a lot of authority in spending. On the other hand, half of the British peacetime army was stationed in Ireland and the Irish parliament was responsible for the upkeep of barracks throughout the country. This was often resented, although the money spent by officers and men and their families undoubtedly benefitted garrison towns. The following decades saw some tensions and disagreements, but nothing too serious until the Money Bill Dispute 1751–1753, when the Irish parliament, despite the undertakers' best efforts, voted to keep Ireland's treasury surplus instead of sending it to England as they usually did. In the 1760s Henry Flood MP, a lawyer, emerged as the head of the 'patriots' – that is, those who insisted on Ireland's right to govern itself without reference to England, and argued for the lifting of trade restrictions brought in to protect English goods (particularly textiles and cattle) from Irish competition. The 'undertaker' system finally broke down after the viceroyalty of George Townshend, 1769–1773, who built up a strong support base by the judicious disbursement of the '3 Ps' – pensions, peerages and places (i.e. jobs) – among those who could be trusted to form a permanent 'Castle' party voting the way England wanted it to. From then on, it was the viceroy and his supporters versus the patriots. In the 1770s the patriot influence grew, especially under Henry Grattan, another lawyer and a powerful speaker. News of the American colonies breaking away from Britain excited patriots and alarmed their opponents. In 1778 the Volunteers were set up as a militia, ostensibly to protect Ireland from invasion by the French (there had been an attempt in 1760 in Antrim) but really as a show of patriot strength. Catholics were excluded from it because they were not allowed to bear arms, but elements in it were sympathetic to Catholic relief. It was Henry Grattan who argued that Irish Protestants could never be free while Irish Catholics were still 'slaves'. The constitution of 1782, often called 'Grattan's Parliament', repealed the Declaratory Act of 1720, modified Poynings' Law of 1494, and allowed the Irish parliament to regulate Irish trade, ending restrictions on a lot of Irish exports. The late 1770s and early 1780s also saw the repeal of most of the penal legislation on property, education and profession of faith; Catholics could now run schools, bishops and regular clergy were now allowed to reside in the country, and secular priests' registration took a more acceptable form. Irish confidence and optimism was at an all-time high. The House of Commons was still in the tight grip of John Beresford and John Fitzgibbon (Lord Clare), who were firmly opposed to reform of any kind, but their viewpoint was challenged more and more within parliament and outside it. Prominent Catholics had, up to this time, placed their trust in the English Crown, who had (from William of Orange onwards) always put a brake on the extreme penal legislation demanded by Irish Protestants. Now it looked as if deliverance could lie nearer home. There had been a Catholic Committee since 1756, quiet and deferential, made up of aristocrats like Lord Kenmare, but the political changes of the 1780s gave it new energy and hope, and a membership that extended far beyond landowners.

4.4 Economy and Society

Irish political economists worried all through the eighteenth century about the apparent lack of growth of the economy, and to discuss their theories and treatises would take a book in itself. The culprits as identified ranged from lazy or demoralized Catholics to greedy middlemen (landlords' agents) to idle or absent landowners, or all of these reasons taken together. Yet, despite the fiercely resented restrictions on the Irish cattle and wool trade imposed by England in the seventeenth century, the eighteenth-century Irish economy throve. Irish exports of provisions (salted beef and butter) remained strong and grain became such a lucrative export crop that many big and small farmers on suitable land found mixed farming (i.e. both livestock and tillage) increasingly profitable, especially from mid century. (Map 4.1)

The fact that the port towns were the fastest growing and liveliest urban centres indicates how important exports were. Cork firms got several naval contracts in the early years of the century, Waterford had a good market (and good fishing grounds) in Newfoundland, and Atlantic and continental sea-roads were as lively as ever. There was some industry, too, with coal mines in north Kilkenny at Castlecomer and north Roscommon at Arigna. There was textile production, mainly linen and wool in the earlier years, and later cotton. Although Armagh, Derry and Donegal dominated, textiles were produced throughout the country especially from the 1730s, and many villages in Munster and Leinster had their 'bawns' or bleaching-greens. Spinning, carding, weaving and knitting enabled many small farmers and

MAP 4.1 Irish counties after the shirings of the thirteenth and seventeenth centuries. Print Collector/Contributor/Hulton Archive/ Getty images. This map, from 1902, shows the county divisions of Ireland which were completed in the seventeenth century and which still exist in the twenty-first century as units of local government in independent Ireland.

Peace? Ireland's Short Eighteenth Century, 1704–1791

labourers to survive, providing cash for rent and, if they were lucky, for some of the increasing variety of consumer goods. The number of markets, already growing in the seventeenth century, rose again with pigs and poultry – usually reared by women – supplementing the traditional dairy produce. There were about 500 livestock fairs in the 1680s, and 3,000 in the 1770s. Flour and grain mills multiplied in the second half of the century, as farmers brought grain not only to sell, but to be milled for their own use and for animal fodder. Brewing also throve in tillage areas: Guinness's, founded in Dublin in 1759, was only one of many. Ironworks and sugar production all took off in this century, as did paper mills, to satisfy the demand from the ever-growing number of printers producing an ever-growing number of books, periodicals and magazines for an ever-growing reading public. By the 1780s there were eighty printers in Dublin alone, and printing presses in most towns and cities.

The 5,000 or so Protestant landowning families on the top of society – nobility, politicians and bishops – were massively wealthy. Archbishop King of Dublin, by no means the richest, was prepared to pay up to £400 (about £33,000 in today's money) for a set of silver plates in the early years of the century, as long as they were made in Ireland. Buy-Irish patriotism originated among the Protestant elite in this century and the buyers were not fussy about the religion of the manufacturers and tradespeople. Builders and all associated trades were thriving throughout the country; the huge mansion at Carton in Maynooth was built by the Duke of Leinster in 1745, but more typical of the gentry houses was the solid and substantial Damer House in Roscrea, Co. Tipperary. (Figure 4.2)

FIGURE 4.2 Damer House, Roscrea, Co. Tipperary. Epics/Hulton Archive/Getty images. Built by John Damer in 1728, this is a good example of a three-storey, unadorned (pre-Palladian) but still substantial gentry house in eighteenth-century Ireland.

The elaboration of household furniture and ware kept carpenters, cabinetmakers, wallpaper-stainers, glaziers, upholsterers, silversmiths and goldsmiths busy: many of the latter supplied ecclesiastical plate to the Church of Ireland, and on the quiet, to the Catholic Church. Jewellers made clocks, ever more popular not only as ornaments, but as timekeepers, as businesses and banks (the Bank of Ireland was founded in 1782) began to keep more regular hours. Those who did not have to work had set hours for the consumption of the popular New World drugs, tea, coffee and chocolate (always a beverage). For the decorative serving of these drinks, china was imported, but there were home-grown potters too. Tailors and dressmakers used Irish wool, linen, poplin and frieze, and imported silks and cambrics. Stays, used mainly to support muscles weakened by childbearing, were gradually adopted by all women who could afford them – Hugh Kelly, later an actor and playwright in mid eighteenth-century London, began his working life as a Dublin staymaker. The male fashion for wearing wigs had begun in the previous century and in the eighteenth century it was expected that all men who presented themselves for public view in urban settings (or who appeared in positions of authority in any setting) would wear them.

Most shopping still took place at stalls and markets, but the end of the century saw a rise in stationary retail establishments with fixed pricing and select entry for customers. All of this industrial and commercial activity was made possible by improved transport networks. Turnpike roads began to be built in the 1730s, and another phase of road building followed thirty years later. The Duke of Leinster in the 1760s, allowed his carters five hours to get from Carton House in Maynooth, Co. Kildare, to his town house Leinster House, in the newly built Kildare St, in Dublin. By 1800, however, the road trip from Dublin to Cork could be achieved in twenty-four hours, and there were twelve coach destinations out of Dublin. The Grand Canal, linking Dublin to the Shannon, was begun in 1779, the Royal Canal, which went in a north-western direction from the capital, in 1790 but neither of these waterways was open to traffic until the early nineteenth century.

Catholics and Dissenters, unable to practise politics and, in the case of Catholics forbidden from investing in land, went into business and many made good money in trade. John Smithwick, founder of the famous Kilkenny brewery in 1710, was a Catholic. Quaker families such as the Odlums, Shackletons and Goodbodys, went into flour milling. The wealthiest merchants and traders were still more likely to be Protestants from the Established Church than Catholics or Dissenters, but Catholics in particular, in every port town, continued to use the national and international trade connections they had developed over generations. A third of Waterford's merchant families were Catholic in the 1770s. More than 10,000 Presbyterians, however, mainly tradesmen from Ulster and their families, took themselves to the American colonies in the earlier part of the century in search of religious tolerance and better economic opportunities. They would settle in the southeastern states and become known as 'Scotch-Irish'.

Income and geographical location (accessibility of markets and shops) determined standards of living and comfort. Everyone with produce to sell – women at markets, men at fairs – got to the town regularly and saw what was for sale and what the 'quality' were wearing, eating, drinking. Upper-class complaints about the fancy fabrics and shoes worn by the poor in Co. Monaghan in the 1760s show that improving living standards filtered to all classes. Prosperous farmers were building good houses in some parts of the country; the thatched farm-house Edmund Ignatius Rice (born in 1762) grew up in, in Callan, Co. Kilkenny, had four bedrooms, a kitchen, a parlour and a hallway. Eíbhlín Dhubh Ní Chonaill's lengthy lament for her husband Art O'Leary, who was murdered in 1773, describes the comfortable home he provided for her – white parlours, painted walls, ovens plural, featherbeds, servants to wait on her.

With all this business and hard work, it is easy to overlook the poor. In the 1790s one-third of the population had annual incomes of between £5 and £20, that is, on a spectrum from persistent poverty to cautious comfort. And these were boom times everywhere, not typical of the century as a whole. The frost famine of 1739–1741 is a more telling indicator of comparative wealth and poverty. Severe frosts in the winter of 1739–1740 were followed by summer drought and then by another severe winter; the potato harvest was low, thawed stored potatoes were inedible, and the grain harvest was also badly affected – animals died from want of fodder. It is estimated that between 310,000 and 480,000 people (out of a population of 2.4 million) died of hunger and of the virulent diseases that resulted from social upheaval – smallpox, dysentery, typhus. Yet those who died were not necessarily the poorest on the worst land, but those (especially in the dairying heartlands of Munster) whose integration into the market economy had led to their dependence on the potato for everyday consumption. Urban working-class people were hard-hit, too, by high prices charged by unscrupulous farmers and merchants. What the frost famine illustrated was the vulnerability of even normally well-doing propertyless people. This mortality of about 13–20 per cent of the population was proportionately greater than that caused by the Great Famine a century later.

4.5 Language and Culture

English was the language of parliament, politics, philosophy and polemics; it was the language of the law, of administration, of schooling and sedition, of pleas for Catholic relief and arguments against it. English was commonly the language of settlers, too, although in Munster and in Ulster many spoke or at least understood Irish. Ninety per cent of the population of Munster and Connacht were Irish speaking in the 1770s, especially in the small towns and rural areas, but Irish was still spoken in rural Meath and Louth and parts of Kildare too. In Dublin city the percentage of Irish-speakers was somewhere between 10 per cent and 19 per cent – one Dominican chapel in Dublin had to have a sermon in Irish at one of its two Sunday masses in 1761. In Cork city, between 40 and 49 per cent of the population spoke Irish and, in Kilkenny city, between 30 and 39 per cent did.

There was very little printed work in Irish in the eighteenth century. Fr Donlevy's bilingual *Catechism* in 1762 was one, and there were a small number of devotional works too. The famous Irish poems and songs of the eighteenth century, although originally written down by the poets themselves, were learned and transmitted orally. The most famous had explicit references to the Stuarts: Aodhagán Ó Rathaille's *An Aisling* (The Vision) and *Mac an Cheannaí* (Son of the Merchant (or Redeemer)), Eoghan Ruadh Ó Súilleabháin's *Ceo Draíochta* (Magic Mist) and Art MacCubhthaigh's *Úirchill an Chreagáin* (The Creggan Graveyard), and Piaras MacGearailt's *Rosc Catha na Mumhan* (The Battle Cry of Munster), all invoke the 'Pretender', sometimes by name. Popular also were invective-packed verses cursing oppressive middlemen, landlords or process-servers, as in Mayo poet Riocaird Bairéad's sarcastic *Eoghan Cóir* (John the Just), about a rapacious land agent in the 1780s. Although the Irish language might have 'hidden' their seditious verse from the ruling classes, these poets did not inhabit a Gaelic underground. They moved with ease between two worlds. Ó Rathaille, born into a prosperous farming family on the Cork–Kerry border around 1675, had fluent English, and made his living as a teacher of Latin and Greek, and a labourer. Ó Súilleabháin, born in 1748, was also a teacher and labourer, and while serving in the British navy was involved in a victorious battle with the French in the Caribbean, after which he wrote a heroic ballad in English, for his commanding officer, Admiral Rodney. Donncha Rua MacConmara's *Bánchnoic Éireann Ó* (The Fair Hills of Ireland), was written while he was sailing between Waterford and Newfoundland, or perhaps on the busy sea-road between Ireland and Hamburg; a teacher and sometime fisherman, he died in 1810 aged ninety-five. The subject matter was not always political or historical, and all the poets mentioned earlier, and many others not mentioned, wrote about love and bereavement and other personal matters, and praised good, generous people – not invariably their patrons, either. Seán Ó Tuama and Aindrias MacCraith, based around the Maigue river in Croom, Co. Limerick, their lives spanning the length of the century, were both known as 'merry' and light-hearted. There was also humour in Clareman Brian Merriman's ribald yet lyrical *Cúirt an Mheáin Oíche* (The Midnight Court), where love-starved women arraign men on the charge of not marrying. Merriman, a farmer and teacher of mathematics, died in 1810. There were laments for good people gone, commissioned by families, or written from the heart by the bereaved. The dominant note in Eíbhlín Dubh Ní Chonaill's haunting lament for her dead husband *Caoineadh Art Uí Laoghaire* (Lament for Art O'Leary) is personal rather than political, though politics comes into it. O'Leary, a captain in the Hungarian Hussars (like many upper-middle-class Catholics he held a commission in a European army) was murdered by a Protestant (in Ireland) in a dispute over a horse.

There were also prolific writers in the English language. Jonathan Swift's polemical writings have already been mentioned, and his *Gulliver's Travels* (1726) was relished both as satire and as fantasy. George Berkeley's *Querist*, published 1735–1737, was a three-volume compendium of knowledge in a question-and-answer format. Other Protestant and Dissenter divines such as John Abernethy in the early part of the century and Francis Hutcheson in the 1730s were early fathers of 'New Light' Presbyterianism. Charles O'Conor, of the famous Connacht high-king family, who wrote his *Dissertations on the antient history of Ireland* in 1753 was a collector of old manuscripts and also, wrote in favour of Catholic relief. Another supporter of Catholic relief was Edmund Burke, who was related to the Nagle family mentioned previously, an MP in the English parliament from the 1760s to the 1790s, and a brilliant polemicist. But there was more than political commentary, theology and satire. Dublin was a theatrical hub, and playhouses were set up in most cities during this period – Belfast, Cork, Limerick, Waterford, Galway – while smaller towns set up temporary theatres for touring companies. Actors and playwrights abounded, and most successful were the Sheridan family of novelists and dramatists – parents Thomas, who managed the Theatre Royal in Dublin, and Frances (who wrote a novel *The Memoir of Miss Sydney Biddulph* in 1761), and son Richard Brinsley, born in 1751, who based himself in England and wrote mainly on English themes. His most successful play, *The Rivals*, 1775, gave the word 'malapropism' to the language and popularized the 'stage-Irishman', Sir Lucius O'Trigger, an excitable Protestant 'squireen'. Twenty years Richard Brinsley's senior was Oliver Goldsmith, (Figure 4.3) a clergyman's son from Co. Longford, whose play *She Stoops to Conquer* was a great success. Goldsmith loved Ireland, but all his literary works, including his one novel, *The Vicar of Wakefield* (1766), are set in England. However, Longford people insist that the 'Sweet Auburn, parent of the blissful hour' of his *The Deserted Village* (1770) is Lissoy, the village between Athlone and Ballymahon where he spent most of his childhood. The verse of the poem about the village schoolmaster

FIGURE 4.3 Oliver Goldsmith (1728–1774). Getty images.
A clergyman's son from Longford/Westmeath, Goldsmith was journalist, novelist, playwright and poet, celebrated on both islands; his 'Deserted Village' would become a beloved staple of Irish anthologies.

was a beloved staple of twentieth-century school poetry anthologies, especially the lines about the local men listening to the 'master' discoursing on various topics: 'And still they gazed, and still the wonder grew | That one small head could carry all he knew.'

The respect for learning gently mocked by Goldsmith was an Irish trait of long-standing, and one that, by the eighteenth century, came to be shared by many of settler stock. Henry Flood left a sum of money in his will for the establishment of an Irish-language chair in Trinity College and collected many Irish manuscripts. William Crawford, a Presbyterian minister in Tyrone, wrote a two-volume *History of Ireland* in 1783 with a strong cultural-nationalist bent. Charlotte Brooke, daughter of author Henry Brooke (a Protestant novelist who called for a relaxation of the Penal Laws) learned Irish and collected many Irish songs and poems from Irish speakers, which she published in translation in *Reliques of Irish Poetry* in 1789. Like the author Maria Edgeworth, who lived with her clergyman father in Co. Longford, Brooke had those advantages crucial to women's intellectual development in the days when they were barred from universities: access to an extensive domestic library, and sympathetic fathers.

4.6 Women

Katherine Conolly, wife of Speaker William Conolly, was a powerful hostess and wielded, like all such women, the kind of 'soft' political influence it is impossible to measure and to record. She was also a philanthropist, employing local labour to build an elaborate obelisk during the bad times of 1740–1741, and a very distinctive granary. Other female names which have come down to us from the eighteenth century – Mary Delany, Dorothea Herbert – were not well known in their own time but the documents they left behind give an insight into the lively, if narrow, social spheres they inhabited.

While wealth had obvious advantages for women, it could be dangerous. 'Abduction' of heiresses was more common here than in other countries, because of tensions around landowning and, perhaps also, because of the remoteness from law and order of many big houses. The woman or girl (at least one was as young as thirteen, but widows were also at risk) would be kidnapped by the prospective 'husband' and his friends, raped, and then forced to submit to a marriage ceremony carried out by an unscrupulous or unfrocked priest or clergyman. A law of 1707 made this a capital offence, but not all cases were brought to trial, because there was shame involved for the victim who had no further utility as a suitable marriage prospect.

But, luckily for them, most women were not heiresses. Marriage for women at any level below the servant-employing classes, in the farming, labouring, trade and even the growing clerical/administrative classes, involved ceaseless work. Despite the frost famine at mid century, the Irish population rose from 2.4 million in 1750 to nearly 4.5 million in 1800, with the biggest increase in the poorer classes. Population increase does not just 'happen'; successful childbearing and child-rearing involves hard physical work and wear and tear, and continuous vigilance. Most women combined physical and cultural reproduction with food provision and preparation, dwelling-maintenance, and, at this particular period, the textile work which drove population growth by enabling early and almost universal marriage among the non-propertied classes. And what about their children? When infant mortality statistics began to be collected in the late nineteenth century, the figures for rural Ireland were between a third and a half of those of towns and cities. This could be also true of the late eighteenth century, although the relentless work of spinning and smallholding maintenance which drove the rising population might also have reduced Irish mothers' ability to care for young babies, as it did in other European countries towards the end of the eighteenth century when infant mortality soared. Still, marriage for females at age twenty or twenty-one among the poorer classes, which made for a twenty- to twenty-five-year childbearing period, ensured that enough children survived to grow up and have children themselves.

Not all women married, and it was not only the independent-minded daughters of the leisured classes who chose the single life. Domestic servants usually stayed single for as long as they remained in service. Prosperous female trades like dressmaker, glove-maker, lacemaker or mantua-maker (all in high demand during this century of ever-elaborate female *toilettes*) made marriage for economic reasons unnecessary. Teresa Mulally, an unmarried Dublin milliner, amassed enough resources to set up schools for Catholic children in George's Hill in Dublin in the 1770s; her associates eventually affiliated with Nano Nagle's Presentation order, but she never entered the religious life herself.

Only twelve or so convents survived the early Penal Laws, always in towns where Catholic merchants and wealthy people equalled or outnumbered Protestant – Dublin,

Galway and Drogheda, rather than Limerick or Cork. The Galway Dominican nuns, who had returned from Spain in 1685 after being exiled there during Cromwellian times, made two foundations, one in Dublin in 1717, and one in Drogheda in 1722. They, like the few scattered communities of Carmelites, Poor Clares and Augustinians, wore civilian clothes and did not advertise their presence. When Nano Nagle invited the French Ursulines to Cork in 1772 to take over the running of her schools, there was strong criticism from some Protestants in the city, even though these nuns were enclosed. It was this enclosure which caused problems for Nagle, leading her to set up her own sisterhood in 1775, the Sisters of the Charitable Instruction of the Sacred Heart of Jesus. Canonically recognized in 1802 as the Presentation Nuns, this was the first of the new, active female congregations which were to make such an impact on nineteenth- and twentieth-century Ireland.

4.7 Conclusion

Unlike England, Ireland had no established poor law, so provisions for the poor took the form of hospitals and charitable institutions. Dublin was well served with Jervis St hospital, Mercer's hospital, Dr Steeven's, the Meath, Sir Patrick Dun's and the Rotunda Lying-in Hospitals; in Cork there was the North Infirmary, and in Belfast (where there were fewer upper-class philanthropists) a charitable dispensary which would later become the Royal Victoria hospital. Images of eighteenth-century Ireland are usually dominated by Dublin's graceful public buildings – the houses of parliament on College Green, Leinster House, the Four Courts, the Customs House and elegant streetscapes of Georgian houses in Cork and Limerick as well as Dublin, but the philanthropic public institutions, some of which still operate as hospitals, were of far greater importance to the people as a whole. (Figure 4.4)

Most of the rich were Protestant, but not all Protestants (even all members of the Established Church) were rich, or even middle class, and while most of the poor were Catholic, there were not only the aforementioned wealthy Catholics but also middle-class Catholics in farming,

FIGURE 4.4 The Rotunda Lying-in Hospital, Dublin. Christopher Loh/Moment Unreleased/Getty images. Founded in 1745 by Dr Bartholomew Mosse as a charity lying-in hospital, this still serves the people of Dublin on its eighteenth-century site. It was one of many charitable hospitals set up in Ireland in this century.

business and trade. Literate Catholics and Protestants read the same newspapers and periodicals and books, which, by the last quarter of the century, reached the skilled working classes in the towns and the big-to-medium-sized farmers in the country. Catholics and Protestants of more or less equal economic status brushed up against each other quite often. In a light-hearted song from this era, '*Iníon an Phailitínigh*' (The Palatine's Daughter), a young woman from the settler (Protestant) Palatine community in Co. Limerick, after kissing the song's narrator, tells him: '*Má thréigeann tú an papaireacht, gheobhaidh tú mé le pósadh*' (If you abandon papistry, you'll get me as a bride). We are not told if the narrator took her up on her offer. What the song *does* tell us, is that in this region, Catholic and Protestant farming people moved in the same circles, meeting on a '*lá breá aoibhinn margaidh*' (a fine market day), which is when the song opens. This would have been true of most of Munster and Leinster and, of course, Ulster, though not Connacht, where there were far fewer middle-class or farming Protestants. Also, in most Irish-language songs and poems of this century, English speech is rendered *in English*, so perhaps the song, by putting Irish in the Palatine's mouth, also tells us that this second generation of settlers picked up enough Irish to flirt in, if nothing else.

Marriages between Catholics and Protestants happened, and Protestant and Catholic of roughly equivalent social standing also met often for sport and recreation. The fact that Catholics could not own horses of racing quality did not prevent them from betting at the Curragh, Galway, and other venues where horse racing was formalized from around the middle of the century. The lively traditional tunes 'The Rakes of Mallow' and 'The Bucks of

Oranmore' take their titles from the boisterous young gentlemen whose antics often shattered the peace of spa towns. Duelling was common among the Protestant and Catholic gentry; it – and its less lethal working-class equivalent, faction-fighting – was regularly condemned by clergy of all faiths.

Clergy also condemned another kind of violence: agrarian agitation. Fr Nicholas Sheehy's bishop was remembered with hatred in Tipperary over a century later for not trying to prevent his priest's execution for alleged complicity in these offences. From the 1760s, the Whiteboys in Munster and the Hearts of Oak (later Rightboys and Hearts of Steel, respectively) in Ulster, protested regularly against tithe, enclosures of land, rising rent, evictions and anything which made everyday rural and small-town life difficult for those without property. Usually tenant farmers (on the smaller side) and tradesmen, in the north they were Presbyterian, in the south, mainly Catholic. All men, they went out at night dressed in white bed sheets or women's clothing; they rarely killed anybody, but intimidated people, maimed livestock and injured offenders. Occasional accidental (or deliberate) murders were given the death penalty, but even the public hangings of several Steelboys in Carrickfergus in 1772 and Whiteboys in Clonmel in 1776 failed to stamp out this kind of protest. This kind of nocturnal rural redress of wrongs happened all over the world, but because Irish social inequalities were given added weight by the formal political exclusion of the protestors (as Catholics and Dissenters), and by tensions between Catholic and Protestant in certain parts of the country, everyday grievances were often expressed in sectarian terms and groups adopted sectarian identities.

Meanwhile a new kind of hybrid Irishness was emerging from a Protestant parliament which, by the 1780s, was offering a tentative and cautious welcome to Catholics, though many within it still strongly opposed any political concessions to those of the majority faith. Conservatives and liberals alike would be challenged by a new kind of Irish nationalist in the 1790s. A century before, Louis XIV of France had thrown his considerable weight behind the Catholic Irish/Jacobite interest, and in the 1790s the French would take a strong interest in Ireland again, though they would not be backed by, or support, any king, or indeed any religious faction, this time.

5
Construction and Destruction

~

War, Peace and Famine, 1791–1851

5.1 Introduction

Three new political ideologies emerged in these six decades. The republicanism of the 1790s demanded full separation from Britain. The Act of Union (with Great Britain) of 1800 gave a new name – unionism – to those who supported that political connection. Thirdly, Daniel O'Connell formed and led the first mass modern constitutional nationalist movement. These sixty years also saw the country's population rise sharply only to plummet dramatically, in the last decade.

5.2 The 1798 Rebellion and the Act of Union

From about the 1780s, there was something of a communications revolution in Ireland. Country people were coming into the towns or moving around the country to collect or deliver textile or garment work, to sell milk and eggs and beasts and corn, to hire labour or to be hired. Living and working conditions, urban and rural, encouraged not only earlier marriage, but greater sociability. In the towns, as workshops and retail outlets flourished, people met each other, on streets, at markets, in shops and public houses, in eating houses and the more genteel coffee houses in the bigger towns. Books and periodicals were bought and borrowed, newspapers were passed from hand to hand and read aloud.

People meeting like this talked about local news, the weather, family news, business and trade – but it is more than likely that, after 1789, the news from France came up for discussion, because there was huge Irish interest in those cataclysmic events. Tom Paine's *The Rights of Man* went into seven Irish (i.e. published in Ireland, not Irish-language) editions in the early 1790s. The relaxation of the Penal Laws and the legislative independence of Grattan's Parliament would have been another talking point. Liberal Protestants and Catholics followed with great interest the doings of the Catholic Committee, who organized a Catholic Convention in 1792 in Back Lane in Dublin. Their secretary was the radical Dublin lawyer, Theobald Wolfe Tone, (Figure 5.1) who had published his *Argument on Behalf of the Catholics of Ireland* the year before. The 'Back Lane parliament', as it was derisively known, was led by John Keogh, Richard McCormick and Edward Byrne. Excluded as Catholics from the professions, all had made their money (or their fathers had) in business or in farming.

The news from France about the Civil Constitution of the Clergy in 1790 worried some Irish Catholics, but it did not stop many others from joining the Society of United Irishmen, founded in 1791 in Dublin and Belfast. The early leaders were Wolfe Tone, William Drennan, also a lawyer, from Belfast, Thomas Russell a Cork (Catholic) journalist, James Napper Tandy, the son of a shopkeeper (Protestant), and Samuel Neilson, a Belfast linen-draper, the son of a clergyman. The broader membership included doctors,

FIGURE 5.1 Theobald Wolfe Tone (1763–1798). Hulton Archive/Stringer/Getty images. The father of Irish republicanism, a lawyer from a Church of Ireland background, he founded the United Irishmen in 1791, having previously been secretary of the Catholic Committee.

printers, teachers, blacksmiths, shopkeepers, millers, publicans, clergymen and priests, all people whose jobs brought them into regular contact with others, which is how the society spread. Presbyterians were to the fore in the society in Belfast and Derry, because as Dissenters they were also excluded from parliament by the Penal Laws, but also because the ideals of their creed found republicanism congenial. There were Church of Ireland Protestants involved, too, Wolfe Tone himself, Lord Edward Fitzgerald (son of the Duke of Leinster) and the Emmets being the most prominent examples. Outside Ulster, Catholics were in a majority in the organization, but no more so than in the population as a whole.

In their founding days, the Society of United Irishmen were a kind of 'fan' organization for the French Republic, and not necessarily separatist or revolutionary. Although closely associated with the radical *Northern Star* newspaper, published in Belfast from 1792, the society's key reform demands were shared by many parliamentarians; universal male suffrage and the removal of all penal legislation against Catholics and Dissenters.

Meanwhile, more of the Penal Laws on Catholics were being dismantled. Catholic men down to the level of 40-shilling freeholder (i.e. medium-sized tenant farmers and some tradesmen) were given the parliamentary vote in 1792–1793, and Catholics were admitted to the legal profession and to grand juries (precursors of county councils). St Patrick's College in Carlow was set up by the government as a seminary in 1793 and an even bigger seminary was begun in Maynooth in 1795. This attempt to prevent trainee priests from going to revolutionary France was also a quasi-official recognition of Catholicism as a religion whose ministers needed education. Catholics were also granted the right to bear arms. These relief measures, which also applied to Catholics in Britain, were imposed from London upon an Irish parliament. But Westminster was only prepared to go so far. In 1795 a Lord Lieutenant sympathetic to further Catholic reform, Lord Fitzwilliam, was recalled after seven months, to the relief of those, headed by Foster, Fitzgibbon and Beresford, who were hostile to Catholic claims.

At this stage Britain (and much of Europe) was at war with France, which heightened the government's security concerns. The Catholic Committee disbanded in 1793, and the Society of United Irishmen were banned in 1794. Driving the organization underground sharpened its republicanism and led it to merge with what was almost a ready-made supplementary army of about 100,000, the Defenders, in 1795. The Defenders were formed in the late 1780s and early 1790s in Cavan, Monaghan and Armagh. Their grievances were the familiar agrarian ones of land, wages and tithes, but the Defenders were influenced by French revolutionary ideology, less local in organization and outlook, and much better armed than the agrarian Whiteboys or Rightboys. The Defenders gave the mainly urban United Irishmen a strong rural base. Between the two forces, by 1796, nearly 300,000 were organized, with over a third of these in Ulster. Just as the mass of French revolutionaries were *sans-culottes* or 'without knee-britches', the United Irishmen/Defender rank and file were 'croppies' because they wore their hair short, without wigs – like most rural working men. (There are several ballads from this period about the 'Croppy Boy'.) Although Catholics and Protestants worked together in the United Irishmen and in the leadership of the Defenders, the Defender rank and file had more of a Catholic character, especially when defending Catholics against Protestant attacks in small-farming south Armagh. Confrontations between Catholics and Protestants were always sharpest where interdenominational differences in income and status were narrow, where Catholic resented Protestant advantage and Protestant feared Catholic encroachment. The anti-Catholic Orange Order was founded after one such confrontation, the Battle of the Diamond, in Armagh in 1795.

The strength of their numbers gave the revolutionaries the confidence to seek French help. The French sent forty-five ships carrying 15,000 soldiers under the command of General Lazare Hoche in 1796, but stormy weather prevented them from landing at Bantry Bay in Cork. This was a tremendous propaganda coup for the United Irishmen whose membership rose by another 10,000, and it gave the government a terrible fright. Habeas corpus was suspended, recruitment in the yeomanry and militia was stepped up and intelligence networks were improved. Curfews, torture, the application of the pitch-cap (burning tar on the head) and the burning of houses were carried out enthusiastically by militias. The excesses of the North Cork Militia in Wexford drove many local people to support the rebellion in 1798, and those of the Wicklow Militia in Westmeath boosted rebel recruitment in the midlands.

This rebellion had four 'theatres'. The Dublin-Kildare-Meath one was the least successful, although it had the most high-profile member, Edward Fitzgerald. An efficient spy network meant that the rebels were apprehended before they reached the seat of power at Dublin Castle, although the action spread as far as Westmeath with over 1,000 rebels staging a rapidly suppressed revolt in Kilbeggan. The rebellion in Wexford was comparatively successful. The rebels, who numbered about 10,000, established a Republic which lasted from 31 May to 21 June under a Directory with four Protestant and four Catholic leaders. Wexford had a very confident Catholic leadership made up not only of continental-educated clergy like Fr Murphy, but of merchants and farmers. It also had substantial Protestant support led by Bagenal

Harvey, a landowner in south Wexford. A minority of Protestant landowners and public officials, however, remained loyal to the government and long-simmering anti-settler tensions at farmer and labourer level gave rise to shocking massacres, by the rebels, of Protestants, including women and children, at Scullabogue and Coolgreaney. The Wexford rebels held out the longest though they were finally defeated by heavy artillery at Vinegar Hill. The United Irishmen of the north-east were far greater in number – 27,000 – and under the leadership of mainly Presbyterian United Irishmen like Henry Joy McCracken and Henry Munro, but they were defeated very quickly in early June. This was partly because of effective government infiltration but also because many working-class and rural Protestants, far more numerous in Ulster than in Leinster, were hostile to the rebels. The rebellion had one last gasp when the French General Humbert landed a force of 1,000 men in Killala, Co. Mayo, in August and, his numbers more than doubled by local United Irishmen, routed crown forces at Killala and Castlebar and took Westport and other Mayo towns. A Provisional Government was declared, but they were forced to surrender when they crossed the Shannon at Longford. The French sent another gunship, the *Hoche*, to Lough Swilly, but this was defeated off Tory Island in October, and Wolfe Tone, who was on board, was captured. Sentenced to hanging, he took his own life in prison.

Even with minimal French aid, therefore, the United Irishmen and Defenders mounted a serious challenge to the government. Because of this, both the king and the prime minister, William Pitt, began to press for an abolition of the Irish parliament, but when this was first put to College Green in 1799 it was narrowly defeated. Opponents of the Union in 1799 were the extreme Protestant interest who trusted in their Protestant Ascendancy 'garrison' to keep Catholics and rebels down. Henry Grattan and his supporters, on the other hand, opposed the Union because they hoped to expand on the legislative independence granted in 1782 to give more relief to Catholics and bring in parliamentary reform. Most politically minded Catholics agreed with the latter group. But influential Catholics like Lords Fingal and Kenmare (who, as Catholics, did not sit in the house of lords) and some Catholic bishops, believed that the Union offered the best hope of eventual repeal of all anti-Catholic legislation including the right to sit in parliament. The Orange interest was gradually won over to the Union with scenarios of Protestants being politically outnumbered in an Irish parliament if Catholic Emancipation were granted. The Irish parliament voted itself out of existence in 1800 when the Act of Union was passed by 158 votes to 115 in the Irish House of Commons, and by seventy-five to twenty-six in the House of Lords. Under the Union, the office of viceroy or Lord Lieutenant remained intact; he would operate his administration from Dublin Castle with the help of a chief secretary and under-secretary. A hundred MPs would be elected in Ireland by Irish voters for Irish constituencies to sit in Westminster, along with twenty-eight Irish peers for the House of Lords and four Church of Ireland bishops.

In 1803, twenty-two-year-old student Robert Emmet, a nephew of United Irishman Thomas Addis Emmet, who had been exiled for his part in the revolution, staged a rising in Dublin city. He and the other leaders were hanged for treason, but Emmet's powerful speech from the dock made him a hero for future generations of nationalists.

5.3 Catholic Emancipation and Repeal

Prime Minister William Pitt had assumed that Catholic Emancipation – that is, giving Catholics the right to be elected to parliament – would follow logically from the Union. But King George III stood fast against it, believing that it would be a violation of his coronation oath. There was opposition to Catholic Emancipation not only in Ireland but also in Britain, where a strong popular distrust of Catholics and a fear of papal interference was reinforced by the prospect of emancipation ushering in the long-called-for parliamentary reform. This would involve the redrawing of constituency boundaries, the extension of the franchise, and the granting of equivalent rights to other groups, including Jews.

It was the Irish who eventually won the Catholic Emancipation which would benefit Catholics of both islands. In 1804–1805 a petition drawn up by a group of Dublin Catholics and presented to parliament by Henry Grattan was defeated by 336 votes to 124 in the House of Commons and by 178 to 49 in the House of Lords. In 1808 and 1810 other bills were presented and defeated. Robert Peel, chief secretary of Ireland from 1812, believed that Catholic Emancipation would be disastrous. Not everyone agreed and a bill presented by William Plunket in 1821 with the conditions of payment of clergy, and a government veto on episcopal appointments passed the House of Commons but was defeated in the Lords.

Daniel O'Connell (Figure 5.2) began to build his campaign for Catholic Emancipation free of all such conditions, shortly after Plunket's bill.

O'Connell was born in 1775 into a Kerry family which had managed to hold onto its land and wealth through the time of the Penal Laws. Educated on the continent (like many other prosperous Catholics) he was one of the first Catholics to be called to the Irish bar in 1798. In 1823 O'Connell and lawyer Richard Lalor Shiel set up the Catholic Association to campaign for emancipation without conditions. The founding members consisted mainly of lawyers and businessmen, with a sprinkling of

FIGURE 5.2 Daniel O'Connell (1775–1847). duncan1890/ DigitalVision Vectors/Getty images. One of the first Catholics to qualify as a lawyer after the Penal Laws, O'Connell ran a successful campaign for Catholic Emancipation (granted in 1829) which mobilized Catholics of all social classes and firmly established constitutional nationalism.

landed gentlemen. O'Connell's association (reborn as the New Catholic Association after it was suppressed in 1825) involved Catholics of all social classes by making them associate members on payment of 1d (one penny) a month to local collectors. This gave many (probably most) Irish Catholics of all classes ownership of the cause, and brought them together regularly in town and country to pay the 'Catholic rent'. Thus was built up not only an effective fundraising mechanism but a country-wide network of supporters. O'Connell held big open-air meetings up and down the country. Economic depression in the 1820s made life hard for everybody, but Catholics, disproportionately represented among the less well-off, naturally traced many of their troubles to the non-representation of those of their religion in parliament. But there were genuine Catholic grievances other than this, such as having to pay tithe to Protestant clergy, Protestant (not Catholic) schools being subsidized by government, and a uniformly Protestant judiciary and magistracy.

Circulating among many rural Catholics were the Pastorini prophecies that the year 1825 would drive out all the Protestants, and there was a surge in agrarian violence, the agitators this time calling themselves the Ribbonmen and followers of Captain Rock. The government was glad to have a reason to suppress the Catholic Association, which it claimed was stirring up this agitation, and no doubt believed it was being even-handed by suppressing the Orange Order too. But O'Connell's campaign had no connection with secret societies. It sought a modern objective, religious equality, through an open, constitutional political organization, not a secret society with oaths, and it was conducted with argument, reason and rhetoric, not pikes, cattle-maiming or flaming torches. In the 1826 General Election several pro-emancipation candidates were successful; Villiers Stuart unseated Thomas Beresford, whose family had held the Waterford seat for generations. However, in 1828 when the anti-emancipation Arthur Wellesley, Duke of Wellington (and hero of Waterloo), became prime minister with the anti-Emancipation Robert Peel in the Home Office, O'Connell forced the government's hand by running as a candidate against Vesey Fitzgerald, a pro-Emancipation candidate, in a by-election in Clare. O'Connell won the election by 2,057 votes to 982. Fearful of another Irish rebellion, Wellington persuaded the king to grant Catholic Emancipation. This allowed Catholics to sit in both houses of parliament and to occupy most of the high offices of the land. No conditions were attached – no payment of clergy, no veto on the appointment of bishops – but the franchise was taken away from the 40-shilling freeholders, who had been granted it in 1793. This does not seem to have affected O'Connell's popularity, probably because the parliamentary vote was still such a novelty and the reality of universal male suffrage still a long way away.

O'Connell had beginner's luck with his campaign for Repeal of the Union in the 1832 election, when 39 (over a third, nearly two-fifths) of the 100 MPs returned for Irish constituencies pledged to support him. Thereafter, the movement simmered slowly, and it was not until 1840 that the Loyal National Repeal Association was set up. Structured on the same basis as the Catholic Association (repeal 'rent' collected at regular intervals, countrywide organization, public debates), it was characterized even more than the previous campaign by mass meetings. Four-hundred-thousand attended one at Tara, Co. Meath, in 1843 which had 42 bands and 10,000 horsemen. At least 250,000 packed the relatively small town of Ennis, Co. Clare for a Repeal meeting in the same year, travelling from the furthest reaches of Clare, Limerick, Tipperary, Galway and even King's County; there were 60 temperance bands and 6,000 horsemen. Such spectacular shows of strength alarmed the government. A big meeting planned in October 1843 for Clontarf (a historic site to match Tara) was proscribed and O'Connell, mindful of staying within the law and wanting to avoid bloodshed, called it off. Imprisoned briefly for sedition, he died the following year.

The very popular *The Nation* newspaper (which sold 250,000 copies in 1843) founded by journalist and poet Thomas Davis and lawyer Charles Gavan Duffy, became disenchanted with Daniel O'Connell after he cancelled the Clontarf meeting. But O'Connell never claimed to be a revolutionary. He always professed loyalty to the crown, worked within the law and, while he kept pressing for Repeal of the Union, welcomed the reforms of the 1830s which opened up public office, local government participation and educational provisions to Catholics and redressed some glaring wrongs.

5.4 Administrative, Legal and Welfare Reforms

The payment of tithe by Catholics to the Established Church was a grievance going back to the Reformation. Catholic Emancipation did not get rid of it, and twelve anti-tithe protesters were killed by yeomanry in Newtownbarry, Co. Wexford, in 1830; the following year, eleven police and soldiers were killed by anti-tithe agitators in Carrickshock, Co. Kilkenny. Only one-third of all tithes were being collected by 1835. The Irish Church Temporalities Act of 1835 and the Tithe Rent Charge Act of 1838 scaled down tithe payments and converted them into a rental charge on landlords, and arrears were written off. The principle of tithe was not completely abolished, but this was a preliminary recognition that Catholics should not have to pay for a church that was not theirs.

Reforms in local government followed upon similar reforms in Britain from 1835 under a Liberal government. In this year all but four of sixty Irish town corporations (i.e. councils, dating back to the Normans) were exclusively Protestant in membership. The Municipal Corporation Act of 1840 reduced the number of corporations to ten (Belfast, Clonmel, Cork, Derry, Drogheda, Dublin, Kilkenny, Limerick, Sligo, Waterford) and Daniel O'Connell was elected as Dublin's first Catholic Lord Mayor since the Reformation in 1840. The abolished corporations were replaced by elective town councils with a far greater representation of Catholics than before, and much local administration devolved upon the elected Boards of Guardians (for which Catholics were also eligible) of the Poor Law, introduced in 1838. More attempts were made to include Catholics in the grand juries who administered county affairs.

Catholics had been admitted to the bar since the 1790s, now, in the 1830s, more Catholics were appointed judges and magistrates and legal advisers to the administration headed by Lord Mulgrave in Dublin Castle, supported by Chief Secretary Thomas Drummond. More Catholics were called to serve on juries, and vigorous (and successful) attempts were made to recruit Catholics to the new police force, the Irish Constabulary.

Permanent police forces were one of the new mechanisms of social control introduced in Napoleonic territories (i.e. most of Europe) from about 1804, but Britain, which prided itself on cherishing civil liberties, did not go about setting up a police force until 1829. All through the nineteenth century, however, exaggerated government perceptions of Ireland as endemically lawless meant Ireland was more heavily policed than Britain, and an armed constabulary introduced into Ireland in the 1820s had 35,000 members by 1828. This became the Irish Constabulary in 1836. ('Royal' was added later.) The Dublin Metropolitan Police was also set up in the same year. At a practical level, this meant plenty of pensionable jobs for farmers' sons, highly valued recruits because of their good general health and strength. Unarmed in their day-to-day patrols, these constables could check weapons out of stores when needed. Most Irish policemen went their entire working lives without ever touching a firearm, though the land agitation of the 1870s and 1880s would make considerable demands upon them.

Another pensionable government job open to all religions – and unlike the constabulary, to both sexes – was that of National teacher, from 1831. Government subsidy of Protestant schools was one of the fundamental Catholic grievances. The National Board of Education, set up in Dublin in 1831, allowed interested parties of any religion to apply to the board for a capital grant for school-building. Teachers' salaries would be paid by central government, standard textbooks would be issued and an inspectorate established. Primary education would not become compulsory until 1892, so the National Board did not establish a countrywide network of schools but acted as an enabling and grant-aiding body for those who wanted to do so. Some Catholic religious orders (notably the Christian Brothers) were unhappy about not being permitted to display religious emblems, and held aloof, but most Catholic parish priests and especially precariously resourced orders of nuns availed eagerly of the National Board's facilities. This explains why the Irish state-funded schooling system remains denominational down to the present day.

The mental asylum, however, did not rely on personal or group initiative. From the 1780s there was great optimism all over Europe about the possibility of curing insanity, and Ireland was part of this wave. In 1817, building in Ireland began in earnest, and by 1850 every county had its large asylum, many of these designed in attractive Palladian style, not as grim-looking as the workhouses. (Figure 5.3) They were administered by the grand juries (local government bodies) who were also responsible for the building of fever hospitals in most major towns from 1797. If philanthropic charitable hospitals are included, there were 171 general (i.e. non-mental) hospitals in Ireland by 1845, and over 600 charitable dispensaries. These were unevenly distributed, with three times as many in Munster as in Connacht, but their existence shows some commitment to public health care and disease containment. The nucleus of Ireland's general hospital network, however, would evolve from the Poor Law workhouses set up in 1838.

FIGURE 5.3 Cork District Mental Asylum. Westend61/Westend61/ Getty images. Built in 1845, this was one of the large district asylums built all over Ireland between 1817 and 1852.

Ireland had many discrete (if not particularly discreet) poor relief institutions – a Foundling Hospital since the early eighteenth century, various Mendicity Institutions, charity hospitals mentioned in the last chapter – and many counties had 'workhouses', relaxed, rough-and-ready places of recourse for the homeless which were quite unlike the regimented workhouses founded by the Poor Law of 1838. This, closely modelled on the stringent New Poor Law introduced to England and Wales in 1834, was the first universal, countrywide system of relief for the destitute and the desperate in Ireland. One-hundred-and-thirty workhouses (more would be added during the Famine) were purpose-built in Ireland by capital grant. Ongoing maintenance and support of the poor was paid for by the ratepayers (i.e. property owners) of the Union, the administrative district served by the workhouse.

Workhouse administration was overseen by the Guardians of the Poor, unpaid officials elected by ratepayers, who hired the workhouse staff – master, matron, porter, nursing staff and tradesmen. The Poor Law was set up against the recommendations of the Commission of Inquiry into the Relief of the Poor in Ireland, which published its report in 1836. Chaired by Dr Richard Whately, the Protestant Archbishop of Dublin, and including the Catholic Archbishop of Dublin, Dr Daniel Murray, this commission travelled all over the country and through its consultations with male and female cottiers and labourers, small farmers, big farmers, doctors, clergy of all denominations, landlords and their agents, concluded that there were about 2 million people in Ireland on the brink of destitution. The commission's report recommended massive public works (roads, drainage schemes, house building) and assisted emigration to relieve immediate population pressure, and some longer-term measures to alleviate poverty. The voices of the pre-Famine Irish poor are preserved forever in this report, but many of them would no doubt have exchanged that historical immortality for a longer time on this earth.

And why were so many Irish people poor at this time?

5.5 Economy and Society

All over Europe between 1780 and 1830 the population of unskilled and labouring people rose dramatically, and controlling this expanding and mobile labouring class was one of the spurs for Napoleon's Civil Code of 1804. This introduced not only police forces but also the new poor relief measures everywhere from the Italian states to the

Low Countries, all over the German lands and all over France, Iberia and in middle and eastern Europe. In England and Wales, a comparatively generous parish-based poor relief system was replaced by the punitive and carceral New Poor Law of 1834 described earlier.

Ireland, therefore, was not exceptional at the dawn of the nineteenth century in either its rising population or in its proportion of potentially destitute people, and the Irish poor did not give much cause for concern until after 1815. From 1794 until then, almost continuous European war boosted demand for agricultural and textile products everywhere, prices for crops, livestock and provisions such as dairy produce rose. Harvestmen and women, herdsmen and women, dairy workers, spinners, weavers, knitters and general labourers embarked on a pattern of early and almost universal marriage (i.e. marriage became more popular than before), and the population rocketed from 5 million in 1800 to 6.8 million in 1821. War meant other kinds of work too; about one in six members of the British forces in the early nineteenth century were Irish, which meant many of the heaviest eaters (males in their prime) were fed and clothed away from the country for extended periods. If they survived, they brought money home with them. Shopkeepers and other services prospered, transport jobs proliferated. The tillage zones of dry, sunny east Munster, Leinster and east Ulster provided plenty of labouring work at set times of the year – harvest-time and to a lesser extent, spring sowing and early summer weeding. Labourers doubled their wages between the 1770s and 1810. The stock-rearing regions (the west midlands and east Connacht) employed less labour, but needed cowherds and shepherds all year round, as did the dairying heartlands of mid- and west Munster, which also provided work for dairymaids and dairymen in spring and summer. Towns in tillage areas were centres of milling and brewing, but there, and also in the areas where pastoral farming predominated, weekly markets where women sold butter, milk and eggs livened up Saturdays, created contact between the town people and the country people, and brought business to the retailers. Barrels, buckets, pans, and other items needed on farms (of all kinds) were commissioned from tradesmen, while those who could afford little luxuries bought tea and sugar at the grocery shop. (Quaker Mary Leadbeater in her *Cottage Dialogues* (1811) warned farmers against giving servants a taste for extravagances like tea, lest they aspire to it when they set up house themselves.) The long reach of O'Connell's penny-a-month levy in the 1820s suggests that even the poorest were handling some cash at this stage. West of a line from Derry to Cork (roughly – leaving out some good lands on its eastern fringes) small farmers eked out a living doing a bit of tillage (oats mainly), a bit of spinning and weaving, stock-rearing for the family use or to sell east, fishing on the coast, hauling sand and seaweed inland to sell, and migrating seasonally to work in eastern counties. From Derry to Belfast and in the towns of Down and Armagh and their hinterlands, flax-growing stimulated textile production in homes and in the new factories and mills which would come to characterize this part of the country, employing in all locales more than 50,000 before 1815.

Townspeople bought whatever food they could afford from farmers' wives at markets, and from provision merchants. In the countryside, oats were eaten in Ulster and north Connacht, wheat and barley in Leinster, eggs everywhere, when they could be spared from sale, milk, butter and buttermilk (but no cheese) likewise, meat a few times a week for the prosperous. Fish, shellfish, puffins and cormorants were consumed in coastal areas and on islands. But in most parts of the country, the potato was the bedrock of the diet, because it took up very little ground and was a nutritious and filling food.

The bad times did not begin just when war ceased in 1815; even in boom times the slightest shortfall in supply plunged people already teetering on the edge, into destitution. A 'minor' famine in 1800–1801 left between 40,000 and 60,000 dead. The famine of 1817–1819, in which about the same number of people died, was exacerbated by the post-1815 depression. Plummeting demand for goods affected not only agricultural labourers but also workers in quarries, textiles, mines, canals and mills. Falling wages, shortage of work and high prices were the common complaints of the 1820s. The rate of population growth slowed down between 1821 and 1841 (See Appendix A.1), partly because of the emigration of almost a million people between 1815 and 1845, many of them small farmers and tradesmen. Ulster people followed a trail already laid down in the eighteenth century to the south-eastern United States, while thousands from Waterford and south Tipperary made their permanent homes in Newfoundland and Nova Scotia, after generations of migrating there seasonally for fishing. In the north of England, the Catholic population of one Tyneside diocese increased from 400 in 1798 to over 4,000 in 1843, due to Irish immigration.

As poverty in Ireland intensified from generation to generation, land which had never supported human life before (e.g. on Erris Head in Co. Mayo, and in parts of west Galway) was painstakingly reclaimed and worked to yield potatoes. By the 1830s, bread, dairy produce, meat and even pulses had disappeared from the diet of the poorest people. The houses of the poor were built of sod or stones, often without chimneys, with barely a chair or a table not to mind a bed; people ate out of communal pots and slept on straw strewn over an earthen floor, covering themselves with coats or shawls. Blankets were in short supply and most of what was knitted was sold, commanding increasingly miserable prices in the 1830s and 1840s. And as if life was not hard enough, the Big Wind which swept through Ireland on Little Christmas (6 January) 1839, when waves overtopped the Cliffs of Moher and water was blown out of canals, levelled many of these homes, and over 300 died. In normal times, visitors to Ireland saw quite a lot of the badly clad and dirty (but, they also noted, good-looking and healthy) poor, precisely because their dwellings were only used for eating and sleeping and sheltering from bad weather.

Those labourers and small farmers who gave evidence to the Poor Inquiry in the 1830s knew their circumstances were worsening; 'It is often we lament', said a Monaghan woman referring to the shrinking income from textile work, 'that we leave the whole burden on the men of supporting the children'. Doing what they could to keep body and soul together, they were not prevented by their struggles from taking an interest in life outside their cabins. The numbers of children going to school rose from 394,000 in 1821 to around 700,000 in 1841, most to the newly established National schools. In the 1830s the crowds who came to towns to hear the temperance crusader Fr Theobald Mathew, and the multitudes who flocked to O'Connell's Repeal meetings, included the dangerously poor. Vulnerable they might have been but ignorant they were not, and their loud lamentations when the potato failed shows that they knew the disaster they had long anticipated was finally upon them. (Figure 5.4)

5.6 The Great Famine

In the late summer and early autumn of 1845 the first signs of potato blight were reported, giving cause for concern. At the onset of the winter, Robert Peel, prime minister of a Conservative government, purchased Indian meal (corn meal) and made it available in depots around Ireland, and opened up public works to provide employment. Peel had not enjoyed his time as chief secretary in Ireland thirty years previously (to put it mildly), but he believed that governments had a responsibility to feed those in danger of starvation. Thanks to the unpalatable 'Peel's Brimstone', as the Indian meal was known, there were no deaths from starvation in 1845–1846, though there was hunger and hardship. And even poor, badly nourished people could get through one year of shortage.

It was when the potato crop failed again in 1846 that the first deaths from starvation were officially recorded. Peel's government fell, giving way to Liberals/Whigs under Lord John Russell. The Liberals believed in the free market, so they closed down the public works and food depots. Although they opened the public works again in October, they did not provide any food relief. Half-starved people

FIGURE 5.4 Bridget O'Donnel and her children. Photo 12/Universal Images Group/Getty images. From the *Illustrated London News* of 1849, this sketch, because it gives the woman's name, insists upon the humanity of Famine victims. By 1849 the soup kitchens which had opened (far too late) in the early summer of 1847 were all closed, and the crisis was officially over, but not for the O'Donnel family.

collapsed on the job, their places quickly taken by others. Meanwhile, people were dying of hunger all over the country, because there were poor, potato-dependent people almost everywhere in Munster, Leinster and Connacht and parts of Ulster, though they were most numerous in the west. Coastal communities were slightly less badly hit, because of the availability of fish and shellfish, and parts of Ulster and north Connacht where oats were commonly cultivated for domestic consumption had lower mortality than other areas. But everywhere, the poorest people succumbed. They died on the side of the road, or more commonly, shut up in their little cabins, whole families together. The new workhouses undoubtedly saved some lives but were completely overwhelmed.

Public works were phased out from January 1847 and the government, with great fanfare, began to build soup kitchens from February, but these did not open until much later. In this cold, starving spring, mortality and weakness prevented many people from sowing their potatoes on or before St Patrick's Day, as was the custom, so, although there was no blight in 'Black '47', the potato harvest was poor. Once soup kitchens were open by early summer, mortality fell dramatically, with about 3 million being fed daily. But weakness and malnutrition and crowds milling for soup led to the spread of typhus and 'relapsing fever', dysentery, cholera and smallpox. Workhouses introduced 'outdoor relief' (contrary to Poor Law regulations) for about 50 per cent of those who sought help. Outside of the workhouse system, the Quakers (Society of Friends) had already opened soup kitchens in 1846, and individual priests, clergymen, doctors and some landlords were also working hard since the beginning of the crisis. Without these people, and without neighbours handing out alms at doors, there is no knowing how many more would have died.

The government soup kitchens were closed in September 1847, when the crisis was deemed to be over.

When potato blight struck again in 1848, the soup kitchens were not reopened and the workhouse system was left to cope with the demands of the hungry. The most vulnerable were nearly all dead at this stage anyway.

People unable to feed themselves could not pay rent, and while many landlords did without, a minority took advantage of the crisis to evict the 'uneconomic' tenants they had wanted to get rid of for years. Between 300,000 and 500,000 people were evicted between 1845 and 1854, their cabins pulled down immediately by gangs of young men called 'scalpeens', hired from the towns. Most evictions happened in Clare, Tipperary, Mayo, Galway and Kerry; in Clare one in every ten persons was permanently evicted. Lord Lucan (George Bingham) in west Mayo and Crofton Vandaleur in west Clare were particularly pitiless, Vandaleur preventing his sitting tenants from harbouring the newly evicted, under pain of being evicted themselves. The evicted, if they were not sheltered by neighbours, went to the overcrowded workhouses, or slept under hedges, or died. The streets of the bright, new town of Belmullet, Co. Mayo, were strewn with corpses in the spring of 1847.

Those who left Ireland permanently in these panicked years were not the starving, but the class just above them, who sold all they had to get out, or were assisted by government or landlords to do so. The 4,000 or so orphan girls sent by Poor Law Unions to Australia under Earl Grey's scheme were among the luckiest, travelling in seaworthy ships, with clothing kits, matrons and conscientious ships' doctors. Landlord-assisted emigration was chancier. Lord Monteagle's tenants from Co. Limerick, helped by him to go to Australia, were so grateful that some sent him back the passage money, but the tenants of Gore-Booth in Sligo and Mahon of Strokestown in 1847 were sent off in appalling conditions. The term 'coffin ship' was used by shocked contemporaries to describe the unseaworthy commercial vessels hastily fitted out by unscrupulous Irish and English firms to meet the unprecedented demand. Of the 100,000 Irish emigrants who travelled to Quebec in 1847, for example, one-sixth died either en route or after arrival.

By 1851 every part of Ireland (except for the cities) had experienced population loss through death and emigration. Taking one county from each province, Tyrone's population fell by 17 per cent, Kilkenny's by 22 per cent, Tipperary's by 26 per cent and Mayo's by 31 per cent between 1841 and 1851. In Mayo, which had 72 per 1,000 average excess death rate 1846–1851 (compared to Kilkenny's 18, Tyrone's 22 and Tipperary's 35), that loss was mainly through death. Other high excess death rates were in Sligo (61), Galway (58) and Roscommon (57.4). Although Carlow, at 8.8, and Wexford, at 6.6, had the lowest excess deaths in the country, even they saw a higher than normal death rate. No part of Ireland was unaffected.

5.7 Conclusion

The Famine mortality was all the more shocking because Ireland had, by the 1840s, a reasonably good transport infrastructure that shrank distance. The Grand and Royal Canals linked the Shannon and other inland waterways with Dublin, and Belfast was also linked by canal with several towns in its hinterland by 1820. Roads were improved and stage-coach travel streamlined; Charles

Bianconi's fast coaches with cheap fares, radiating from Clonmel, Co. Tipperary from 1815 onwards, covered most of Leinster, Munster and Connacht by 1840. The road connecting Castlebar in Co. Mayo to Erris was built by the late 1820s and it was one of many such roads to hitherto 'remote' parts of the country. During the Famine, crusading journalists from Dublin and London newspapers reported vividly, in words and sketches, on the crisis as it was unfolding in Cork and other parts of the west.

These improved communications were one reason why a revolution was even attempted in July 1848, when Young Ireland, or the Irish Confederation, under the leadership of William Smith O'Brien, carried out a small, quickly suppressed rebellion in Ballingarry, Co. Tipperary. Labour interests and trades councils in the towns backed them, and the English Chartists under Feargus O'Connor offered moral support. But many of their members (including John Mitchel) had already been found guilty of sedition, and their most famous intellectual, Thomas Davis, had died in 1845.

The Young Irelanders are much derided by historians. Yet, for them and their few hundred poorly equipped supporters (who included the nearby Castlecomer miners), government mismanagement of the Famine was a fundamental part of what was wrong with the way Ireland was governed. This belief would motivate both constitutional and militant nationalists for the next seventy years.

6

Modernization

From the Famine to the Farmers' Victory, 1850–1903

6.1 Population, Emigration and Marriage

The single most important fact about Ireland after 1850 is its continuously falling population, from 6.5 million in 1851 to 4.4 million in 1911. (See Appendix A.1.) Ireland's population after 1850 did not fall because of the population loss of the Famine. The population could have recovered within a generation, as it did after the (proportionately) higher mortality of the 1740s. There were two causes of long-term population decline: emigration and low marriage rates.

Between 1856 and 1914, 4.5 million people left Ireland permanently. Eighty-four per cent of these emigrants went to North America, 7 per cent to Australia and 9 per cent to other destinations – New Zealand, South Africa, South America and India. There was also a constant stream eastward across the Irish Sea, although, as Ireland was part of the United Kingdom at the time, this was not considered emigration.

Between 1854 and 1871, emigration was highest from Munster and Leinster. From 1881, greater numbers people left from Connacht, with west Munster still heavily represented. Emigration from Leinster and Ulster slowed down, but emigration never died out completely from any part of the island.

Apart from the assisted schemes, most emigrants were the non-inheriting sons and daughters of middling to small farms, shops and trades, who were more use to their families far away earning money to send home, than at home unemployed. They left homes anchored by parents, parents' heirs, and one or two other children or adults. Post-Famine emigrants were overwhelmingly young (aged between eighteen and twenty-four) and single. Once established in the New World, they sent money home to their parents, and also to help pay the passage of a brother, a sister or a cousin, both to relieve pressure at home and to establish a new income stream for the home place.

Although men predominated among emigrants in the 1850s and 1860s, thereafter there were always slightly more women than men leaving Ireland; from 1901 to 1911, there were 82 emigrant males for every 100 females. There were fewer job opportunities for women than men in Ireland, but, also, daughters were more trusted than sons to maintain links with home and to send money. Vere Foster's assisted emigration schemes in the west of Ireland in the 1850s and again in the 1880s, favoured young women for this reason.

Although Catholics predominated among emigrants at this stage, not all were Catholic and not all (not even all Catholics) were the young, single offspring of farmers. Many were drawn by the possibility of individual improvement rather than driven by family needs. Entrepreneurs went to the newly settled western regions of North America and Western Australia, governesses and female teachers (particularly Protestants) were in great demand in Australia and New Zealand, white-collar and professional workers took the British imperial trail to India and South Africa, and certain localities built up contacts in South America – communities from west Cork and Westmeath, for example, went to Argentina. Another significant emigration was the departure of over 20,000 young women (mostly after 1850) for convents on all five continents.

About 10 per cent of all emigrants from the 1850s onwards were 'assisted' in some way, by philanthropists like Foster, Bishop John Ireland and others. Some were single, some in family groups. Over 3,000 north Mayo people, most of them families, left Blacksod Bay for America between 1883 and 1884 in good, seaworthy ships, assisted by the philanthropist James Hack Tuke. Although deplored as 'extermination' by nationalists at the time, these schemes were eagerly competed for.

Ireland after 1850, therefore, lost not only the 4.5 million people who went but also their potential children and grandchildren. Another reason for the steady population decline, however, was the low marriage rate. In Ireland in 1851, 10 per cent of males and 12 per cent of females had never married by age forty-five to fifty-four, which was about average for most countries. But by 1911, 27 per cent of men and 25 per cent of women in this age category had never married, which deviated from the European norm. At this date also, the median age at marriage for women was twenty-nine, compared to twenty-three-and-a-half in 1861. A well-nourished woman who marries at twenty-nine or thirty however, can still have up to eight children, and, despite late marriage, completed Irish families remained large by European standards up to the 1970s. The real cause of low population growth was not late marriage but 'rare' marriage. A *small* number of *big* families are not as favourable to population growth as a *big* number of *small* families, because people cannot marry their brothers and sisters.

Rates of singleness for both sexes were highest in the prosperous big-farming and urbanized areas of Munster and Leinster in both 1881 and in 1911, and lowest in Connacht and Ulster, the provinces which had the greatest proportion of small farmers and industrial workers per head of the population. Poverty did not prevent marriage but the realistic expectation of a higher standard of living if marriage was postponed (or foregone) did. Connacht and west Ulster caught up with demographic trends in the rest of the country, in the early twentieth century, but only slowly, and early (and almost universal) marriage continued in the towns and cities among young men and women whose wages were not going to get any better if they remained single.

Singleness rarely meant solitude. Unmarried people nearly always lived in extended families with ageing parents or married brothers or sisters, with nieces and nephews growing up around them. Except for the chosen celibacy of priests, brothers and nuns, religious denomination was not a decisive factor in non-marriage, and areas of the country where Protestants predominated had as many middle-aged single people (and sometimes more) than Catholic. Patterns of earning, however, especially in the new administrative posts of the expanding machinery of state eagerly sought after by people of farming and artisan backgrounds, often discouraged marriage.

6.2 Work and Education

In 1851, 23 per cent of the adult workforce (both sexes) was engaged in agriculture (as farmers, farmers' assisting relatives, and labourers) and by 1911 this had fallen to 17 per cent. On neither date were farmers' wives counted (they were assumed to be 'engaged in home duties'), nor were children under twelve. Yet, rural National schools opened half an hour later than urban ones in recognition of the early-morning farm work children had to do, and farms could not operate without women's work in house, farmyard and fields. A fifty-acre pasture farm could be managed by parents and five or six children, with the aid of a part-time labourer for the hay-making and other busy times of the year.

The number of acres under tillage shrank from 4.6 million in 1851 to 2.2 million in 1911, as pasture farming became more common. Putting cows or sheep out to graze had always been the only option for farmers on wet, stony, mountainous or boggy land. Now, some big farmers on flatter, drier land – in Meath, and parts of east Munster – turned their good tillage land over to beasts too. One reason for this was the difficulty of getting labourers, whose bargaining power had increased now that they had the alternative of emigration. Labourers' wages rose from 54 per cent of the British industrial wage in 1845, to 83 per cent in 1913, and labourers formed several unions between 1884 and 1913. Some farmers, like those in 1870s Kildare, got over the local labour shortage by hiring gangs from west Cork or Kerry for the harvest, who worked from 5 a.m. till dark on 8d a day and wheaten bread and buttermilk. Others hired teenage servant boys at fairs, whose living conditions were satirized in an 1880s ballad, 'The Galbally Farmer', in which the hired boy on the Tipperary-Limerick border is given food that would 'physic a snipe | or give you the woeful disorder'.

Farming got a little easier towards the end of the century, with the introduction of modern implements like harrows, sprayers and 'tumbling paddy' rakes for hay. Threshing machines were another novelty in tillage areas. There was also an increase in draft animals. The donkey had been introduced to Ireland at the time of the Napoleonic wars, and the number of asses, mules and jennets rose from 100,000 in 1851 to 250,000 in 1911. This quarter of a million patient (if occasionally wilful) draft animals were helping a much smaller population to a more comfortable working life.

The number of women counted in the census as farmers in their own right (not 'engaged in home duties' or 'assisting relatives') grew from 6.8 per cent of all farmers in 1861 to 14 per cent in 1911. Mostly on the big farms of Leinster, Munster and Ulster, some of these were single, but most were widows. It is sometimes assumed (on no evidence whatsoever) that these widowed farmers' domination prevented their male heirs from marrying. One might just as well suggest male inertia as a cause of permanent bachelorhood. A more likely explanation for rural late marriage or non-marriage is that male heirs' potential spouses – other farmers' daughters – were increasingly attracted away from the farm either by paid work in the towns, or by emigration, or (in the case of Catholics) by the religious life.

Although some farmers consolidated lands into ranch-style holdings by the end of the century, two-thirds of all

Irish farms were of thirty acres or less. (The average-size farm in 1911 was 38.9 acres.) Whether tillage, pasture or 'mixed', the work was hard, and 'gentleman farmers' whose womenfolk never milked a cow or helped in the fields (such as Mrs O'Brien in Mary Carbery's *The Farm By Lough Gur*) were exceptional. Even in the big-farming counties of Meath and Westmeath, less than a quarter of all farms were over fifty acres.

6.3 Non-agricultural Work

Ulster was Ireland's industrial heartland, and by the 1890s over 100,000 people, many of them women, (Figure 6.1) worked in the spinning and weaving mills, the garment

FIGURE 6.1 Millworkers, Belfast, c.1890/1900. Ilbusca/DigitalVision Vectors/Getty images. Girls and women made up 76 per cent of the 83,000-strong textile workforce in the north-east of the country. These weavers and spinners had a measure of economic independence, although twelve-hour days in damp atmospheres took a toll on their health.

factories and the Belfast shipyards and ancillary industries. There was some industry, though not on the same scale, in the rest of the country. The number of woollen mills all over Ireland multiplied by ten between 1851 and 1902 – Blarney Woollen Mills in Cork employed 600 in the 1870s. Tait's, the world's biggest military outfitter, employed 2,000 Limerick people in the 1860s, and there were other small clothing firms. In general, industry in Ireland outside of Ulster centred around the five 'b's; bacon, butter-blending, biscuits, bread and beer. The numbers employed rose only slightly over time, because jobs were passed on within families from generation to generation. The trades of the towns were buoyant, but they were not expanding either, and some trades (weaving, coopering, and branches of blacksmithing) were threatened by cheap mass-produced items in shops. There was 1 shop per 143 people in 1851, and 1 per 79 in 1911, and therefore more people working in shops. These jobs, especially in country towns, were often apprenticeships to the trade in question (grocery, drapery, ironmongery), although bigger 'general stores' and department stores in the major towns from about the 1880s employed large numbers of waged male and female assistants. Retailing brought a rise in jobs in transport, not only in carting and portering but also in the expanding rail network in the 1860s and again in the 1890s. Unskilled males found jobs in construction – in Dublin city the numbers working in building rose from 2,639 in 1881 to 8,625 in 1901 – and in transport work.

The posts most sought after by the offspring of the lower-middle/farming/skilled/working class were Post Office clerk, government clerk, policeman, mental asylum attendant, prison warden, National teacher and nurse, all of which demanded a little more than basic literacy and numeracy. National teachers trained on the job at first, and then sat examinations, or won scholarships to the teacher-training colleges established from about the 1880s. Aspirants to other government posts either got private tuition or managed a few years of teenage education at designated schools to prepare them for entrance examinations or interviews. Even if such schooling was provided free by brothers, nuns or parochial grammar schools, or if scholarships were availed of, parents had to be able to do without these children's earnings for a few years. Small farming, labouring or working-class parents sometimes managed to do this for one child. Among small farmers this was usually a daughter, whose agricultural earning potential was nil, and this was how female National teachers outnumbered male by the end of the century.

There was little to stop National teachers, male or female, from marrying (no marriage bar against female teachers), but other occupations were not so accommodating. Policemen could not contemplate marriage until they were in their thirties, and even then, were not always granted permission. Assistants in shops big and small lived in, which ruled out marriage for many years, sometimes forever, if they did not move on to independent trading. District nurses employed by the Poor Law could be married but hospital nurses, like prison wardens and asylum attendants, lived on site. Also, many of these workers were supporting the parents who had made sacrifices to prepare them for the jobs they got and could not afford either to give up work for marriage (as daughters in many jobs would have had to do) or to support two households. It is easy to see how marriage, postponed indefinitely, might not have happened at all.

All jobs which involved dealing with the public demanded a presentable appearance, which was good news for the tailoring, dressmaking and millinery trades. Working from their homes or from small sweatshops, they held their own in the face of competition from ready-made clothing in drapery shops and market stalls. The second-hand clothing market was also buoyant, particularly in Ulster. Sewing machines, available from the 1860s on hire-purchase terms accessible to all but the very poor, were used not only to dress the family but also, just as frequently, to make money dressmaking, or doing alterations or mending. Cobblers, however, were worse hit by the ready availability of cheap boots and shoes in every town and country shop, and turned their hands to mending. The sizing of ready-made footwear was hit-and-miss, and labouring men often developed a plodding gait, not to mention corns and bunions, from the cheap, ill-fitting boots they had to wear all their lives.

Many women in the spinning mills of the north-east kept on their jobs after marriage, if their husbands were casually employed or unemployed, giving them up when an oldest daughter could take their place. (Figure 6.1) Male shipyard workers, like male skilled workers, earned (just about) enough to enable their wives to stay at home, though as in most working-class single-income families, female malnutrition was masked by the 'respectability' of white lace curtains and scrubbed front steps. North and south, the largest percentage of female workers throughout the period was in domestic service, although their numbers declined by 30 per cent (actually 45 per cent, but population declined by 15 per cent in the same period) between 1881 and 1911. Female domestic servants in towns and cities had many opportunities to meet potential husbands, as illustrated in the comical song from the 1870s, 'Courting in the Kitchen': 'When I was seventeen | Apprentice to a grocer | Up near St Stephen's Green | Where Miss Henry used to go, sir.' Miss Henry was the 'belle out of Captain Kelly's kitchen', and the title 'Miss' indicates the social status of a servant in a 'good house'. Servants got their bed and board, and could save money, so they were attractive marital prospects. Still, with its buckets of water and coal carried up and down stairs, heavy pots and pans heaved on and off fires and ranges, and toddlers and small children hauled onto hips, domestic service was almost as taxing as construction work, and most women gave it up by their late twenties.

The Queen's Colleges of Belfast, Cork and Galway, state-funded universities, opened their doors in 1849, and attracted many students from a variety of backgrounds. The Catholic University of Dublin was set up in 1854 by John Henry Newman. At a more basic level the numbers of children attending primary school rose decade on decade, until schooling was made compulsory for all in 1892. In 1878 the Intermediate Education Act established a school-leaving examination on an equal basis for boys and girls, which gave an impetus to the spread of secondary schools with low fees. Secondary education was voluntary, and staying at school beyond twelve or fourteen was for the minority. Literacy levels rose rapidly, however, among a populace which took an increasingly keen interest in public life and in politics.

6.4 Politics: The Fenians, the Land Struggle and the Home Rule Party

The founders of the Irish Republican Brotherhood (IRB), on St Patrick's Day in Dublin in 1858, were James Stephens, a civil engineer, Thomas Clarke Luby, the journalist son of a Church of Ireland clergyman, Jeremiah O'Donovan Rossa, a grocer from west Cork, John O'Mahony a Gaelic scholar and former Young Irelander, John O'Leary, a former medical student turned journalist, and Charles Kickham, a shopkeeper's son. Popularly known as the Fenians after Irish legendary warriors *na Fianna*, they were modelled on European secret societies of the time and heavily influenced by Mazzini's Italian nationalists. Half of the 80,000 or so Irish members were artisans or tradesmen, others were shop assistants, porters, National teachers, soldiers or factory workers. Small shopkeepers and professionals assumed leadership roles and many soldiers also took the Fenian oath. Fenians were town-based working-class or lower-middle class men who had time in the evenings and on Sundays to meet each other and organize. The movement had very few farmers' sons, for whom (or for whose fathers) the concept of formal 'free time' had yet to develop.

Through their actions, like the show of strength at the funeral of old Young Irelander Terence Bellew MacManus in Dublin in 1861, and their newspaper *The Irish People*, the IRB drew attention to their movement. This need for publicity clashed with the requirements of a secret society and made it easy to infiltrate. Fenianism spread rapidly among the Irish abroad, with tens of thousands of members in Britain and the United States. Michael Davitt, (Figure 6.2)

FIGURE 6.2 Michael Davitt (1846–1906). Print Collector/ Contributor/Hulton Archive/Getty images. Born in Straide, Co. Mayo, at the height of the Famine, he emigrated, with his family, to Lancashire as a child. Imprisoned for Fenian activities 1870–1877, he emerged in time to take joint leadership of the land movement with Parnell. He later became a Home Rule MP.

whose family had left Mayo after the Famine, joined the Fenians in Lancashire in 1865 when he was nineteen. Up to 1,500 American-based Fenians, most of whom who had served in the Union army in the Civil War, used their military experience in their invasion of Canada at Ridgeway, near Fort Erie, in 1866, in a struggle that went on for several days and involved heavy engagement, although it ended in defeat for the Fenians. Bombs in London and Chester brought the Fenians to the attention of the British public. The Fenian revolts which took place in

1867 in Cahirciveen, Midleton, Cork city, Tallaght, Kilmallock, Waterford and Limerick Junction were suppressed by the constabulary (who were bestowed with the title 'Royal' for their efforts), but they showed the strength of the organization in Munster and Leinster.

One of the many songs written retrospectively about the Fenians (this one by Peadar Kearney) has the lines, 'And wise men have told us their cause was a failure | But they loved dear old Ireland and never feared danger', which is hardly a ringing endorsement for any revolutionary force. Yet failure was immediately converted to the 'success' of suffering and endurance, and thus, a new and powerful element entered Irish physical-force nationalism, which can be traced all the way through 1916 to the IRA hunger strikes of the 1980s. The hanging in Manchester in December 1867 of Fenian activists William Allen, Michael Larkin and Michael O'Brien is a case in point. Shooting at the lock of a prison van to release two Fenian prisoners (who escaped), they accidentally killed a policeman, Charles Brett. Their execution (one of the last public executions in Britain) caused nationalists to call them the Manchester Martyrs. (Figure 6.3)

Many Fenians arrested in the wake of the rising were released before completing their sentences because of the efforts of the widely supported Amnesty Association founded in 1868, led by Isaac Butt, a prominent Irish lawyer. Butt had debated the Repeal question publicly with Daniel O'Connell, but his views had changed since then.

Fenian activity also made a deep impression on William Gladstone, prime minister of a Liberal parliament in 1868, who declared that his mission was to 'pacify Ireland', and addressed himself to perennial Irish grievances. In 1868, he

FIGURE 6.3 The 'Manchester Martyrs'. Universal History Archive/ Universal Images Group/Getty images. Allen, Larkin and O'Brien were the three Fenians hanged in Manchester for the murder of a policeman in 1867. This picture comes from an American Fenian publication; the song about the Manchester Martyrs, T. D. Sullivan's 'God Save Ireland' was sung to the air of the US Union Army's 'Tramp, Tramp, Tramp'.

got a bill through the Commons and Lords which disestablished the Church of Ireland. In 1873 he attempted unsuccessfully to establish an Irish university that would be acceptable to Catholics. But most important of all for the future direction of Irish nationalism was his Land Act of 1870.

Tenant right had been a slow-simmering issue on the agenda of Irish politicians in Westminster since the 1840s, promoted by James Fintan Lalor and Charles Gavan Duffy. Tenants, they demanded, should have the three 'f's – fair rent, free sale and fixity of tenure. As things stood, most Irish tenants had very insecure leases, and no protection against eviction, or compensation for improvement. Richard Deasy's Land Act of 1860 compensated tenants for certain improvements but its other provisions provided little additional security for tenants. Under Gladstone's 1870 Act, the 'Ulster custom' – whereby tenants, mainly in Ulster, had some traditional security of tenure – was given a legal basis, and all tenants wherever they were, could claim compensation for improvements more easily than under Deasy's Act. Furthermore, tenants evicted for any reason other than non-payment of rent, had to be compensated for disturbance. There were also clauses whereby a tenant who put up one-third of the purchase fee of his holding could borrow the remaining two-thirds from the government at favourable terms. The Act had many flaws, but the compensations for disturbance and improvement recognized tenants' interest in their holdings, which alarmed landlords. If they were also members of the recently disestablished Church of Ireland – and many were – they felt that their world was collapsing around them, and many flocked into Isaac Butt's Home Government Association set up in 1870.

The Home Government Association brought together conservatively minded men perturbed at how far Gladstone had gone and liberally minded ones who believed he had not gone far enough. By 1873 the conservatively minded had left, and the association became a firmly nationalist Home Rule Party, winning over half of all Irish seats (59 out of 103) in the general election of 1874. The Conservatives' comfortable victory under Benjamin Disraeli made them secure enough not to need the Home Rule Party's support, and the Irish party was not tempted to ally with the Liberals, so it developed at its own pace. That pace was too slow for a younger element in the party, represented by John O'Connor Power, an English-based tradesman, from a small farmer background in east Connacht, and Joseph Biggar, a Presbyterian shopkeeper from Belfast. They practised obstructionism, giving long speeches to hold up parliamentary business and draw attention to the Home Rule issue. Both men had been expelled from the Fenians for getting into constitutional politics, but as the Home Rule Party's profile began to rise, the IRB began to soften towards them, and to look also to a rising star in the party, the Wicklow landlord's son, Charles Stewart Parnell (Figure 6.4). But it was the land issue which brought the IRB (Fenians) and the Home Rule Party together. John Devoy, a labourer's son from Kildare who had taken part in the Fenian rising, met Michael Davitt, just out of prison after serving seven years for Fenian activities, and they decided on what historians would call the 'the New Departure' in revolutionary nationalism – co-operation with constitutional politicians.

FIGURE 6.4 Charles Stewart Parnell (1846–1891). William Lawrence/Stringer/Hulton Archive/Getty images. From a Protestant landowning family in Co. Wicklow, Parnell was elected as a Home Rule MP for Co. Meath in 1876 and assumed leadership of the Home Rule/Irish Parliamentary Party in 1880, having already assumed leadership of the growing land movement.

Three bad summers in a row, which destroyed the hay and grain harvest, shot the tenant right question to the top of the political agenda in the late 1870s. Irish farmers, big, middling and small, had one burden in common, the rent, and they all resented it when times were hard. And when farmers suffered, so did the shopkeepers in country towns whose bills went unpaid. Better rail transport and widespread distribution of newspapers meant that journalists, chief among them James Daly of the *Connaught Telegraph*, were able to bring town and country together. The Irish National Land League was founded by Daly and Davitt at

Irishtown, near Claremorris, Co. Mayo, in April 1879, and in June, Parnell addressed a huge meeting at Westport (also in Mayo) where he urged people to keep a tight grip on their homesteads. By October 1879 he was president of the Land League and, the following year, leader of the Home Rule Party.

The Land League was a non-violent constitutional organization whose tactics were mainly rent strikes, non-violent resistance to evictions, and ostracism. Social isolation of a rack-renting landlord or a someone who took land from which a tenant had been evicted was called boycotting, after an offending Mayo landlord Captain Charles Boycott, who was given this treatment. Faced with this movement, Gladstone – back in government in 1880 – granted the long-awaited three 'f's in the 1881 Land Act – fair rent, free sale and fixity of tenure. This step was a ground-breaking interference with landed power and a significant surrender to a popular movement, but it did not satisfy either Parnell or Davitt, because there were no provisions for tenants in arrears of rent, who could still be evicted, or for the many tenants who could not pay any rent at all. Parnell gave speeches against the Act while quietly advising tenants to work with it, or to pay 'rent at the point of a bayonet' (i.e. only at the point when the police and bailiffs came to evict). In response, Gladstone had him and Davitt and other leaders arrested and put in prison in 1881, at which point the Ladies' Land League took over, led by Anna Parnell, sister of Charles. Gladstone came to terms with Parnell in an agreement known as the Kilmainham Treaty in 1882 (Parnell was in Kilmainham jail at the time), whereby tenants in arrears would be admitted to the acts, and land courts would be set up for arbitration. The main 'Land War' seemed to be over.

It established Charles Parnell as leader of nationalist Ireland and the Home Rule Party as its main mouthpiece. The Land League became the Irish National League, a constituency organization for the party. A disappointed Davitt, who had hoped for the abolition of landlordism and the equitable redistribution of holdings, called this 'the overthrow of a movement and the enthronement of a man'. Anna Parnell, who had shared Davitt's hopes, never spoke to her brother again.

Even after 1882 many impoverished tenants found it impossible to pay rent, and some landlords were fighting back ferociously. The Plan of Campaign was spearheaded in 1886 by Home Rule MPs William O'Brien and John Dillon on estates where landlords continued to evict tenants. Tenants would agree a fair rent, offer it to the landlord, and if he refused to take it, put it into a fighting fund for court proceedings. The organizers' keen eye for publicity and government overreaction, such as the massacre of peaceful protestors in Mitchelstown, Co. Cork, in 1887, kept the cause in the public eye. The Plan was wound down in 1890, but out of it grew the United Irish League, set up by O'Brien in 1898, to fight for the redistribution of land especially in the west. By this time a series of land acts being brought in by both Conservative and Liberal governments were steadily eroding landlord rights, and in 1903 the Wyndham Act (called after George Wyndham, the Chief Secretary of the day) made sale of lands to tenants compulsory, turning tenants into owner-occupiers and abolishing landlordism once and for all. To understand why all this happened it is necessary to explain the political background.

In 1885 the strength of the Conservative and Liberal parties in the House of Commons was about equal, and each needed the Home Rule Party to make up a majority. Accordingly, both parties made overtures to the Irish MPs. Over the Christmas of 1885–1886, Gladstone, the Liberal leader, decided to support Home Rule for Ireland. The First Home Rule Bill was introduced and defeated in 1886, because some Liberals voted with the Conservatives on this issue. Gladstone was out of government again, and Lord Salisbury, the Conservative leader, was prime minister.

Going into alliance with Gladstone and the Liberals reduced the Home Rule Party's bargaining power, but it gave their cause the support of about half of the British electorate. Electorates in both Britain and Ireland almost trebled when the Third Reform Act of 1884 gave the vote to all male heads of households, and in this age of mass communication, parliamentary politics was everybody's business. British Liberal voters supported Home Rule for Ireland because they saw it as a just and moral cause. Those who voted Conservative, however, regarded Home Rule as a first step in the break-up of the empire upon which they believed Britain's prosperity depended.

An indication of how threatened Conservatives were by the Home Rule Party's success was the series of articles in *The Times* newspaper in 1887, 'Parnellism and Crime', which indicated that Parnell had approved of the infamous Phoenix Park murders. In May 1882, Chief Secretary Frederick Cavendish and Under-Secretary Thomas Burke had been brutally done to death in the Phoenix Park in Dublin by a group called the Invincibles, which had no connection to Parnell or the Home Rule Party.

When the key evidence for *The Times*'s allegation, letters purportedly written by Parnell, were proved to be forgeries, he was vindicated, and Home Rule's popularity soared. The Liberal Alliance, with all the sentimentality of the era, was called the 'Union of Hearts' and there were commemorative plates and pictures with Gladstone's and Parnell's portraits on them.

These plates cracked and fell asunder in 1889–1890, when Parnell was named as co-respondent in a divorce case brought by William O'Shea, a former Home Rule MP. Parnell and O'Shea's wife, Katherine, had been living together in discreet domesticity in England since 1880, with her husband's full knowledge. Very few people knew of the relationship, and when the story emerged, the Home Rule Party, in shock, voted initially to keep Parnell as leader, though many were apprehensive. They had every reason to be. The Catholic bishops of Ireland, Home Rulers to a man, could not tolerate an unrepentant adulterer as party leader. Just as importantly, Gladstone's middle- and working-class support base throughout Britain, many of them Nonconformist Protestants, considered Parnell's behaviour not only immoral but redolent of the kind of aristocratic licence they deplored. Gladstone threatened to break the Liberal Alliance unless the party dropped Parnell, and so the Home Rule Party split in two, with the majority calling on Parnell to resign, and a minority siding with him. In 1891 Parnell fought two by-elections in Ireland, and he died in Brighton in October, at the age of forty-five. His body was brought back to Ireland for burial in Glasnevin in Dublin, and some Irish nationalists, especially in Dublin and Roscommon, remained fiercely loyal to him.

Despite the split, the Home Rule Party still voted together, and the second Home Rule Bill of 1893 passed the House of Commons, though it was vetoed by the House of Lords. In 1900 the party reunited under the Parnellite John Redmond. By this stage, however, Unionist opposition to Home Rule was strong and organized.

The 1886 election had seen eighty-six Home Rulers and seventeen unionists elected for the country as a whole. Unionists held only about 16 per cent of the Irish seats. There were unionists all over the country, but they did not manage to elect MPs outside of Ulster except in Cork and in Dublin (the Trinity College seat). It made sense, therefore, for the Conservative party to concentrate its efforts on Ulster where unionism was concentrated. Randolph Churchill, a leading Conservative, called this playing 'the Orange card'. But there was nothing cynical about the strong opposition to Home Rule among Ulster Protestants of all classes. The north-east's comparative economic success, it was believed, was based on the Union, and Home Rule would not only see an end to naval shipbuilding contracts but could also put tariffs on textiles. There was also a fear that Home Rule would mean 'Rome Rule', that Irish Catholics, who made up the majority on the island as a whole, would strengthen the Pope's political and cultural influence. From its beginnings under Colonel Edward Saunderson in the 1880s, Irish unionism found its most effective expression in the north-east, culminating in the Ulster Unionist Council of 1904–1905.

Meanwhile Conservative governments invested time and money in Ireland, a process contemporaries called 'killing Home Rule with kindness'. The successive land acts described earlier, which eventually turned tenants into owner-occupiers in 1903, were part of this process; the Conservatives had no problem ditching the Irish landlords to court popular support. Light railways from the mid-1880s provided much-needed transport and stimulated tourism and trade in west Clare, west Kerry, west Galway, Mayo and Donegal. The Congested Districts Board, set up in 1891, concentrated on the chronically poor regions of the extreme west, making grants available for small industries and fisheries, solid, slated houses (many of which still stand), piers, bridges and jetties. The Irish Agriculture Organization Society of 1894 raised agricultural standards, and the Department of Agriculture and Technical Instruction became an important resource for agri-businesses and industries. A countrywide network of rural apostles of health, the Jubilee nurses, was inaugurated 1888–1891, followed by the Lady Dudley nurses in 1903. Women could become Poor Law Guardians from 1896, and those who met the property qualifications got the local government franchise in 1898, when county councils and urban district councils were set up. None of these initiatives 'killed' Home Rule, but they made farming and fishing more efficient all over the country, provided local employment, and greatly improved housing, health and welfare.

6.5 Religion

In 1861 Ireland was 77.6 per cent Catholic, 11.9 per cent Church of Ireland and 9 per cent Presbyterian, with the remainder taken up with other Protestant denominations and Freethinkers. The removal of the privileges of the Church of Ireland in 1868 brought it closer to other Protestant denominations, particularly Presbyterians and Methodists. The Church had been reforming all through the century, in any case, with a clampdown in the early decades on absenteeism and pluralism, and a new emphasis on missions at home and abroad. The 'Second Reformation' to convert Catholics, begun in the early nineteenth century, developed over the next two decades with Irish-language texts and Bibles and Protestant 'colonies' established on Achill island, in west Galway and west Kerry. Most conversions were temporary, and the Irish Church Missions to the Roman Catholics, set up in 1849, did not result in massive conversions either, but all these initiatives energized the Church of Ireland.

The General Assembly of the Presbyterian Church in 1840 called for wide-ranging reforms, although some divines were a little perturbed by the religious revival throughout Ulster from 1859. This took the form of frequent meetings and experiences of personal conversion, and gave a new freedom of religious expression to lay people, especially women. The more usual Protestant female experience was involvement in welfare organizations – charity clothing groups, Bible distribution, temperance societies, Sunday schooling and fund-raising for the churches and for the missions abroad, evening classes and day-schools.

Under the leadership of Archbishop, later Cardinal, Paul Cullen, from 1852, the Catholic Church's clerical discipline was improved, bishops' authority was strengthened, and new devotional practices like novenas and forty-hours adoration supplemented older devotions like the

Rosary. Most of the old, multi-purpose Penal-era chapels had been used for schools and catechism classes as well as religious services (in Irish-speaking areas up to the 1970s the church was still called *'teach a' phobal'* –the people's house), but these were replaced by large, imposing, single-purpose buildings, heavily decorated and ornate. In the countryside, the parish priest was the major religious authority who managed, among other things, the Catholic National school. In towns all over the country, although to a lesser extent in north-east Ulster, nuns were the main agents of Catholic modernization. Irish congregations, the eighteenth-century-founded Presentation, the Brigidines (founded in 1807), the Irish Sisters of Charity (1815), the Loreto (1821) and the Sisters of Mercy (1828) were the most widely-distributed, but foreign orders like the Sacred Heart, the St Louis Sisters and the French Sisters of Charity (to name but a few) also put down roots in the country after 1840. The Dominicans and Poor Clares (who were active rather than contemplative at this time) also flourished. Women religious taught, nursed, visited the sick poor, ran hostels and evening classes and industrial schools, and nursed in Poor Law workhouses. There were over 8,030 nuns in Ireland by 1901 compared to 3,700 priests, and 1,100 religious brothers. Women, therefore, made up over three-fifths (62.7 per cent) of all Catholics under religious vows.

In 1901 there were 3,898 Jews in Ireland, 75 per cent of them concentrated in Dublin and Belfast. Most arrived in the late 1880s and 1890s, fleeing oppression in eastern Europe and Russia, and most were small-scale businesspeople. In Limerick city, a concerted anti-Jewish campaign by a Redemptorist priest reduced the 170-strong community (unfairly singled out as moneylenders) to a handful by 1904. This was unusual, and Jews were at home enough in urban Ireland by the early twentieth century for the memorable and convincing main character of James Joyce's *Ulysses*, set in Dublin city in 1904, to be the insider-outsider Jew, Leopold Bloom.

6.6 Conclusion

As well as regular attendance at services, all religions agreed on certain core values: literacy, hard work, cleanliness, sobriety, sexual continence and service to the poor. All these traits facilitated associational culture, too, and the number of Irish people who belonged to some group other than their family or church grew from decade to decade. Every town had two or three musical bands, often with overtly political identities (Orange bands in Ulster, Parnellite and anti-Parnellite bands in Cork), and garrisons had popular bands too. They played at races and the newly popular regattas: 'The *Derry Standard* came to us and it bore a special notice | That on July the 21st comes off the Coleraine Regatta', ran a song set in 1872. Every river town had at least one rowing club for its 'commercials' (a general term for office, shop and industrial employees), and the Irish Amateur Rowing Union was founded in 1899. Soccer took hold in Leinster and Munster towns from the 1880s, as did rugby; the small east Clare parish of Parteen fielded a rugby team made up of farmers' and shopkeepers' sons and tradesmen and labourers, in the early twentieth century. Cycling clubs, for women as well as men, sprang up all over the country. Although Michael Cusack, one of the founders of the

Gaelic Athletic Association in 1884, had played cricket with some skill, his organization banned its members from playing (or even attending) cricket, soccer, rugby and other 'foreign games' until well into the twentieth century. The Gaelic Athletic Association revived and codified hurling, football, handball, and other sports. These sports were all for men, but camogie, hurling for women, developed from 1903.

The Gaelic League, by contrast, was apolitical, though it, too, developed into a nursery for revolutionaries. Founded in 1893 and admitting women on equal terms with men from the very beginning, it had 600 branches countrywide (and several paid employees) by 1903. A genuinely popular movement, it held Irish classes for factory workers and inner-city children as well as office workers and teachers and published simple, accessible textbooks. Its weekly newspaper, *An Claidheamh Soluis* (The Sword of Light) began in 1899. Its founders were Eoin MacNeill, a Gaelic scholar from Antrim, and Douglas Hyde, a Roscommon clergyman's son born in 1860.

Another culturally influential Roscommon Protestant born six years before Hyde was William Percy French, whose light-hearted songs on topics as diverse as unrequited love ('Pride of Petravore'), and unreliable railways ('Are You Right There, Michael?') are still loved and sung by Irish people of all classes and creeds. French was also a commentator on current affairs, and his comical verse 'The Queen's After-Dinner Speech', about Queen Victoria's visit to Dublin in 1900, mentioned the man who would later be acclaimed as Ireland's pre-eminent poet in the English language: 'And I think there's a slate, sez she | Off Willie Yeats, sez she ... Paradin' me crimes, sez she | In the *Irish Times*, sez she.' (To describe someone as having 'a slate off' was to say they were mad.) Yeats, one of the milder opponents of the queen's visit, was already coming together with Lady Gregory, Edward Martyn, William Fay, Willie Rooney and others to produce a distinctive Irish literature in the English language. These efforts resulted in (among other things) the founding of the Abbey Theatre in 1904.

Ireland at the dawn of the twentieth century was acutely conscious of cultural and political identity, nationalist or unionist. But it had also seen sweeping changes in living conditions and public health since 1850, and these will introduce the next chapter, setting the scene for the decades of war and revolution.

7
Revolution

∾

Twenty Decisive Years, 1903–1923

7.1 How the People Lived, 1903–1923

Life improved a lot for rural people in Ireland in the second half of the nineteenth century. The basics of diet remained what they had always been: potatoes, oatmeal, butter and milk, and home-cured bacon, with fish near coasts and rivers, and eggs if they could be spared from sale. Tea (in every house by the 1890s) and sugar broke the monotony. Another shop-bought item, the raising agent bicarbonate of soda, led to the baking of wheaten soda bread with regional variations – soda farls and boxty (flour mixed with grated raw potato) in Ulster, griddle bread and soda cake in Munster, seedy bread in Leitrim and Sligo. (Figure 7.1) The labourers' housing acts which accompanied the Land Acts of the 1880s and 1890s, the Congested Districts Board in the 1890s and other enabling legislation for the newly founded local authorities after 1898, led to the Irish small-farming /labouring class being the best housed in Europe by 1914. Slated roofs, back doors, good fireplaces and chimneys, glass windows and solid walls and floors gave some comfort to hard working lives. Country people also had clean water from springs and wells, and could dispose

FIGURE 7.1 Mother and child, Tyrone c. 1902. Reproduced by kind permission of the Ulster Folk and Transport Museum, Cultra, Co. Down. Good health and well-being shine forth from this rural mother and baby, despite their rather basic living conditions.

safely of waste. Rural poverty persisted. On Achill island, Co. Mayo, the struggle to maintain a standard of living caused a rise in the number of seasonal migrants to Scotland every year, at a time when these numbers were falling elsewhere, and in Donegal, there were near-famine conditions in some parts in the 1890s. In Co. Meath in the 1890s, the widowed Anne Ledwidge worked for 2s 6d a day for local farmers to rear her large young family. But at least she had a new three-bedroomed, solidly built county council cottage to return to in the evenings.

Some urban district councils built artisan dwellings, usually with two rooms upstairs, two downstairs, a water tap in the kitchen and a toilet out the back, or single-storey houses with the same number of rooms. These were most common in Belfast, Derry, Dublin, Cork, Limerick, Waterford and – to a lesser extent – Galway.

Every town with a sizeable railway station had its 'railway cottages' for transport employees and many mental asylums and other institutions had tied houses for workers. But too many of the urban working class, even in small towns, clustered in small unsanitary cabins on the fringes of the town, or in lanes, courts and tenements. One-third of Dublin's population lived in tenements, one- or two-room dwellings in multiple-occupancy urban houses. (Figure 7.2) By 1900 they had access to clean water at regularly placed pumps or pipes, and ground-level water closets for the disposal of waste, but often only one of

FIGURE 7.2 Dublin tenements. Reproduced by kind permission of Dublin City Libraries Archive. About one-third of Dublin's population in the early twentieth century lived in un-serviced one or two-roomed apartments in old Georgian or Victorian houses. Ceaseless housework (note the lace curtains) made tenement living just about respectable, but good health was out of reach for all but the sturdiest and strongest.

these for several families. Living with dignity under these conditions demanded continuous cleaning and carrying of vessels in and out. Elderly Dubliners in the 1980s who had been born in the tenements proudly remembered their care-worn mothers' pride in having everything 'spotless'. They also remembered the 'unfortunate girls' in the 'kip-houses' (brothels) of inner-city Dublin as well dressed and pretty, and kind to the poor children of the locality, but their delicate descriptor speaks for itself. Sex work was dangerous and dirty, and if sexually transmitted disease did not kill these women, pleurisy, tuberculosis or alcoholism would. 'Poor old Dicey Reilly, she has taken to the sup | And poor old Dicey Reilly, she will never give it up', goes the popular ballad about an aged-out prostitute.

Urban working-class diet depended on what was cheap in the shops, and what could be cooked on a small fire or stove. Every town had its own specialties usually based around offal: coddle in Dublin; skirts and kidneys in Limerick; crubeens (pig's feet) in Cork; the Ulster Fry with its sausages and puddings; tripe everywhere. Shop bread had health-giving yeast, but butter was hard to come by, and the much-criticized bottle of cold, sugared tea was far safer for a toddler than milk whose provenance and quality could not be ascertained.

The death rate for Ireland stood at 7 per 1,000 of the population in 1911 (lower than that of Britain) and this broke down as 8.7 for Leinster, 7.5 for Munster, 6.3 for Ulster and 4.9 for Connacht. In 1851, dispensaries (free or cheap doctors' clinics) had been set up on a systematic basis throughout the country, and in 1861, Poor Law workhouses opened their infirmaries to the general public. A very successful inoculation programme against smallpox was rolled out from 1858 as Irish people, always quick to embrace the new, queued for injections. Registration of births and deaths, begun in 1864, not only counted arrivals and departures but charted causes of death and incidence of diseases. The Public Health Act of 1874 divided the country into sanitary districts, with officers responsible for supplying clean water, preventing air pollution, keeping streets clean and maintaining cemeteries.

By 1900, smallpox, cholera, scarlatina, typhus and gastroenteric diseases were no longer major killers, but a deadlier plague than all of these, tuberculosis, was killing an average of 12,000 per year between 1899 and 1908. Consumption, as tuberculosis was also called, flourished in crowded, dusty working environments, with tailors, dressmakers, stonemasons and porters particularly vulnerable. Rates of pneumonia and bronchitis also rose. A vigorous programme of preventive education reduced the rate of tuberculosis infection by 1910, or maybe the bacillus exhausted itself. Connacht had the lowest incidence of tuberculosis, but even there, the rate was more than half that of Leinster, illustrating that the modernization of the westernmost province was coming at some cost. The influenza epidemic of 1918–1919 claimed around 10,000 lives in Ireland and took its heaviest toll in the towns and cities, where disinfected trams, empty streets and horse-drawn hearses queueing at cemetery gates, were sights never forgotten.

While living some distance from towns was usually better for general health, women about to give birth were safer near towns where they could access medical expertise if necessary. Maternal mortality was higher in 1910 in Mayo, the county with the second-lowest overall death rate in the country, than it was in the cities of

Dublin, Limerick or Belfast, which had very high overall death rates. However, maternal survival rates were improving everywhere, partly due to the trained district nurses who traversed difficult rural terrain on foot or bicycle in all weathers. Some of Annie M. P. Smithson's best-selling novels (and her autobiography) describe vividly her experiences as one such nurse in the first decade of the century. Infant mortality was another matter. In 1914 infant mortality in Ireland was 87.3 per 1,000 births; in Dublin and Belfast the rates were 143 and 128. The safest place to be a baby in 1914 was Roscommon, where the rate was 37.7, and after that Cavan (40.4) and Leitrim (41.9). These counties had some of the smallest, poorest farms in the country but clean air, pure water and the milk of local cows or goats for newly weaned children helped toddlers to thrive. (Figure 7.1)

At the other end of the life-cycle, the Old Age Pension, introduced on 1 January 1909, was a boon not only to the over-seventies, but to the families they lived with. This additional household income stream improved household food intake and probably played its part in the overall reduction of vulnerability to tuberculosis. However, old people without extended family or secure lodging could still end up in the dreaded 'Union' workhouse.

There was less reason to dread this place than before, by 1900. Workhouses had become less punitive since around the 1870s; the nuns who managed most Irish workhouses and, in Protestant parts of the country, the lady visitors, insisted on toys and treats for children, tea and buns for the elderly, curtains on the windows, mats on the floor, and better clothing and bedding for all. Many orphaned children were not in workhouses at all, but in industrial

MAP 7.1 Irish Railways 1906. Viceregal Commission on Irish Railways Including Light Railways. The existing cross-country lines laid down in the 1850s and 1860s were supplemented by 'light railways' in the late 1880s and 1890s, until very few parts of Ireland were unreachable by trains. Rail travel facilitated not only commerce and business, but excursions and holidays too.

schools, run by nuns, brothers or Protestant committees. These schools, in operation since 1868, were run on voluntary initiative but funded and inspected by the state. Although some would become bywords for brutality and neglect in the twentieth century, in their early days, industrial schools were often criticized for 'pampering' the offspring of the poor, because they taught them trades. Reformatories, an alternative to prison for criminal teenagers aged fourteen to sixteen, had been operating on a similar basis since 1858. The mental asylums founded at the beginning of the nineteenth century were still going strong, one in each county. These were enthusiastically availed of by the rural as well as the urban Irish, probably because of the alternative they offered to more heavy-handed ways of managing insanity or senile dementia in small thatched dwellings with open fires. An asylum in a town was a small industry, employing up to 150 people (many of whom had small farms on the side) and providing custom for local trades and provision merchants. Prisons employed fewer people but were just as important in the local economy. Mountjoy in Dublin and Maryborough (now Port Laoise) in Queen's County (now Laois), were the convict prisons but most cities and large towns had local prisons for petty crime – minor theft, vagrancy, disturbing the peace.

Industrial work of all kinds, especially the textiles and shipbuilding of the north-east, boomed during the war years 1914–1918 when demand soared. Demand for agricultural produce also increased dramatically, and these were good years for farmers, shopkeepers and food processors all over Ireland – half of the entire British armed forces' processed meat was produced by Dennys of

Waterford. Wages rose, but unemployed or badly paid working-class town dwellers struggled to pay the higher prices for eggs, bread and milk. About 200,000 men joined the British forces, and the wives of serving soldiers or sailors received 'separation allowances', which was the first money some wives and mothers ever controlled in the family exchequer. Women teachers, nurses, office workers, shop assistants and factory workers took part in all the activities a war brings – first-aid classes, knitting and sewing circles, bandage-rolling. The Agricultural Wages Board set up by the government in 1917 established minimum pay and conditions for agricultural labourers and, encouraged by this, by 1918, 60,000 of these workers had joined unions. Building workers, craftsmen, and office workers got organized, and the membership of the Irish Transport and General Workers Union (ITGWU) rose to 120,000 by 1920. Trade unionism was politicized in these years, which also saw other significant political developments.

7.2 Unionism, Nationalism and Trade Unionism, 1903–12

Although there were unionists all over Ireland, their activity was concentrated on the north-east of the country, co-ordinated in the Ulster Unionist Council of 1904–1905. Ulster Unionists included landowners, farmers, tradesmen, professionals and white-collar workers, and factory workers. Yet their leader, from 1910, was a Dubliner, the celebrity barrister Edward Carson. (Figure 7.3) All shades of political opinion, Conservative, Liberal, labour and suffragist, agreed upon the preservation of the Union

FIGURE 7.3 Edward Carson (1854–1935). Bettmann/Contributor/Bettmann/Getty images. A Dublin lawyer, and MP for Dublin University (Trinity) from 1892 to 1918, Carson also held several high legal offices during that period. Leader of the Irish Unionist Party from 1910, he ceded leadership to his deputy, James Craig, in 1921.

and the refusal of Home Rule. A strong, simple message, it overrode other loyalties.

Because nationalism involved planning for a new Ireland rather than maintaining the status quo, there were many competing ideas about the shape this new Ireland should take. The Home Rule Party, re-united under John Redmond and secure in its alliance with the Liberals at Westminster, wanted Ireland to have its own parliament but to remain in the British Empire for defence and foreign affairs. Most Irish nationalists supported this party up to 1916. Nationalists who wanted a greater degree of independence – Arthur Griffith's

Cumann na nGaedheal, the Dungannon Clubs (founded in Ulster in 1905), Inghinidhe na hEireann (Daughters of Ireland), a women's nationalist organization founded by Maud Gonne in 1900, and others – came together in one loose organization in 1904–1906. Novelist Mary Butler (a cousin, as it happened, of Edward Carson) came up with a name for it, Sinn Féin, which means, simply, ourselves. Griffith proposed dual monarchy, whereby Ireland and Britain would enjoy the same kind of relationship with each other as Austria and Hungary. Non-constitutional or 'advanced' nationalists also included republicans; the IRB, while not formally a member of Sinn Féin, was always hovering around the edges. Cultural nationalists, many of them members of the Gaelic League, found a welcome in Sinn Féin too. All agreed that Irish people should work out independence for themselves, on their own terms.

The Irish trade union movement had already set the example of working out Irish problems in Ireland, when the Irish Trade Union Congress (ITUC) broke with the British Trade Union Council in 1894. It represented only about 5 per cent (membership dipped and rose) of Irish waged workers by 1901, and it was increasingly challenged (or rendered irrelevant) by the rise of new trade unionism. Ireland's mini-boom since 1881 had brought about a sharp increase in unskilled workers, agricultural labourers, transport workers, construction workers and women workers in various sectors, all hungry for representation. The May Day parade organized in Dublin in 1893 brought 20,000 onto the streets. The Irish Land and Labour Association, founded in 1894, was giving a stronger voice than before to agricultural labourers. The pace picked up in the first decade of the new century.

The British-based National Union of Dock Labourers (NUDL), of which Liverpool-Irish James Larkin was an organizer, was one of the 'new' unions for unskilled workers sweeping across the globe since the late 1890s. After organizing strikes among textile workers, dock labourers and even bringing the police out on strike in Belfast in 1907, Larkin turned his attention south, threw off the NUDL, and founded the ITGWU in 1908. This 'new' labour activism utilized the strike, the sympathetic strike and the ban on 'tainted goods' (i.e. goods produced or handled by non-union labour). Membership of the ITGWU alone rose from 5,000 in 1908 to 18,000 in 1912, while trade union membership in general rose to 41,000 in that year. Politicians had been taking notice of labour since the broadening of the franchise in 1884, and by the early twentieth century J. P. Nanetti MP was the Home Rule Party's liaison with the ITUC. The year 1912 also saw the foundation of the Irish Trade Union Congress and Labour Party in Clonmel. Not all trade unionists were socialists, by any means, but James Connolly, one of the most inspiring and charismatic labour organizers, was. An Edinburgh-born labour organizer who had founded the short-lived Irish Socialist Republican Party in 1894, he had brought female workers out on strike in Belfast. Unusually, he also recognized, in his persuasive writings, the burden of women's unpaid household work, and unlike many mainstream trade unionists, he unequivocally supported women's suffrage.

The Irish women's suffrage movement encompassed all shades of political opinion. Members of the Munster Women's Franchise League included the novelists Somerville and Ross (whose political sympathies were broadly unionist), and the nationalist Mary MacSwiney. Suffrage societies were dotted all over the country in the first decade of the century, and there was even one in Annaghdown, Co. Galway. Inghinidhe na hEireann's *Bean na hEireann* (Woman of Ireland), a newspaper which ran from 1908 to 1911, was pro-suffrage, though its main focus was nationalism. Suffragism was quite respectable; when militant English suffragist Christabel Pankhurst gave a speech in Galway in 1911, the Town Hall was packed with the city's political, academic and commercial elite. The Dublin-based Irish Women's Franchise League comprised mainly nationalist graduates (male and female) in Dublin, with the radical Sheehy Skeffingtons (Francis and Hanna) at its core. But feminists did not ignore working-class women. The Irishwomen's Reform League under Louie Bennett was as devoted to trade unionism as it was to the suffrage, and the Irish Women Workers' Union, founded in 1911 by Bennett and Delia Larkin, represented poorly paid and sweated workers. All these organizations, like Sinn Féin and the Gaelic League, attracted nationalist women because there was nowhere else for them to go. The Home Rule Party, unlike the British Conservative and Liberal parties, did not have a female auxiliary organization. Some nationalist MPs, Stephen Gwynn, T. M. Healy, William O'Brien and Willie Redmond among them, supported votes for women, but when Asquith, hostile to the suffrage, assumed leadership of the Liberal party, the Home Rulers would not go against him. Carson, leader of the Unionists, was anti-suffrage, though his right-hand man and successor, James Craig, was sympathetic to it. A number of different Irish organizations came together in the all-island Irish Women's Suffrage Federation in

1911, only to disband the following year when nationalist–unionist tensions became irreconcilable.

The Third Home Rule bill was introduced in the House of Commons in 1912 and passed in January 1913. It was defeated in the House of Lords, but the Lords' veto on legislation was due to be abolished anyway, so Home Rule seemed imminent. In response to this prospect, over 237,000 Ulster Unionist men came out en masse to sign a Covenant against Home Rule in September, and around the same number of women signed a separate Declaration to the same effect. Now, as Irish unionism became Ulster Unionism, the political partition of the island – the exclusion of at least some Ulster counties from a Home Rule Ireland – was discussed publicly for the first time.

On the eve of the Great War, about four-fifths of Ireland's population supported Home Rule, and about one-fifth were implacably opposed to it. That one-fifth, however, was concentrated in one area, and had the backing of a major British political party and about half of the British electorate. The Ulster Volunteers, a male military force, were formed early in 1913 to resist Home Rule if it was forced upon them. By 1914 they numbered about 100,000. Nationalists who wanted more than Home Rule watched everything with great interest but were not, as yet, planning any separatist activity. John Redmond was still regarded by most as the Irish prime-minister-in-waiting. The next four years would change everything.

7.3 Politics, 1913–1923

In Dublin in 1913, Larkin's ITGWU – 30,000 strong countrywide – brought many unskilled workers out on strike in August, and the event known as the Dublin Lock-Out (members were locked out of their jobs) lasted until February 1914. As an industrial action it was a failure, but because it drew attention to the appalling living conditions of Dublin's unskilled workers, it drew sympathy from a broad range of Irish advanced nationalists, intellectuals and artists, and British trade unions. After two workers were killed by police during a labour demonstration on 31 August, the Irish Citizen Army was founded by Jack White and James Connolly as a workers' defence force. It was small, and Dublin-centred, with only about 350 members at its height. It admitted women, among them medical doctor Kathleen Lynn, a clergyman's daughter from Galway, and Constance Markievicz. From a landowning family in Sligo, Markievicz was a close associate of Connolly, and a sister of British-based trade unionist Eva Gore-Booth.

The Irish Volunteers were formed in spring 1914 by Eoin MacNeill, partly as a response to the Ulster Volunteers' mobilization; if unionists had a militia, then so should nationalists. Although Redmond was wary at first, he made the best of it, and soon the movement grew, numbering 188,000 by the summer. One prominent Irish Volunteer was Patrick Pearse, a barrister, teacher and Irish-language scholar. Unlike the Ulster Volunteers, the Irish Volunteers had a female auxiliary force from the start, Cumann na mBan [literally, the women's organization], under the leadership of Agnes O'Farrelly, one of the first Irish female academics, and Jennie Wyse-Power, a shopkeeper who had been (as Jennie O'Toole) a member of the Ladies' Land League twenty-five years earlier. The Irish Volunteers drilled and trained openly and were not a secret society. The Ulster Volunteers imported its arms in April 1914 through Larne in Co. Antrim without any fuss; the Irish Volunteers' parallel effort in July of that year at Howth culminated in troops called in by the Dublin Metropolitan Police shooting four people dead in a Volunteer demonstration in Bachelors Walk in the city centre. Nationalists of all shades of opinion were outraged by the Curragh 'mutiny' earlier in the year, when a number of British army officers stationed in Ireland's biggest garrison in Co. Kildare declared that they would not enforce Home Rule even if ordered to do so by their government. Another worry for nationalists was that the House of Commons had passed a bill in June which could exclude Ulster from Home Rule on a temporary basis. As there were over half a million nationalists/Catholics in the nine Ulster counties taken as a whole, and they made up the majority population in five of these counties (Cavan, Donegal, Fermanagh, Monaghan and Tyrone), this was worrying.

The outbreak of the European war in August 1914 did not budge nationalists or Unionists from their positions, but it postponed direct confrontation. Home Rule was shelved for the duration of the conflict, and John Redmond in September 1914, at a speech in Woodenbridge, Co. Wicklow, strongly advised Irish Home Rule supporters to support the war effort. About 200,000 Irishmen joined the British forces, half of these from Ulster. The Irish Volunteers split on this issue, with the majority following Redmond's advice and calling themselves the National Volunteers. The Irish Volunteers (the minority retained the original title) who numbered about 13,000, vowed to 'serve neither king nor kaiser, but Ireland'. Cumann na mBan, which numbered about 3,000 also split, with the majority of the women staying with the Irish Volunteers, although the founder of Inghinidhe na hEireann, Maud Gonne, went to France with an ambulance unit.

The Easter Rising of 1916 was the work not only of the Irish Volunteers but also of the now-resurgent IRB, and the Irish Citizen Army, with Cumann na mBan nursing, catering, doing signals and despatch-riding. But why was there a Rising at all? Advanced nationalists feared that Home Rule would never happen, given the strength of Unionist opposition. More importantly, they were not satisfied with the limited independence which Home Rule promised, which would leave foreign affairs and defence under the control of the British Empire. Those on the left wanted a republic which would give a strong voice to workers and their representatives. The Republic which was proclaimed outside the General Post Office (GPO) on Easter Monday was a social democracy which promised the equality of all traditions on the island, and gender equality. But why did it happen in 1916? Looking back, we can see that this was the mid-point of the Great War, but contemporaries had no way of knowing this. The much-anticipated Allied 'Big Push' planned for early summer would, it was hoped, end the European conflict, and the revolutionaries wanted to proclaim a republic of Ireland before the war was over so as to gain a seat at the peace negotiations. They were not unusual in the Europe of their time. Revolutions broke out, or were planned, in several belligerent countries, notably Russia but also Germany and Finland.

Plans to import ammunition from Germany were made by Ulster Protestant Sir Roger Casement, who had been knighted for his human rights activism in the Congo and Peru. Although Casement's plan failed and he was arrested on Banna Strand in Co. Kerry on Good Friday, the Dublin revolutionary leaders ignored Eoin MacNeill's order not to proceed with the revolution and staged a revolt on Easter Monday without sufficient arms and with only minimal support outside Dublin.

After the defeat of the rebels, the Rising was portrayed as a heroic failure, and it is tempting now to view it through the lens of W. B. Yeats's stirring poem, 'Easter 1916', which describes its outcome as a 'terrible beauty'. George Russell (AE), James Stephens, Seumas O'Sullivan and Francis Ledwidge also wrote memorable poems about the Rising which stressed sacrifice, heroism and youth. But the Rising's organizers, especially Tom Clarke and Seán MacDiarmada of the IRB, fully expected the Rising to succeed. Seizing and fortifying key buildings in a city, especially the centre of communications, the GPO, was standard revolutionary procedure, and the rebels managed to hold Dublin city centre for five days and to divert British men and ammunition away from the front. They could have held out longer, had they been less responsible about the death toll. By the time of the surrender, 450 combatants and civilians were dead, and most Irish people, even nationalists, were angry with the rebels. Yet, popular sympathy throughout most of the island (except the north-east) was not long in swinging behind the rebels in the spring and summer of 1916, for a number of reasons.

One reason was the excessive reaction of the British forces and administration. The massacre by soldiers of sixteen civilians in North King Street, and the murders of well-known pacifist Francis Sheehy Skeffington, journalists Thomas Dickson and Patrick McIntyre, and mechanic James Coade by Captain John Bowen-Colthurst, operating out of Portobello barracks, shocked many. News outlets were paralyzed during Easter Week, so most people did not hear of these atrocities until around the same time as they heard about the executions.

The 1916 leaders were rebelling against a government which was supported by democratically elected Irish nationalists – the Home Rule Party – and, moreover, solicited aid from the enemy against which many Irishmen were fighting. Arguably, therefore, the executions by firing squad in Kilmainham Jail of the Proclamation signatories Patrick Pearse, James Connolly, Thomas Clarke, Thomas MacDonagh, Joseph Plunkett, Seán MacDiarmada, Eamonn Ceannt and of seven others, five of whom were commandants of garrisons, were militarily justifiable. Two garrison commanders were spared the death penalty, Eamon de Valera (Boland's Mills) probably because of his American birth, and Constance Markievicz, (Royal College of Surgeons), because she was a woman. The execution of British nurse Edith Cavell by the Germans in Belgium the previous October had caused widespread revulsion, and the British did not want to risk provoking a similar reaction. However, even if the rebel leaders' executions could be justified, the strapping of a dying James Connolly to a chair to be shot disturbed even his firing squad. And there was widespread disquiet at the executions of rank-and-file rebels Willie Pearse (because he was Patrick's brother) and John McBride (because he had fought against the British in the Anglo-Boer War). Home Rule MP John Dillon had every reason to be angry with those who had usurped his party's leadership of nationalist Ireland, yet when he protested about the executions in the House of Commons he was widely supported. The hanging of Roger Casement (a traitor's, not a soldier's death) in London in August 1916 – preceded by a stripping of all his well-earned honours – was seen as particularly vengeful.

There is also the fact that Ireland was a small country, and Dublin a small city where many people knew, or at least knew *of*, each other. Joyce has Molly Bloom in *Ulysses* (Figure 7.4) commenting on Arthur Griffith in 1904 as 'the coming man', though she adds that he doesn't 'look

FIGURE 7.4 Arthur Griffith (1871–1922) and Eamon de Valera (1882–1975) at the Peace conference in Dublin, 1921. Hulton Archive/Stringer/Hulton Archive/Getty images. One of the last pictures taken of these two men together. Griffith would take the pro-Treaty side in the ensuing split and Civil War and de Valera would lead the anti-Treatyites.

it'. The men who took part in the Rising were clerks, teachers, small shopkeepers, shop assistants, jobbing journalists, tradesmen, factory workers, general labourers and railway workers. De Valera (Figure 7.4) and MacDonagh were academics, Pearse a barrister and Plunkett a highly educated poet, but they were a minority among the men. Educated women made up a proportionately greater part of Cumann na mBan and the Irish Citizen Army, but there were also drapers' assistants, milliners, shirt-makers, factory workers and laundresses imprisoned in Richmond Barracks after the Rising, and a good proportion of the female workforce of Jacobs Mills operated under the command of Thomas MacDonagh (who sent them home before the surrender so that they would not be arrested). The 1916 rebels, male and female, were few in number but they were a seam that ran through all of society.

It was after the Rising that the women's organizations took charge, disseminating a vigorous cult of the dead and the imprisoned (about 1,000 were interned straightaway in Frongoch in Wales), running prisoners' welfare funds and numerous commemorative events, many with strong religious overtones. Thomas Ashe's 1917 poem 'Let Me Carry Your Cross for Ireland, Lord', made an explicit connection between the Passion of Jesus Christ and the Rising, continuing the cult of suffering and endurance that began with the Fenians. The 1916 propagandists, however, received unbidden help from unlikely sources. Advertiser-publishers Wilson Hartnell, not noted for their nationalism, published *The Brochure of the Rebellion: Dublin and the Sinn Fein Rising – An illustrated Record of the 1916 Insurrection* a month after the Rising and advertised it in their magazine *The Lady of the House*. This thirty-two-page collectors' album had pictures of Volunteer badges and detailed maps of the revolutionary garrisons, and although it showcased the Trinity College Officers' Training Corps which had stood ready to help put down the rebels, its publication of a poem 'by Mr P.H.Pearse to his mother written immediately prior to his execution' showed where its sympathies lay.

Meanwhile, Irish men were fighting on the battlefields of Europe, and over 40,000 would die before the Armistice. Home Rule MP Thomas Kettle's poem 'To My Daughter Betty' shows that many saw the Great War as a fight for Christian civilization and social justice: 'for a dream, born in a herdsman's shed | And for the secret Scripture of the poor'. He died at the Somme. Poet and nationalist Francis Ledwidge died at Ypres two years later. Fighting in the Great War entrenched unionists in their British identity, but it did not destroy nationalists' dreams. Many battle-scarred Irish soldiers returned to Ireland to find that the caravan had moved on in their absence. Some Great War veterans hopped nimbly aboard, like Tom Barry, the architect of the bloody ambush of Auxiliaries in Kilmichael, Co. Cork in 1920, and Emmet Dalton, who was with Michael Collins when he was ambushed in 1922.

In 1918 all shades of nationalist opinion on the island, including Home Rulers, were mobilized in a successful campaign against conscription; bishops, trade unions and local authorities (outside the north-east), and women's organizations campaigned tirelessly. In the general election held throughout Great Britain and Ireland in December 1918, all men over twenty-one were able to vote and so, too, were women over thirty of adequate property qualifications. These first-time voters might have been partly responsible for the Sinn Féin success; Griffith's organization, now the party representing the heirs of 1916, won seventy-three seats, the Home Rule Party six seats, and the Unionists twenty-seven seats. Constance Markievicz was the first woman ever elected to the House of Commons, but she never took her seat, because the Irish parliament, or Dáil, met for the first time in Dublin's Mansion House on 21 January 1919. Its members were (and are) called *Teachtaí Dála*, (Dáil deputies), or TDs for short. Several deputies were in prison at the time, such as Eamon de Valera, who was elected president of the Dáil and managed to escape from Lincoln Jail in April. On the run, he went to America to raise funds, leaving Michael Collins (Minister for Finance) and Cathal Brugha (Defence) in charge of the new government and the Irish Republican Army, the new name for the Irish Volunteers. The British proclaimed the democratically elected Dáil an illegal organization in 1919. Thereafter it could only meet secretly and irregularly, and this gave militants the upper hand.

The War for Independence (1919 to 1921) was never a total war. Commercial and social life continued. In 1920 thousands of people from all over the country descended on Tipperary town by train and charabanc to see a weeping statue of Our Lady. They might have encountered on their way patrols by the 13,000-strong 'Black and Tans' and Auxiliaries, two ill-disciplined but well-resourced paramilitary forces sent in to supplement the police force. The events of 21 November 1920 are an extreme example of the attack–reprisal pattern of the War. Eleven unarmed British intelligence officers were murdered in their lodgings in Dublin by Collins's elite assassination squad early on that morning, and in reprisal, that afternoon Auxiliaries drove into Croke Park, the Gaelic Athletic Association's sports ground in Dublin where Dublin were playing Tipperary, and opened fire, murdering fourteen unarmed match-goers. By the following January most of Munster was under martial law. The 'Tans and Auxiliaries' rather than the Royal Irish Constabulary (RIC) or British army were now the main targets for IRA attack, and their reprisals – burning entire towns including Balbriggan, Cork and Mallow, and shooting unarmed civilians – were losing the propaganda war for Britain.

As guerilla fighters, the IRA depended heavily on the (now) 21,000 members of Cumann na mBan, who not only carried messages and ammunition (even the 'Tans' were slow to search women) but also routinely provided meals, accommodation, bandages and clean clothes in the farmhouses which served as barracks for the 'flying columns' of IRA guerillas. Women also took part in the law courts and local government machinery set up by the Dáil; forty-three were elected to county councils in 1920. Agricultural and unskilled labourers set up soviets – workers' co-operatives – throughout 1919 and 1920, among them the Limerick soviet of April 1919 and that of Knocklong (a town in the heartland of the dairying Golden Vale) in 1920, and there were 'red flags over the Suir valley' (South Tipperary and Waterford). The first Irish soviet, however, was in January 1919, when the male and female staff and patients of Monaghan District Lunatic Asylum came together to demand better working and living conditions – a story of co-operation that could cast a new light on these institutions. The fact that soviets were founded at all showed both keen awareness of international developments and a belief that the workers' republic was imminent.

The war also spilled into the north of the country, where there was an active IRA campaign and a strong reaction from police and from Orange interests. Sectarian tension that was never far from the surface resulted in hundreds of civilian deaths and many Catholics were burned out of their homes. In December 1920 the Government of Ireland Act set up two states on the island, Northern Ireland and Southern Ireland. It was envisaged that the two states would come together in a Council of Ireland, to decide key matters. Southern Ireland never came to be, but Northern Ireland exists to this day. Embodying Antrim, Armagh, Down, Fermanagh, Londonderry and Tyrone, it had its own assembly, and a relationship with Westminster similar to that envisaged for a Home Rule parliament. In its first elections, held in May 1921, unionists won forty out of fifty-two seats, and James Craig succeeded Carson as leader.

July of the same year saw an end to the War for Independence and a truce, and negotiations for a treaty began in the autumn.

The five Treaty delegates who travelled to London included veteran Arthur Griffith and relative newcomer Michael Collins, already making his name as a skilled administrator in his role as minister for finance. Eamon de Valera did not go. They came back to the Dáil in December with an agreement which they hoped the Dáil would ratify. The proposal was for dominion status for a twenty-six-county Ireland, with a far greater measure of independence than that offered by Home Rule.

A battle-weary Collins admitted to the Dáil that this was not freedom, but 'freedom to achieve freedom'. The British, with vastly superior resources, had threatened resumption of war if the Treaty was not accepted. The Treaty debates raged over the Dáil session of Christmas and New Year 1921–1922 and the main objection to it was the oath of allegiance to the British Crown. The exclusion of the six counties was hardly discussed at all, because the Treaty delegates had been promised a boundary commission to sort all this out, but also because nationalists believed that the small state of Northern Ireland could not last long. In January 1922 the Dáil ratified the Treaty by a slender majority of seven; de Valera and Cathal Brugha went against it. De Valera led the anti-Treaty side, Collins and Griffith led those who upheld it. Moderate labour interests and a majority of voters supported the Treaty parties (pro-Treaty Sinn Féin and the Labour Party led by Thomas Johnson) who won the general election comfortably in June. Griffith, elected president of the pro-Treaty Dáil, died of a brain haemorrhage (some said a broken heart) in August the same year, and later that month Collins was shot by Republican (anti-Treaty) forces in west Cork. At this stage the Civil War was in full swing, Republicans versus Free Staters.

TD Mary McSwiney's lengthy speech against the Treaty during the Dáil debates suggested that if this was the best the male delegates to London could do, they should 'send the women next time'. (Figure 7.5) Nearly 90 per cent of Cumann na mBan opposed the Treaty, as did most prominent female nationalists – Markievicz, Kathleen Clarke (widow of 1916 leader Thomas and

FIGURE 7.5 Mary MacSwiney (1872–1942). Topical Press Agency/Stringer/Hulton Archive/Getty images. One of the first female graduates and a suffragist and nationalist from the early twentieth century, MacSwiney was elected to the Second Dáil in 1920 and was sister of Terence MacSwiney, the Lord Mayor of Cork who died on hunger strike in Brixton Prison in the same year. She was one of the most vocal opponents of the treaty.

a lifelong activist in her own right), Kathleen Lynn, Ada English (a psychiatrist and a TD), and many more, although the most senior female activist of all, Jennie Wyse-Power, supported it. Those on the far left like Donegal teacher Peadar O'Donnell and Galway socialist Liam Mellows also went against the Treaty. Rank-and-file anti-Treatyites, nonetheless, represented all shades of socio-political opinion, and the Free State National Army was made up of men of all social classes. All the establishment powers from the British government to the Catholic bishops supported the Free State, and the Republicans finally laid down their arms in May 1923.

The Civil War claimed between 1,500 and 2,000 lives (810, or 40–54 per cent of these were soldiers of the pro-Treaty Free State), making it one of the least lethal European civil wars of that time, and life returned to normal fairly quickly after it. If the Civil War divisions determined the major political loyalties for the remainder of the century this was not because of significant ideological differences but because of long and unforgiving memories of atrocities perpetrated by both sides. The murder of Republican Noel Lemass was still being commemorated in the 1980s on the spot in the Dublin mountains where his body was found in 1923, and similar commemorations all over the country continue to the present day.

7.4 Conclusion

'When we get what we want, we'll be quiet as can be | Where the mountains of Mourne sweep down to the sea', was the Ulster nationalist exile's concluding promise in Percy French's song, 'The Mountains of Mourne', written in 1904. But, by 1923, had any political group on the island of Ireland got what it wanted? Ulster Unionists were still not ruled directly from Westminster, which was what they (and Carson in particular) clamoured for originally, but their movement had developed sufficient momentum and independence to be satisfied with its own parliament. Their numerical supremacy over the one-third of nationalists in the six counties was clear, but not comfortable enough to enable them to be in any way gracious in victory.

Saorstát Éireann, the Irish Free State as established in 1922, was not Pearse's republic or Connolly's workers' republic, nor even Griffith's dual monarchy (although Griffith had moved on from this ideal); neither was it Redmond's or Parnell's Home Rule Ireland. Nor was it the total separation envisaged by the IRB since the 1860s, nor the Young Irelanders in the 1840s, nor even Wolfe Tone's republic. But although cynics commented that only the flags on public buildings had changed, the Saorstát had a greater degree of independence than that promised by Home Rule. Britain retained three naval ports (Beara Island and Cobh in Cork, and Lough Swilly in Donegal) and there was still an oath of allegiance to the British monarch, but all other British armed personnel and civil administrators left the twenty-six counties. The Free State had autonomous defence forces and civil service, and was responsible for its own foreign policy.

As for the flag, the Tricolour of the Free State, later Republic, promised the white of peace between the green of nationalism and the orange of unionism, an aspiration that went back to the 1790s. Such a dream was impossible to realize in the short-term, and over the next half-century, if the Free State/Republic as a whole often forgot about the orange part of the flag, Northern Ireland often acted as if independent Ireland did not exist either.

8

Stability, 1922–1969

8.1 Introduction

For the remainder of this book, the twenty-six-county state which won its independence from Britain in 1922 will be called Ireland, independent Ireland, or (after 1948) the Republic, to distinguish it from the six-county statelet which remained within the United Kingdom. This will be called Northern Ireland, or sometimes 'the North', with a capital N. 'The island' or 'both jurisdictions' will be used to refer to the country as a whole. (Map 8.1)

8.2 Ireland, 1922–1969

8.2.1 Politics

The Free State Constitution established the standard bicameral parliament comprising the Dáil, the lower house, and the Seanad (or Senate), the upper house. The 153 members of the Dáil were elected by proportional representation, or the single transferable vote – voters vote one, two, three, and so on in order of their choice, and the surplus votes of those elected are distributed according to preferences. Imposed by the British as one of the terms of the Treaty, proportional representation survives to this day. The Seanad of 1922 had sixty members, some appointed by the president of the Dáil, some

MAP 8.1 Partitioned Ireland, 1922. Interim Archives/Contributor/ Archive Photos/Getty images. Six of the nine Ulster counties were incorporated into Northern Ireland in 1922. Donegal, Monaghan and Cavan remained in independent Ireland.

elected by its members. It could discuss and delay, but not veto, legislation presented by the Dáil.

Until 1937 the head of the governing party in the Dáil was called the president. The ceremonial head of state was the governor general, the king's representative. Under de

Valera's new constitution of 1937, the head of government or prime minister was called the Taoiseach, the deputy PM was the Tánaiste, and the houses of parliament as a collective entity were called the Oireachtas. The office of governor general was abolished, and the ceremonial head of state was an tUachtarán, the President. Douglas Hyde, the founder of the Gaelic League, served in this role until his retirement in 1943; Seán T. Ó Ceallaigh, a republican veteran, succeeded him until 1958, then Eamon de Valera took over until 1973. In 1948 Taoiseach John A. Costello declared Ireland a republic and left the British Commonwealth.

The Free State established universal adult suffrage (over twenty-one) with both sexes eligible to vote and to be elected or appointed to the highest political office, thus giving Irish women complete political equality six years before their British and Northern Irish counterparts. This would be as good as it got for Irish women's public and political status for the next half-century.

The oldest political party was Labour, founded in 1912. In 1922 it supported Cumann na nGaedheal, the pro-Treaty party under W. T. Cosgrave, but winning twenty-two seats in the 1927 election gave it the confidence to turn its back on the government party with which it was becoming disenchanted.

Fine Gael (the extended family of Gaels) was formed in 1933 from a combination of Cumann na nGaedheal under W. T. Cosgrave, and the militant Army Comrades Association, also known as the Blueshirts. Fine Gael gained a reputation as the law-and-order party. However, the police force they founded in 1922, the Garda Síochána (Guardians of the Peace) was unarmed, and they managed to curtail the political power of the army generals in 1924. They also managed not to overreact when their former Civil War opponents took their Dáil seats in 1927.

These opponents — most of them at any rate — had become the political party Fianna Fáil (the soldiers of *Fál*, an ancient name for Ireland) founded in 1926 by Eamon de Valera. In 1922 the forty-four elected Republican TDs refused to take their seats because of their objection to the oath of allegiance to the king, but after the 1927 election de Valera led them into the Dáil, declaring that the oath was an empty formula, and could be taken by Republicans. Fianna Fáil, supported by the Labour Party, took office in 1932, but were returned the following year with an overall majority, no longer dependent on Labour. De Valera, now president (as the office of Taoiseach/prime minister was then known), abolished the oath of allegiance, downgraded the office of governor general, and refused to pay the land annuities (repayments to the British for loans incurred during tenants' purchase of their lands between 1903 and 1908). The British abdication crisis in 1936 proved an opportune moment to remove all references to the monarch from the constitution. De Valera's Constitution (Bunreacht na hÉireann), a more nationalist one than that of 1922, was accepted by a majority of the electorate in 1937. In 1938, as part of a deal on trade, de Valera got the British to vacate the three ports it had retained as part of the Treaty settlement.

Fianna Fáil broke definitively with its paramilitary past when de Valera declared the IRA an illegal organization in 1936. This was broadly in line with public opinion, which was unsympathetic to the IRA bombing campaign carried out in British cities in the late 1930s — nine civilians were killed in Coventry in August 1939. There was little or no public opposition to the internment of 500 IRA prisoners in the Curragh camp in the 1940s, though there was some muted disquiet at the hanging of six IRA men charged with capital offences. Later, the IRA border campaign of 1955–1962 was not widely supported on the island.

De Valera's policy of neutrality in the Second World War was supported across party lines. During the Emergency, as the years 1939–1945 were known in Ireland, tens of thousands of Irish people emigrated to a Britain that was crying out for workers, and Irish food exports to Britain were more important than ever. Ireland's neutrality favoured the Allied forces, despite the impression given by de Valera's notorious visit of condolence to the German ambassador on the death of Hitler in 1945. On Erris Head in Co. Mayo, the word ÉIRE was spelled out in large rocks for the benefit of Allied airmen, and from Blacksod post office and weather station not too far away, the vital weather forecast for the Allied invasion of Normandy in June 1944 was supplied via Dublin. Three years earlier, Dublin and Louth fire engines had rushed north to help out when German air raids devastated Belfast in April and May 1941. Urgently requested and gladly given, this co-operation marked a high point in cross-border relationships. A few weeks later a lone Luftwaffe pilot dropped a number of bombs on Dublin in the early hours of 31 May, killing more than forty people in the North Strand and destroying hundreds of homes.

Wartime privations, rising unemployment and a Wages Standstill Order in 1943 made the Fianna Fáil government unpopular, but Labour could not capitalize on this electorally because it had split into the National Labour Party under William O'Brien and the Labour Party under

Jim Larkin. Meanwhile de Valera's small-farmer support base was being undermined by a new party, Clann na Talmhan (the Children of the Land), founded in 1938. Republicans dismayed at what they saw as Fianna Fáil's betrayal found a voice in Clann na Poblachta (the Children of the Republic) founded by Seán McBride in 1946. These parties joined with Labour and Fine Gael under its leader, John A. Costello, to form the first Inter-Party Government in 1948, when sixteen years of Fianna Fáil rule were brought to an end. Fianna Fáil came back briefly from 1951 to 1954, and came back again in 1957 to remain in power until 1973. In 1959 de Valera stepped down as leader of Fianna Fáil, and Seán Lemass took over. He was replaced in 1966 by Jack Lynch.

The Labour Party reunited in 1948 under William Norton in the first Inter-party Government, and from then on, usually supported Fine Gael in government, with the Labour leader as Tánaiste to the Fine Gael Taoiseach.

The Labour Party represented trade unionists and working people all over the country, especially in parts of rural Ireland where labourers' organizations had been strong in the early twentieth century, such as Tipperary, north Kerry, Wexford and Westmeath. It was usually socially conservative, and could not be called left-wing, but distinguishing 'left' from 'right' is a difficult exercise in mainstream Irish political history. Fianna Fáil was dubbed 'Communist' by Cumann na nGaedheal in the run-up to the 1932 elections, and, indeed, de Valera continued to recognize the Spanish Republic until it finally fell in 1939, and the Fianna Fáil newspaper the *Irish Press* (set up in 1931) had a more left-leaning slant on news than its main rival, the 'Blueshirt' *Irish Independent*. Fine Gael had elements of a right-wing party – a militant quasi-fascist wing the Blueshirts (however short-lived) in the 1930s, and a horror of public spending. In the reforming Inter-Party Government of 1948 dominated by Fine Gael, it was the smaller parties, Clann na Poblachta, Clann na Talmhan and Labour who made the running on economic and social issues. What with this, and Fine Gael's John A. Costello declaring Ireland a republic and leaving the British Commonwealth, it seemed Fianna Fáil's clothes were being stolen. But Clann na Poblachta and Clann na Talmhan died out in the mid-1960s, and it was Fianna Fáil's turn to accuse Fine Gael of being 'red' when the latter brought out a programme for a 'Just Society' in 1965; they also levelled this accusation at Labour when the latter declared that the 1970s would be socialist.

Throughout this period women never made up more than 3.5 per cent of elected members of the Dáil. This was not far behind percentages in other non-Nordic European countries where women had the vote – in 1960, 3.9 per cent of members of the British House of Commons were female, when the Dáil's proportion was 3.4 per cent.

Seán Lemass's historic meeting with Northern Irish Prime Minister Terence O'Neill in Belfast in 1965 sprang from a new confidence on Ireland's part. The fiftieth anniversary of 1916 was celebrated with great pride throughout the country, with pageants, concerts and parades, and its soundtrack was Seán Ó Riada's stirring *Mise Eire*. The blowing-up by a fringe republican group (not the IRA) of Nelson's Pillar in Dublin was regarded by most people as a prank (nobody was hurt) rather than an act of civic vandalism or indeed, a blow to British imperialism.

Ireland joined the United Nations in 1955, and the Irish Defence Forces began to take part in peacekeeping missions. Nine Irish soldiers were killed in an ambush in Niemba, in the Congo in 1960, and Irish peacekeepers saw heavy action in Jadotville the following year. The army also served in Cyprus as UN peacekeepers from 1964.

The rise of the civil rights movement in Northern Ireland and the unfolding events of 1969 would pose a new challenge to the Irish government and its security forces.

8.2.2 *Economy and Society*

Cosgrave's government reduced government spending from £42 million in 1924 to £24 million in 1927, by not expanding existing health and welfare services, and notoriously, by taking a shilling off the Old Age and Blind Pensions in 1924. Minister for Industry and Commerce Patrick McGilligan set the tone in 1923 by stating ruefully that Irish people might have to die of starvation. No starvation deaths were recorded, but levels of malnutrition and deprivation remained high. This government concentrated on business and infrastructure. The hydro-electric power plant at Ardnacrusha, in Co. Clare, known as the Shannon Scheme, (Figure 8.1) was completed by 1929 and the Electricity Supply Board, set up in 1927, was the first of many 'semi-state bodies' set up over succeeding decades which nationalized certain services and resources: Comhlucht Siúcra Éireann managed sugar beet; Aer Lingus, the national airline, was founded in 1936; Coras Iompair Éireann (CIE), the transport authority, in 1945: Bord Iascaigh Mhara, the fisheries authority, in 1952; and many others.

FIGURE 8.1 Ardnacrusha Hydro-electric power station, Co. Clare, under construction. Popperfoto/Popperfoto/Getty images. The flagship project of the new Irish state, this power station was complete by 1929, and its building involved thousands of workers, the importation of some materials and expertise from Germany and huge government investment.

Industrial output rose from £55 million in 1931 to £90 million in 1938 under Fianna Fáil, behind a protectionist wall. Many new factories were set up throughout the country, manufacturing everything from boots and shoes to textiles. Acreage under wheat rose in the 1930s, although prices for cattle fell under protectionist policies, but towards the end of the decade there were relaxations on both sides. Ireland's agricultural exports to Britain during the Second World War were crucial for both countries. During the 1940s several campaigns to harvest tillage crops attracted enthusiastic urban volunteers. A seaplane port at Foynes, Co. Limerick on the Shannon from the late 1930s led to the building of a transatlantic airport at Rineanna in Co. Clare, Shannon Airport, from 1947. The development of the surrounding area as a low-tax investment zone for industries from 1959, was a huge boost for the region, attracting hundreds of industries over the years.

Fianna Fáil built an average of 12,000 local authority houses and flats a year between 1932 and 1942, giving many working-class people the dignity of solid buildings and sanitary facilities. In fits and starts from then to the early 1970s, and under all governments, all the inhabitants of tenements, lanes and courts were eventually rehoused in local authority estates or blocks of flats, but this was sometimes a frustratingly slow process.

Fianna Fáil introduced unemployment assistance in 1932, extended it to small farmers the following year and increased it in scope in 1938. Free milk for over 67,000 children was introduced in 1933. Widows' pensions were introduced in 1936. In 1944 children's allowances were brought in, a great boon to families. However, infant mortality – the deaths of babies aged between six weeks and two years – then, as now, was a key indicator of living conditions. In the late nineteenth century Irish babies and toddlers, outside of the cities, had been the healthiest in Europe. In 1934, the Netherlands had an infant mortality rate of forty, while Ireland's was sixty-three, and this was when one of the two biggest blackspots, Belfast, was taken out. In 1943, infant mortality in independent Ireland reached eighty-three, compared to wartime Britain's rate of fifty. Infant mortality fell definitively in the 1960s because of improved living conditions.

Babies and more particularly, their mothers, were on the agenda of the new Department of Health from 1945, but the defeat of tuberculosis, a resurgence of which was cutting down young adults mercilessly, was the more immediate priority. The new Minister for Health under the Inter-party Government, Dr Noel Browne, built sanatoria all over the country, providing over 4,000 tuberculosis beds. However, when Browne proposed free medical care for all mothers and all babies and children up to the age of sixteen (regardless of income) in 1950, doctors and the Catholic Church objected, the former because they wanted to keep their professional independence, the latter because of a fear of socialized medicine and a fear that the provision of information to women about their bodies might lead to birth control. De Valera's government successfully introduced a modified version of this bill in 1953, providing free care for mothers and for children up to six weeks, sidestepping the doctors' and Church's objections. Maternal mortality, already falling due to improved social welfare, began to plummet. Free or low-cost hospital care was made more accessible and a massive hospital-building programme provided 2,400 new medical and surgical beds between 1949 and 1956. Orthopaedic and paediatric services were also developed, and the Schools Medical Service uncovered congenital defects in children and remedied them at no cost to parents.

Services for people with intellectual disabilities were slower to develop. The 1953 Health Act allowed some state support for voluntary services for persons with a mental handicap, but neither the state nor local authorities actually set up these services. There were not enough places in voluntary institutions (run by the Brothers of Charity, the Hospitallers of St John of God and the Daughters of Charity) and, all too often, intellectually disabled people ended up in mental hospitals. The Disabled Person's Maintenance Allowance, introduced in 1954–1955, supported people living outside of institutions, but because it was partly delivered and funded through local authorities, many applications were refused. The Association of Parents and Friends of Mentally Backward Children, founded in 1955, had an uphill struggle.

The 1960s was a decade of freedom for young people in particular, but the changes it brought had been evolving for decades. The numbers working for wages in towns big and small increased every census year from 1926, which meant free time and pocket money for young single people, even after they 'handed up' at home. Cinemas were popular, and dancehalls were everywhere. Jazz and swing (heard on the American Services' waveband from 1941) were irresistible to young people, dancing till the early hours to bandleaders like Mick Delahunty who added these melodies to their repertoire. Dances in rural houses continued all through these decades in defiance of clerical condemnation, with music (both modern and traditional) provided either by musicians or by the battery wireless or wind-up gramophone. Modern fashions were everywhere; young women wear sleeveless dresses and have permed hair at a rural Kilkenny dancehall in Patrick Purcell's novel *Hanrahan's Daughter* (1942). The Gaelic League, and new social Catholic organizations the Legion of Mary and Muintir na Tire, flourished, attracting as many women as men, as did Macra na Feirme and Macra na Tuaithe, farming organizations founded in the 1940s and 1950s. The Pioneer Total Abstinence Association had over 350,000 members by 1950 and a lively schedule of social activities for its members. Amateur dramatics took off from the late 1940s, and from 1953 an annual week-long competition in Athlone drew entrants from all over the country.

All this sociability did not invariably lead to marriage, before the 1960s anyway. As in many traditional dances, young women and men took a quick swing around the floor before being scattered far away from each other. The trickle of young women leaving the land for jobs in towns in the 1920s and 1930s became a fast-flowing river in the 1940s. From 1939, Britain's building sites, mines and industries attracted young Irishmen from town and country. Young women were drawn to offices, shops and factories in Ireland and across the water, and more and more, to paid nurse-training in the big British hospitals of the NHS, which recruited vigorously in Ireland and demanded a lower standard of completed education than Irish training hospitals. Emigration, most of it to Britain, but a small trickle still to America, reached 40,000 a year by the early 1950s. Concern was expressed in a government Commission on Emigration in the 1950s, and books with words like 'vanishing' and 'dying' in the title, advanced all kinds of anthropo-cultural reasons for Irish non-marriage. Marriage, however, was delayed or foregone for the same reasons it had been delayed or foregone since around 1850; the nature and location of the paid work available in Ireland did not facilitate the dual earning necessary for a small farming or working-class couple to attain a comfortable living standard.

The statutory marriage bar against women in the public service, some restrictive legislation affecting women in industry introduced in 1936, and informal marriage bars in the private sector also caused women to delay marriage, so as not to give up their jobs. The marriage bar on female

National (i.e. primary) teachers which was only put in place in 1932, was lifted in 1958, but other public servants (including secondary teachers) had to wait until 1973. In 1961 only 5 per cent of Irish married women were in the paid workforce, compared to 35 per cent in the United Kingdom, and by 1971 the Irish figure had risen, but only to 7.5 per cent. Still, from the early twentieth century women ran hotels, guesthouses, shops and even factories in their own names (i.e. not as wives). Butlers and Urneys chocolatiers were run by women. Appearance-related female entrepreneurship throve from the 1940s. Dress designers Sybil Connolly and Irene Gilbert won international acclaim, but there were many smaller female-led fashion and cosmetic firms, regularly showcased in Irish women's magazines. Female hairdressers, who numbered only 241 in 1926 (1 to every 6,079 females), numbered 4,655 in 1966 (1 to every 308 females), catering to the demand for neat hair from the growing numbers of women working in schools, shops, offices, hospitals and factories, of whom there were over 97,000 in 1926, and almost 158,000 in 1961.

Seán Lemass's Programme for Economic Recovery, inaugurated in 1957, attracted foreign investment. Gross National Product increased 4.5 per cent between 1959 and 1964; 418 foreign firms were established in Ireland between 1960 and 1973, and over 3,000 new jobs were created annually in this decade. In 1966 trade restrictions with Britain were lifted. The average industrial wage doubled between 1966 and 1973, and farm incomes also rose. Improved public transport and the greater affordability of cars, made town-situated jobs more accessible to rural dwellers. Irish workers' confidence led to a sharp rise in industrial action, and the Republic had more strikes in the 1960s than any other western European country. Small wonder that James Plunkett's epic novel of the 1913 Lock-Out, *Strumpet City*, was such a bestseller when it appeared in 1969.

Free secondary education for all was introduced in 1967. Cosgrave's government had established high-quality free vocational schools in 1931, and had it not been for these schools, and religious-run free secondary schools, lower-middle and working-class Irish people would have had to do without post-primary schooling altogether. Although the numbers at second-level and at university trebled between 1922 and 1961, before 1967 too many children finished their schooling for good at twelve or fourteen, and often headed for the boat in their mid-teens.

Some children missed out even on primary school. The 1963 *Report of the Commission on Itineracy* revealed the poor living conditions of Ireland's 'itinerants', as Travellers were officially known. Numbering between 5,000 and 6,000, Travellers comprised only about 0.2 per cent of the Irish population, but they became more visible as their way of life diverged from that of the settled population, without schooling, housing and the various welfare benefits that depended upon fixed abodes. Some Travellers were housed, but most lived in carts and tents, horse- or motor-drawn caravans. Moving around was crucial to their livelihoods (tinsmithing, animal and scrap trading), with business transacted at annual fairs like those in Spancilhill in Co. Clare, and Ballinasloe in Co. Galway. Up to 1963 government attention to Travellers was minimal and, after it, inadequate. Non-Travellers were sometimes hostile, but a little more sympathetic in this decade, when The Johnstons' cover of Ewan MacColl's 'The Travelling People' reached No. 1 in 1966.

Travellers generally steered clear of the institutions which remained a feature of Irish life up to the 1970s. In 1958 the number of inmates of mental hospitals reached 21,000, or 0.7 per cent of the population. Despite not being violent or suicidal, nineteen-year-old Hanna Greally was committed by her mother to St Loman's hospital in Mullingar for eighteen years. She was not unusual. In addition, there were 6,000 children in industrial schools in 1950, 4,000 in 1960 and 1,500 in 1970. These, like most Irish institutions except for the mental hospitals, were run by nuns and brothers.

8.2.3 Religion

If the Shannon Scheme was the flagship industrial project of the young Irish state, its flagship public event was the Eucharistic Congress of June 1932. Masses in the Phoenix Park had children in white, Children of Mary in blue, soldiers in green, while yellow Papal flags and tricolours and streets bedecked with bunting were seen all over the country. Every Irish Catholic wanted to participate, and over a million did so directly. A magnificent spectacle, it signalled firmly that Ireland was a Catholic country.

The population of independent Ireland in 1936 was 92 per cent Catholic, with the remaining 8 per cent Church of Ireland, Presbyterian, Methodist, Baptist, Society of Friends and Jewish. Freedom of religion was guaranteed under the Free State Constitution of 1922 and de Valera's Constitution of 1937. No bishops or clerics sat in Dáil or Seanad and Church and state were separate. Article 44 of de Valera's Constitution recognized the 'special position' of the Roman Catholic Church as the religion of the majority of Irish people, but also officially recognized all the minority religions by name. This disappointed some ultra-Catholics who had hoped Catholicism would be established as an official state religion.

But Catholicism in Ireland was a kind of unofficial state religion anyway. It is almost impossible to overstate its permeation of everyday life up to 1970. Patterns of Catholic observance were acknowledged in all institutions and most workplaces, and determined the rhythms of social life and street life. Dancehalls were closed during Lent (musicians went to England for the six weeks), people blessed themselves routinely when passing churches, and men removed hats or caps when the Angelus rang out at midday. The British NHS hospitals which recruited student nurses in Ireland were careful to promise nearby 'RC chapels' and time off for Sunday observance. For most Irish Catholics, Sunday Mass was the bare minimum. In John D. Sheridan's very popular 1940s verse, 'Joe's No Saint', the poem's working-class Dublin narrator considers himself a lukewarm Catholic because he 'only' goes to Sunday Mass and to his weekly Confraternity.

Religious rituals, feasts and devotions often brought colour and consolation to people's lives. To the traditional feasts of Christmas, Easter and St Patrick's Day were added the feast of Our Lady of Lourdes (February 11), the Nine First Fridays, the month of October for the Rosary, November for the Holy Souls and many other calendar observances. There were parades for Corpus

FIGURE 8.2 Edel Quinn (1907–44). By kind permission of the Legion of Mary. Quinn left her secretarial post in Dublin and turned down a proposal of marriage to become an energetic lay missionary with the Legion of Mary in east Africa, dying in Nairobi in 1944. Her life choices would have been appreciated and applauded by most Irish Catholics of her generation.

Christi in June and mass public consecrations of the new local authority housing estates built from the 1930s to the 1960s. Women were often the most vigorous promoters and practitioners of devotion. (Figure 8.2)

But the sphere where women exercised the greatest authority of all was the religious life, in which they were mainly teachers and nurses, though a minority ran the institutions which would later become notorious. There were 9,000 nuns in 1926, over 15,000 in 1961, and another 15,000 or so entered convents abroad between these two dates. Women eagerly embraced the religious life, despite the wrench of leaving home and friends; on Áine Stack's first, strange night as a postulant (pre-novice) in the Presentation convent in Cahirciveen, Co. Kerry in 1931, the tune that rang out from the nearby dancehall, breaking into the convent's 'Great Silence', was 'Horsey, keep your tail up'. Nuns were both part of 'the world' and apart from it.

In the 1960s Vatican II reforms such as Mass in the vernacular encouraged even more enthusiastic participation in the sacraments. Daily Masses in towns were still packed, and missing Sunday Mass unheard of. Religious retreat houses (purpose-built in the 1950s) attracted thousands of lay people annually, well into the 1970s. Teilifís Éireann (Irish Television), which started broadcasting in 1961, regularly questioned Catholic authority, but it also gave Irish ecclesiastics a respectful ear and a more powerful platform than ever before.

Catholic authority, therefore, arrived at the 1970s almost unscathed, but a new creativity in Catholic social activism was already forming a generation which would hold the Church's institutions up to greater scrutiny. Pioneering priests, brothers and nuns popularized the teachings of Vatican II, and spearheaded activism for homeless people, the intellectually disabled and others. In 1963 Peter Birch, bishop of Ossory, set up the multi-purpose Kilkenny Social Service Council, which established branches all over the country, and his was only one of several similar initiatives. The popular *The Word* magazine, published by Divine Word Missionaries, contained in one year (1968) articles which criticized apartheid, described (positively) women's lives in the USSR, praised Bob Dylan, questioned clerical celibacy. It carried, moreover, very positive articles by, and on, Protestants of various denominations.

Like their Catholic counterparts, Protestants were late and 'rare' marriers, though they had an extra reason for foregoing matrimony. The decline of 48 per cent in Protestant numbers in Ireland between 1926 and 1991 was partly due to the *Ne Temere* Catholic ruling of 1909, which made Protestant partners in mixed marriages promise that the children would be reared Catholic. Such marriages happened because Protestants mixed freely with Catholics in rural (not so much urban) Leinster and Munster, playing hurling, handball and Gaelic football, in rural development organizations such as Muintir na Tire, and in national and local politics. Mrs Frances Condell, a Protestant and the first female mayor of Limerick city in 1963, was held up as an example to schoolgirls of all faiths. In literature, the 'decaying big house' experience vividly evoked by M. J. Farrell (Molly Keane) and others has overshadowed more popular Protestant writers like Temple Lane and Sheila Pim, who wrote pragmatically and proudly of the new state in novels featuring middle-class and farming Protestants and Catholics.

But non-Catholics were tolerated only up to a point. At Doonass, Co. Clare, in 1956, ten Catholic men, including a priest, assaulted two Jehovah's Witnesses who had been calling to houses in the locality. Charges brought against the attackers were thrown out due to widespread public indignation, and it was the two assaulted Witnesses, and not their attackers, who were bound to the peace.

8.3 Northern Ireland, 1922–1969

Under the Government of Ireland Act of 1920 Northern Ireland was intended as a partner state to Southern Ireland, with a council from both states working towards eventual unity. Because Ireland won full independence, this did not come to pass, and the smaller state was left to itself. Northern Ireland sent twelve MPs to Westminster but, unlike the other constituent parts of the United Kingdom – Scotland and Wales – it also had its own parliament, situated from 1932 in the imposing building of Stormont. (Figure 8.3)

The Boundary Commission comprising representatives from the entire island, and from Britain, examined the possibility of Ireland reclaiming some parts of the six counties. In 1925, however, the 1920 border was agreed by Ireland, Britain and Northern Ireland. It consisted of the counties Antrim, Armagh, Down, Fermanagh, Londonderry and Tyrone.

FIGURE 8.3 Stormont Buildings Belfast. The Edge Digital Photography/Moment/Getty images. Completed in 1932, this very big parliamentary and administrative building for a very small state signals the self-confidence of Northern Ireland unionism from the 1920s to the 1970s.

8.3.1 Politics, 1920–1969

The politics of Northern Ireland in this forty-nine-year period are starkly simple; the Unionist party dominated all the way from James Craig to Terence O'Neill.

The police force, later known as the Royal Ulster Constabulary, had places set aside for Catholics, but it was born in the turbulent years of 1920–1922 when Protestant–Catholic conflict resulted in 557 deaths (303 of them Catholic), 23,000 Catholics driven from their homes and hundreds of Catholic businesses destroyed. Irish Republican Army units tried to destabilize the new state by attacking police barracks and other props of government rule, and attacked Protestants too. With its 'B' and 'C' Specials (partly voluntary auxiliary forces) drawn from the former Ulster Volunteers, the police was heavily biased against Catholics, who were all assumed to be nationalist and opposed to the state.

Catholics made up one-third of the population of the six counties, but the abolition of proportional representation at local and parliamentary level between 1922 and 1929, and the redrawing of electoral boundaries in 1924, gave Protestants a clear majority even in areas where the majority population was Catholic. In 1921 Co. Fermanagh (with a majority Catholic population) had sixty-three nationalist councillors and fifty-seven Unionist, but after the electoral changes, the number of nationalist councillors was forty-three, and that of Unionists, seventy-four. At parliamentary level, Catholics under proportional representation got 33 per cent of the parliamentary representation outside of Belfast, but after it was abolished, 28 per cent. Furthermore, the local government franchise was based on property, and a disproportionate number of property owners were Protestants because Protestants were, in general, wealthier than Catholics. Some businesses also had multiple votes, which had the same effect.

In the 1920s and 1930s Northern Irish nationalists were divided among themselves about whether to reject the new state altogether – this was the Sinn Féin view – or to try to work with it, the view of the former Home Rule, now Nationalist, party under Joseph Devlin. Abstention from parliament became common. Viewed by Unionists as defiant non-engagement with the state, it was also despair at an administration heavily weighted against Catholics in nearly every way. Catholics also insisted (as they always did, in every state) upon their own educational institutions, which gave a further impression of retreat from the mainstream culture. Although there were junior Catholic civil servants, some departments boasted (literally) of having few or none. In local authorities dominated by Unionists (most councils), preference in non-executive /blue-collar public employment was invariably given to Protestants. There was also casual inter-community violence in urban areas. Catholics boarding trains to the Eucharistic Congress in Dublin in 1932 were set upon by stone-throwing and stick-wielding loyalists.

Northern Ireland's Second World War proceeded as it did in Britain, although conscription was never introduced. Thirty-eight-thousand or so people enlisted, many of them Catholics. Because of its shipbuilding and strategic importance, Northern Ireland was targeted, and over 1,000 people were killed in the terrible Belfast blitz of April and May 1941, when 53 per cent of the city's housing stock was destroyed.

After the war an Anti-Partition League, comprising mainly middle-class Catholics, received support from some British Labour MPs, but this died out around 1951. The IRA meanwhile was gathering strength, but its border campaign, which lasted from 1955 to 1962 and resulted in nineteen fatalities, was not widely supported by Catholics in Northern Ireland any more than in Ireland.

Terence O'Neill, prime minister from 1963, was the first to try to attract Catholic voters and to propose reforms in local government and administration. His public expression of sympathy to Cardinal Conway on the death of Pope John XXIII, and his meeting with Taoiseach Seán Lemass, which had not been discussed beforehand with his cabinet, alarmed some, though it reassured moderate unionists as well as Catholics. Nationalists were now optimistic enough to become the official opposition in Stormont in 1965 under the leadership of Eddie McAteer, and confident enough to turn out in their thousands for the 1916 commemorations in Belfast the following year. All these developments displeased more extreme Protestants like the Reverend Ian Paisley, who founded the Ulster Constitution Defence Committee in 1966.

Meanwhile, the Campaign for Social Justice, begun by Conn and Patricia McCluskey in Dungannon, Co. Tyrone, in 1963 and spreading to Belfast in 1964, focused attention on discrimination against Catholics in public employment and housing. Fermanagh, for example, between 1945 and 1967, allocated 82 per cent of its new council houses to Protestants, despite a majority of Catholics in the population being eligible for such housing. The campaign also called for a redress of the local authority franchise anomalies, calling for 'one man [sic] one vote'. The Northern Ireland Civil Rights Association was founded in 1967 by republican socialists Roy Johnston and Anthony Coughlan, and its main demands concentrated on housing, policing and voting. It did not demand an end to partition or a united Ireland. A student protest group, People's Democracy, led by Bernadette Devlin and Eamon MacCann among others, marching from Belfast to Derry in January 1969 were set upon by 200 stick-and-baton-wielding people at Burntollet in Co. Derry. This was one of the first images of the Northern Ireland conflict flashed around the world. Not long after this the notoriously sectarian 'B' Specials, formed in 1920, were disbanded. In February 1969 O'Neill resigned, and James Chichester-Clark took over as prime minister. The summer of 1969 saw widespread civil unrest, particularly in Belfast, where 1,500 families, mainly Catholic, were driven from their homes. The British army was called in to restore order. The Troubles had begun.

8.3.2 *Economy and Society*

Northern Ireland's industries were badly hit by the worldwide depression, and unemployment in Northern Ireland rose to 30 per cent in the 1930s. In 1932 Protestants and Catholics marched together in Belfast to protest at the cut in unemployment benefit. Protestant or Catholic, newly unemployed industrial workers had little to fall back on after generations of debilitating physical toil. A study by Dr James Deeny in Lurgan in the late 1930s found that 54 per cent of employed middle-aged male Protestant weavers, a labour 'elite' if ever there was one, were seriously under-nourished. In Belfast in 1941, infant mortality was 91.5 per 1,000, identical to Dublin, and much worse than in comparable British industrial cities.

Country life was healthier for those who could make a living from it, although the flight of young people from the land happened in Northern Ireland as it did everywhere. With fewer mouths to feed, the agricultural sector throve in the 1920s and 1930s, especially in the dairying and pig-production sectors. The Second World War saw Northern farmers barely able to keep up with British demand for wheat and livestock, milk and eggs. Shipbuilding and aircraft manufacture also boomed. But once the full employment of the war years was over, neither linen production, shipbuilding nor shirt-making ever regained their former strength, though all continued on a smaller scale. Unemployment in Northern Ireland never fell below 7 per cent in the 1950s, a time of full employment in the 'mainland' UK Agricultural employment also fell by a third in this decade. Some new industry was attracted but it did not absorb all the unemployed.

On the positive side, the recommendations of Britain's post-war Beveridge report were implemented wholeheartedly, and Northern Ireland became a welfare state like the UK. Health services were vastly improved, benefitting both Catholics and Protestants. The same was true of the Butler Education Act of 1944, which made free secondary schooling available to all. By 1961 a fifth of the student body at Queen's University Belfast was Catholic. At this stage Ulster Television had been in operation for a few years, and it developed into an important resource for information and discussion.

Many aspects of everyday life in Northern Ireland throughout these decades were broadly similar to life anywhere on the island. The tight-fisted Fermanagh farmer in Anne Crone's *My Heart and I* (1955), who uses old iron bedsteads to stop gaps in hedges, had his counterparts in Munster, Leinster and Connacht. Janet McNeill's harassed housewife Hilda, who knows to a penny the price of everything from a cold in the head to a day at the seaside (*The Other Side of The Wall*, 1956), was the kind of woman the Irish Housewives Association, founded in Dublin in 1943, drew attention to, the middle-class woman coping with rising prices and the permanent disappearance of cheap household labour.

8.4 Conclusion

Apart from the bombings of 1941, the island of Ireland between 1922 and 1969 had a better twentieth century than most European countries. But stability came at a cost. Northern Ireland maintained it by keeping Catholics down in a disgracefully blatant way, while Ireland, for its part, tolerated high institutionalization and disturbing levels of violence towards the defenceless. Frank Crummey, Cyril Daly and others who campaigned against corporal punishment in schools in the 1960s were widely ridiculed, and a man who beat his six-year-old foster-daughter to death in 1967 was found guilty of manslaughter, and received only a twelve-month prison sentence.

Extreme judicial violence, however, ended in independent Ireland after 1954, when Michael Manning was hanged for the brutal murder of retired nurse Catherine Cooper. In 1964, the year the last executions took place in

Britain and three years after the last hanging in Northern Ireland, capital punishment in Ireland was abolished for all offences except capital murder (i.e. the murder of a member of the Garda Síochána or a prison officer), treason and offences under military law. No death sentence would ever be carried out for these crimes.

Independent Ireland's strict censorship regime up to 1967 meant that Irish readers were deprived not only of international authors but also of many Irish writers who described Ireland in a way that powerful Irish people did not like. Maura Laverty's *Lift Up Your Gates* (1946), for example, was banned because of its too-frank description of life in the Dublin tenements. (Figure 8.4) But Ireland was not closed off entirely from outside influences. Most publications, Irish or foreign, were not banned. There was a ready domestic market for books by Irish writers, and American and British films and newsreels played nightly in the cinemas, which even the smallest towns had. Anglo-American popular songs were heard on wireless or gramophone, picked out on the piano from song-sheets, or learned from the singing of others. Around the house and the farm, Irish people sang about the beautiful Isle of Capri and the Yellow Rose of Texas, and south of the border was 'down Mexico way', not the twenty-six counties.

None of these international influences prevented Irish singers like Delia Murphy and Bridie Gallagher from gaining huge followings in the 1940s and 1950s, and the 1960s brought showband stars Big Tom, Brendan Bowyer, Joe Dolan, Paddy Cole, and many others, who played an eclectic mix of jazz, swing, American country, Irish traditional and pop music. The Beatles, the Hollies, the Kinks, Manfred Mann and Herman's Hermits were as

FIGURE 8.4 Maura Laverty (1907–1966). Photograph courtesy of the late Sr Conleth Kelly, sister of Maura Laverty. Pictured here with her son James in the early 1950s, Laverty was a very popular broadcaster, cookery writer, children's writer, playwright, television scriptwriter and journalist from the early 1930s, but this did not prevent two of her novels from being banned in the 1940s.

popular in Birr as they were in Birmingham, but, in 1966, Irish acts (Dickie Rock, Larry Cunningham and others) topped the Irish charts in thirty-one of the fifty-two weeks. Strong interest in England's World Cup victory of 1966 did not mean declining interest in hurling and Gaelic football. 'Thank God we're surrounded by water', went the chorus of a song by the Ludlows which topped the charts for four weeks in the spring of that year, but never had the boundary of the Irish Sea mattered less.

9
The Thirty Year 'Troubles', 1969–1998

9.1 Introduction

Northern Ireland comes first this time, as a recognition of the 3,663 lives lost during these three decades.

9.2 Northern Ireland, 1969–1998

9.2.1 Politics

The civil unrest described in the previous chapter resulted in the deployment of the British army in active units on the streets and roads of Northern Ireland. They were not trained peacekeepers and their presence added another explosive element to an already volatile situation. There were various elements active in the conflict. At either extreme of the political spectrum were loyalists and republicans.

'Loyalist' was the term used to describe militant unionist organizations like the Ulster Volunteer Force (UVF), which traced its origins to 1912 but was newly active again from 1965), the Ulster Defence Association (UDA, founded 1971) the Ulster Freedom Fighters (UFF), the Red Hand Commando and other, smaller organizations. Their loyalty was both to the British connection and to a Northern Ireland politically dominated by Protestants.

The Orange Order, founded by Ulster Protestants in 1795, is an active and uniformed, though unarmed, unionist organization. It is supported by marching bands and, throughout this period, carried out regular public demonstrations of strength. Its elite wing is called the Royal Black Preceptory.

'Republicans' were chiefly the IRA and its political wing, Sinn Féin, whose long-term goal was a united Ireland. It split in 1970 into Official Sinn Féin/IRA, and Provisional Sinn Féin/IRA. The initial disagreements were not about militancy (the Aldershot bombing which killed seven people in 1972 was an Officials operation) but about socialism, abstention from parliament, and other matters. When in 1974 the Official Sinn Féin/IRA gave up the armed struggle, a group broke away from it, calling itself the Irish Republican Socialist Party (IRSP), with a militant wing, the Irish National Liberation Army (INLA). There would be smaller, splinter groups of republicans over the succeeding decades, but these were the most important ones, although the 'Provos' – Provisional IRA, hereafter known as the IRA – were bigger and more active than the INLA.

On the constitutional front, the Official Unionist Party, or Ulster Unionist Party (UUP), headed by Brian Faulkner from 1971, was the single biggest unionist party. This was the party of the reforming Terence O'Neill. Other parties included the Northern Ireland Labour Party (NILP), which had hitherto claimed many urban Catholic votes. Three new political parties were formed in 1970–1971. The Social Democratic Labour Party (SDLP), founded by Ivan Cooper, Austin Currie, John Hume, and others, was more or less the heir of the NICRA, a non-militant nationalist party. The Alliance Party, formed by Bob Cooper, Oliver Napier, and others, was a moderately unionist non-sectarian party committed to political reform. The Democratic Unionist Party (DUP), founded in 1971 by the Reverend Ian Paisley, was on the extreme end of political unionism. The Progressive Unionist Party, formed in 1979 by Billy Hutchinson, comprised loyalists who had moved away from violence and towards dialogue with republicans.

The security forces in the North were the police force, known as the Royal Ulster Constabulary (RUC), the British army, and the Ulster Defence Regiment (UDR), formed in 1970 as an auxiliary to the police.

The years from 1969 to 1971 were characterized by riots, bombings and attacks from all sides, but the British reaction focused overwhelmingly on republicans and suspected republicans. In August 1971, 342 men were arrested and interned without trial, (Figure 9.1) and on January 30 1972 the British Paratrooper regiment shot and killed fourteen unarmed civilians (thirteen died immediately, one later) on a peaceful march in Derry's Bogside, in an event thereafter known as Bloody Sunday. 'Paras 13, Bogside Nil', read the loyalist graffiti afterwards, and Prime Minister Edward Heath's unrepentant reaction suggested that he was in broad agreement with this brutal triumphalism. British treatment of internees and prisoners around this time, most of them republican – hooding, sleep deprivation, physical abuse – would be described by the European Court of Human Rights in 1976 as 'cruel and inhuman', just short of torture.

However, the British government also undermined unionists, by imposing 'direct rule' in 1972, abolishing the Stormont parliament and replacing it by the Northern Ireland Assembly (NIA). This was more or

FIGURE 9.1 Bernadette Devlin. Pierre Manevy/Stringer/Hulton Archive/Getty images. An MP for mid-Ulster from 1969 to 1974, Devlin was at that stage the youngest woman ever elected to Westminster. She is pictured here outside 10 Downing Street, London, with Frank MacManus, protesting against internment.

less the same size as Stormont but elected by proportional representation, and because it gave nationalists a stronger voice than before, it was called 'power-sharing'. British authority was represented by a Secretary of State for Northern Ireland, the first of whom was William Whitelaw, and MPs from Northern Ireland continued to sit at Westminster. Power-sharing was supported by Faulkner's Official Unionists, the SDLP, the Alliance

Party, the NILP and others, who made up three-fifths of the votes cast for the first NIA in 1973. Brian Faulkner was the Chief Executive, the SDLP's Gerry Fitt his deputy. Later that year, an agreement was reached at Sunningdale in Berkshire between an executive committee of the NIA, and representatives of the British and Irish governments. Direct rule and power-sharing would continue and a Council of Ireland, made up of representatives from both Dublin and London governments, and other consultative bodies, was set up. The DUP and the Unionists who had split with Faulkner opposed it, as did republicans, because it did not deliver a thirty-two-county republic. The unionist-dominated Ulster Workers' Council called a two-week strike in May 1974, crippling energy supplies in the region. Bombs in Dublin and Monaghan (discussed in Section 9.3) may also have been part of this reaction.

There were so many murders and attacks perpetrated by republicans, loyalists and the security forces in these three decades that to mention them all would take up the rest of this book. The main IRA/INLA targets were the British army, police, UDR, loyalists, and the Gardai and the Defence Forces when they got in the way of bank robberies and kidnappings carried out in the Republic. However, they targeted Protestant civilians, too, in the murder of eleven Protestant workmen in Kingsmill, Co. Armagh, in 1976 and several other actions. Loyalists had nothing against the security forces so they directed their violence indiscriminately at Catholics. The most extreme were the Shankill Butchers, some of whom were UVF members, who tortured and killed at least twenty-two Catholics chosen at random, in the late 1970s.

Many Catholics and Protestants in Northern Ireland did not actively support either republican or loyalist militants. Everyday life continued, though it was watchful; Seamus Heaney refers to the 'turned observant back' in his poem 'Casualty'. American anthropologist Henry Glassie, who stayed for extended periods in rural Fermanagh for over a decade during the worst of the conflict, noted the mutual affection between Catholic and Protestant rural neighbours, alongside an unshakeable sense of cultural difference that came out in song and story.

Dismay at the ongoing loss of life on all sides led Protestant Betty Williams and Catholics Mairéad Corrigan and Ciarán MacKeown to form the Peace People in 1976, an organization which attracted up to 30,000 Catholics and Protestants in public demonstrations. Although Corrigan and Williams were awarded the Nobel Prize the following year, the movement was overwhelmed by internal divisions, and died out by 1978. However, clergy of all faiths, trade unionists and community activists kept Protestant–Catholic lines of communication open throughout this time. Leaders of the Protestant churches on the island had a secret meeting with the IRA leadership in Feakle, Co. Clare, in 1974, which resulted in a short ceasefire. Catholic ecclesiastics also talked to both sides. Most cross-community activity was cultural rather than political, such as the oral history project on women's health run by the National Union of Public Employees and involving both Catholic and Protestant women.

By the late 1970s the British had decided on a strategy of 'normalization, Ulsterization and criminalization' – Northern Ireland was 'normal', that is, not at war, any problems could be contained within the six counties, and political detainees were common criminals. Internment without trial was ended in 1976, but the British army and British intelligence were still deployed in the North.

Despite some high-profile political assassinations by the IRA and INLA between 1976 and 1979 (Christopher Ewart-Biggs, the British ambassador to Ireland, Louis Mountbatten, the last governor general of India, and Airey Neave, an English politician), republicans were finding it hard to combat the superior resources of the British. It was time to reintroduce the tried and trusted nationalist tactic of suffering. Denial of political status to IRA prisoners led first to the dirty protest – where prisoners refused to wash – and then led to the biggest hunger strike, which began in February 1981, and lasted till October. Ten H-Block/Maze prisoners died, including Bobby Sands, elected as Westminster MP for Fermanagh-South Tyrone while on hunger strike. There was huge sympathy for the strikers across the entire nationalist community, although prominent churchmen like Cardinal Tomás O Fiaich, Bishop Cahal Daly and Fr Denis Faul eventually persuaded the men to end it. Of the five demands of the hunger strikers, four were granted by the end of 1981, as James Prior, the Northern Secretary, was far more conciliatory than Margaret Thatcher, the British prime minister.

Thatcher also came out strongly – in her famous 'out, out, out' speech – against moderate proposals by the cross-border nationalist New Ireland Forum in 1983–1984 for tentative joint governance of Northern Ireland. It was only because of pressure from United States President Ronald Reagan that she came to an agreement with Taoiseach Garret Fitzgerald in Belfast in November 1985, the Anglo-

Irish, or, as it was more commonly known, Hillsborough Agreement. Unionists would never be forced into a united Ireland, but the Irish government would have a consultative role in the future of Northern Ireland, and the nationalist tradition would be recognized in Northern Irish institutions. The Irish government and the SDLP were encouraged by this, but both moderate and extreme unionists were not (Ian Paisley called Thatcher 'a wicked, lying and treacherous woman') and the Ulster Says No campaign mustered huge demonstrations across the six counties. Sinn Féin also condemned Hillsborough because it accepted partition. Peace was still a long way off and republican and loyalist violence continued from the late 1980s into the early 1990s, with tit-for-tat killings of mostly Catholic and Protestant civilians who had no connection with either paramilitaries or the security forces.

In 1993 Taoiseach Albert Reynolds and Prime Minister John Major laid down a framework for the development of a peace process, welcomed by all parties except the DUP and Sinn Féin. Over the next few years George Mitchell, an American congressman, acted as peace-broker and other prominent Irish-Americans played a role, as did US President Bill Clinton. Loyalists declared a ceasefire, but non-militant unionism was still a formidable force; tensions came to a head in 1995–1996 when Orangemen insisted on marching through Catholic areas on the Twelfth of July, with flashpoints at Portadown and Drumcree. (Figure 9.2)

Meanwhile, the broadcasting bans on Sinn Féin were lifted in both the UK and Ireland, which allowed more open discussion and dialogue. Despite intermittent ceasefires, IRA activity continued up to 1997 with bombs in Northern Ireland and Britain (those in

The Thirty Year 'Troubles', 1969–1998

FIGURE 9.2 Gable-end, Sandy Row, Belfast. NurPhoto/Contributor/ Getty images. Gable-ends commemorating historical figures from both traditions are a common sight in parts of Belfast; this one celebrates William of Orange's victory at the Battle of the Boyne in 1690, commemorated every year on the Twelfth of July by Ulster Unionists.

Warrington in 1993 killed two children) and ongoing attacks on security forces.

A permanent ceasefire was agreed with the IRA after a lot of hard work and negotiation. On Good Friday, 10 April 1998, an agreement was signed in Belfast. Tony Blair was the Prime Minister, Bertie Ahern, the Taoiseach and Marjorie ('Mo') Mowlam, the Northern Secretary. Social Democratic Labour Party leader John Hume, Ulster Unionist Party leader David Trimble and Sinn Féin's Gerry Adams and the Alliance Party were the main Northern Irish actors in the process. (Figure 9.3) Paisley's Democratic Unionist Party was the only party which opposed the agreement in Northern Ireland.

FIGURE 9.3 David Trimble and John Hume with the joint Nobel Peace Prize 1998. Micheline Pelletier/Sygma/Getty images. Trimble, of the Official Unionist Party, and Hume, of the SDLP, exemplified the constitutional traditions of both their communities, and were, among others, jointly responsible for the peace process which culminated in the Good Friday Agreement of April 1998.

Weapons of all paramilitary groups were to be decommissioned. Cross-border co-operative and consultative bodies were to be set up. Reforms of policing and amnesty arrangements for political prisoners were promised, and reconciliation would be attempted. A parades commission would curtail provocative displays, and the cultures of both communities would be respected. When the Agreement was put to the Northern Ireland electorate, 71 per cent were in favour and 28.9 per cent against it; voter turnout was 81 per cent. The Agreement also passed in Ireland, which relinquished its historic claim to Northern Ireland (Articles 2 and 3 of the 1937 Constitution). Northern Secretary Peter Brooke had already declared, in 1992, Britain no longer had any 'selfish strategic or economic interest' in the six counties. It was up to the people of Northern Ireland to decide who they were and what they should be. Unionists remained unionist, and nationalists were reluctant to let go the hope of a united Ireland, so the future looked uncertain. However, two unrelated incidents in the summer of 1998 confirmed most people on all sides in their determination never to return to the bad old days. Three little boys of the Quinn family in Ballymoney, Co. Antrim, were killed by a loyalist firebomb in their house in July, and on 15 August, one of the year's traditional holidays when country towns are thronged, twenty-nine people were murdered by a bomb in Omagh, Co. Tyrone. Catholics and Protestants, locals and tourists were among the dead. The perpetrators were the so-called Real IRA, who had rejected the Good Friday Agreement.

In 1996 Monica McWilliams (Catholic) and Pearl Sagar (Protestant) formed the Northern Ireland Women's Coalition (NIWC), to boost female political activity and to get 'a seat at the table' in the peace process that was to come. They achieved this aim and more, performing well at the Assembly and Westminster elections. Their existence, although short-term (they wound down in 2006), was a sign of women's growing confidence in Northern Ireland.

9.2.2 *Economy and Society*

Throughout the Troubles, people went to schools, shops and social events, and loved and laughed and laboured. 'Normal' life continued. Northern Ireland in the 1970s and 1980s was buffeted by the same global economic forces as everywhere else. The disappearance of tens of thousands of shipbuilding, textile and engineering jobs in Belfast and Derry between 1971 and 1991 threw Protestants as well as Catholics onto dole queues. In the 1980s, one in six of the adult labour force was unemployed. On the plus side, however, the Housing Executive, set up in 1971, took housing decisions out of the hands of local councils, and vastly improved the living conditions of working-class people in town and country, building over 80,000 new homes all over the six counties by 1986.

Unemployment fell to one in fourteen in the early 1990s, with a rise in jobs mainly in the services sector, and women came to outnumber men in the workforce. The marriage bar against female public servants had been lifted in 1971, and in Protestant and Catholic schools alike by the late 1980s, more girls than boys were completing secondary education.

Although some feminists from Dublin travelled to Belfast in 1971 in a highly publicized excursion to purchase contraceptives, Northern Ireland was no utopia for women of any religion, and their status was about on a par with that of women in independent Ireland. Contraception, although legal, was often difficult to acquire and to use, not only in small towns and rural areas but also in tightly knit urban communities. The UK's 1967 Abortion Act was never extended to Northern Ireland, where abortion was legal only under very special circumstances. Northern Irish women, like women in Ireland, grew gradually to greater freedom and independence through greater workforce participation, improved living conditions and community activism.

9.3 Ireland, 1969–1998

9.3.1 Northern Ireland in Irish Politics

In 1969 Taoiseach Jack Lynch spoke for many Irish people when he said that Ireland would not 'stand by' while fellow-countrymen and women were being attacked, and by 1972 nearly 10,000 Northern Catholic refugees were being accommodated in camps in Louth and Meath, Waterford, Wexford and other parts of the country. Some settled permanently, notably in the new town of Shannon, Co. Clare, but most returned eventually to the North.

Some politicians felt Ireland should be more proactive in its support of Northern nationalists, and a cabinet sub-committee in 1970 chaired by Neil Blaney and Charles Haughey, both government ministers, planned to import arms to supply to the IRA. Lynch maintained that he knew nothing about this, the army officer who acted as liaison was scapegoated, Blaney and Haughey lost their seats at cabinet, and nothing came of the plan. Shock at the killing of an unarmed Garda, Richard Fallon, by the fringe republican group Saor Eire during a bank robbery in 1970 in Dublin made a lot of Irish people unsympathetic to the armed struggle. Gardai would remain targets of the IRA until 1998, and over the thirty years, twelve Gardai were killed by republicans.

Nonetheless, songs sympathetic to Northern nationalists (one of them Paul McCartney's 'Give Ireland Back to the Irish') topped the charts at various points in 1972. Many children (including this writer in a not particularly nationalist household) knew the Barleycorn's 'The Men Behind the Wire' off by heart. At this stage, widespread indignation at internment in 1971 had been followed by shock and dismay not only at the massacre of unarmed civilians in Derry, but at the British government's immediate justification of it. But when an angry crowd burned the British Embassy in Dublin three days after Bloody Sunday (no lives were lost), the Irish government grew alarmed and its everyday preoccupation from then on seemed to be the repression of anti-government subversion by the IRA. The non-jury Special Criminal Court was set up in July 1972, and an amendment to the 1939 Offences against the State Act, giving the Gardai extensive powers of arrest and detention, was passed in December of the same year. The same month saw loyalist bombs kill two bus drivers in Busaras, in Dublin, and a car bomb on nearby Eden Quay injure dozens. In 1973 the newly elected Fine Gael–Labour coalition carried on these hardline policies but also successfully negotiated the Sunningdale agreement with the British government later in that year. The IRA murder of Fine Gael senator Billy Fox, a Protestant, in Monaghan in March 1974, seemed to confirm the government's worst fears about armed republicans. Two months later, when loyalists (nobody was ever brought to justice, so this is conjecture) detonated bombs in Dublin and Monaghan killing a total of thirty-four people, the Irish government's immediate reaction was to clamp down on the IRA. It became impossible for any politician or journalist to question security measures without being accused of being soft on 'subversives'. In 1976, Minister for Defence Paddy Donegan criticized President Cearbhall Ó Dalaigh publicly as a 'thundering disgrace' at an army function, because the President referred the Emergency Powers Bill to the

Supreme Court. (He subsequently signed it into law.) This Emergency Powers Act gave Gardai the power to detain suspects of terrorist offences for seven days without charge. In the same year Section 31 of the Broadcasting Act of 1960 was vigorously invoked to prohibit interviews with any members of illegal organizations on RTÉ radio or television. Bands like the Wolfe Tones who specialized in nationalist or 'rebel' songs were banned.

Although popular support in Ireland for the IRA began to fall away from the late 1970s onwards, even Irish political commentators who were firmly anti-IRA were chilled by Thatcher's intransigence at the hunger strikes in the early 1980s. Kieran Doherty was elected to the Dáil for Cavan-Monaghan (he died on the strike) in the 1981 elections, Paddy Agnew (a prisoner, but not on hunger strike) was elected for Louth, and Joe McDonnell, who died on strike, narrowly missed being elected for Sligo-Leitrim. Charles Haughey, who had taken over from Lynch as leader of Fianna Fáil in 1979, liked to position himself as the nationalist leader of Ireland. He opposed the Hillsborough Agreement of 1985, because it moved away from the ideal of a united Ireland, but both he and Thatcher were burned in effigy at nationalist demonstrations in Co. Louth.

The steps towards the peace process have already been described. In the referendum on the Good Friday Agreement, Ireland voted 94.4 per cent yes, and 5.6 per cent no; turnout was 55.6 per cent. The vast majority therefore, voted to give up Ireland's constitutional claim to Northern Ireland but only somewhere between a half and three-fifths of the Irish electorate voted. This was not abstention on principle, it was apathy. It was possible to live in Ireland (outside of the border counties) during these three decades and to ignore 'the North' completely. There were other political issues.

9.3.2 Political Parties

The three oldest political parties survived these years more or less intact, with some breakaways and add-ons. Fianna Fáil's last overall majority was in 1977, and apart from a shaky nine months in 1982, it would never govern again without going into coalition. Charles Haughey led the party from 1979. Des O'Malley broke with Fianna Fáil in 1985 to set up the Progressive Democrats (PDs), liberal on social issues and conservative on economic ones. Fine Gael remained strong under its leader (until 1987) Garret Fitzgerald, a kind of Gladstone to Haughey's Disraeli. Official Sinn Féin became Sinn Féin the Workers Party and then, simply, the Workers Party, until a breakaway group became Democratic Left in 1992, and was absorbed into the Labour Party in 1998. Another left-wing party founded by Limerick TD Jim Kemmy in 1981, the Democratic Socialist Party, also merged with Labour, in 1990. The Green Alliance (*Comhaontas Glas*) was formed in 1983 and its first TD, Roger Garland, was elected in 1989.

Ireland voted (69 per cent to 31 per cent) for closer union with Europe by accepting the Maastricht Treaty of 1992, which changed the name of the federation to the European Union and paved the way for a single European currency, the euro, which was introduced in 2002.

9.3.3 The Economy and Living Standards

The average industrial wage doubled between 1966 and 1973 and the 1971 census recorded the first rise in population in 130 years. On this wave of optimism Ireland voted overwhelmingly (83 per cent) to join the European Economic Community (EEC) in 1972. The Labour Party and those further left (e.g. anti-apartheid activist Kader Asmal) opposed joining. But most people, and especially farmers, were in favour of it, and agricultural incomes rose significantly over the 1970s.

The worldwide depression of the 1970s affected Ireland grievously. Unemployment reached 8 per cent in 1972. In 1970 the government recognized the instability of the economy when it embarked on National Pay Agreements with the unions, whereby pay rises kept pace with inflation. Fine Gael were in government from 1973 to 1977, but Fianna Fáil returned with an overall majority in 1977 with an ambitious programme of high public spending and borrowing, paid for by increased taxation of certain sectors. Employees whose tax was taken out by employers – PAYE workers – launched the first of several mass demonstrations in the late 1970s, bringing tens of thousands out onto the streets of cities and towns. These were the lucky ones. Dole queues stretching out onto streets from unemployment offices became a familiar sight as unemployment reached 15 per cent by 1986. Emigration more than doubled, from 14,000 in 1983 to 29,000 in 1986–1987. In 1987 the government invested heavily in the Irish Financial Services Centre in Dublin, to attract foreign financial institutions by offering low tax rates, but this never delivered the number of jobs it promised, partly because some Dublin firms relocated there to avail of the low tax. The Programme for National Recovery from 1987 to 1990 introduced the idea of 'social partnership', by limiting pay rises and negotiating with unions. Some state assets were privatized, but public spending was also cut.

Nonetheless, there were improvements in some areas of life. Going to secondary school became the norm, with the number of pupils rising from 239,000 in 1974–1975 to 362,230 twenty years later. In National/primary schools, average class sizes fell from over forty-five in 1970 to twenty-six in 1998, as more teachers were employed. Eleven regional colleges of technology were set up between 1968 and 1980, and the National Institute of Higher Education (NIHE) was set up in Limerick in 1972 (later the University of Limerick) with a strong European focus. NIHE Dublin (later Dublin City University) followed in 1980. Numbers at university rose from 15,000 in 1965 to over 44,000 in 1991, though many graduates, in the 1980s, no matter how highly qualified they were, could not get work – any kind of work – in Ireland.

Despite the uneven pace of economic growth, real incomes doubled between the 1960s and the 1980s. Telecommunications improved from the late 1970s with the roll-out of Subscriber Trunk Dialling (i.e. direct dialling rather than going through the operator) all over the country, and the number of telephone subscribers increased dramatically. (Up to the 1970s the question 'Are you on the 'phone?' meant 'Have you been connected to a telephone line?') Hardly any fixed dwellings, urban or rural, lacked piped water and electricity by 1976. In 1971 less than half of all houses (46 per cent) had more than four rooms (excluding bathrooms), but by 1991, 71 per cent did. However, government investment in social housing slowed down in this period, as private building boomed, spurred by tax concessions.

In 1980 it was estimated that a third of the population was living on or below the poverty line, and in 1986, a state agency, Combat Poverty, was set up to address this. Over the next two decades, however, Ireland, which had come into the EEC as the poorest of the nine member states, outstripped them all in economic performance. Between 1988 and 1995 the economy grew quicker than in any other EU country, borrowing fell and employment grew at 4 per cent per year.

But this improvement took time to make itself felt. The numbers of people in work in Ireland grew by 45 per cent between 1987 and 2001, but the acceleration happened from the mid-1990s. In 1991 many parishes in the west of Ireland could not put together a football team, because so many young people had gone. A chart-topper at Christmas 1990 was the Sawdoctors' anthem 'N17', where an emigrant yearns for the road from Galway city to his home town of Tuam. There was fierce competition for the US visas negotiated by Congressman Brian Donnelly from the late 1980s. The first use by an economist of the term the 'Celtic Tiger' was in 1994, but the 16,000 Irish people, many of them professionals, who emigrated on Morrison visas to the USA between 1991 and 1994, not to mention the thousands who went to Australia in the same period, had never heard it.

9.3.4 Social and Cultural Life

Ten-thousand people descended on Carnsore Point in Co. Wexford in August 1978 to protest against a nuclear power station. These were decades of activism. (Figure 9.4) From

FIGURE 9.4 Action for the Homeless meeting, Dublin 1986. Independent News and Media/Getty Images News/Getty images. From left, Sr Una McCourtney SCJP, Mary Higgins, Nell McCafferty and Peter McVerry SJ. The socio-political activism of the 1980s brought nuns, priests, feminists and socialists together; this would have been a typical grouping of the time.

the early 1970s, thousands of Irish medical workers, teachers, engineers and other professionals volunteered abroad with agencies like Concern, founded in 1968, and Trócaire, founded in 1973. Many came back radicalized, swelling the ranks of those who opposed American policies in Central and South America and marched (alongside many priests and nuns) in their thousands to protest against US President Ronald Reagan's visit to Ireland in 1984. Refusing to handle South African oranges brought twelve Dublin Dunnes Stores workers, led by checkout operator Mary Manning, out on a punitive strike that lasted from 1984 to 1986. The Simon Community, working with homeless people from 1969, had a representative, Brendan Ryan, elected to the Seanad in 1981. In 1985 Pavee Point was set up by Travellers (and partly government-funded) as a pressure and support group, and the Irish Traveller Movement incorporated this and other Traveller organizations in 1990. Sean Maher's *The Road to God Knows Where*, which appeared in 1972, and Nan Joyce's *Traveller*, published in 1985, highlighted both the differences and the similarities between Ireland's nomads and settled people, as did the distinctive musical style of the Furey Brothers, settled Travellers from Ballyfermot in Dublin who were in the top four of Irish folk/traditional acts in the 1970s and 1980s.

Irish music found new audiences nationally and internationally from the late 1960s with the Fureys, the Chieftains, Planxty, Clannad, Horslips, Scullion, the Bothy Band and many more. Irish rock and pop musicians included Belfast-born Van Morrison, Rory Gallagher, Thin Lizzy, Derry band The Undertones and Dublin bands The Boomtown Rats and U2. Ray Lynam, the Swarbriggs, Sandy Kelly, Philomena Begley, Daniel O'Donnell and many other country/showband/eclectic singers attracted huge audiences all over the island. Music always crossed the border, and even the massacre of the Dublin-based Miami Showband in Co. Armagh in 1975 by loyalists (with some security force collusion) did not put an end to this. On the global stage, Ireland won the Eurovision Song Contest seven times during this period, from Derry woman Dana's ground-breaking 'All Kinds of Everything' in 1970 to Eimear Quinn's 'The Voice' in 1996. At the 1994 contest, hosted in Dublin, the brilliant interval act Riverdance, written by Bill Whelan and performed by Michael Flatley and Jean

Butler, Anúna vocal group, and a troupe of talented dancers, blended the new and the old in Irish dancing and singing.

The Irish language also got a boost. Raidio na Gaeltachta was set up in 1972 specifically for the *Gaeltachaí* (Irish-speaking areas) of Donegal, Mayo, Galway, Kerry, Cork and Waterford, but was listened to by *Gaelgeoirí* (enthusiasts for Irish) all over the country. *Údarás na Gaeltachta* (the Gaeltacht Authority) was set up in 1980 as a successor to *Gaeltarra Eireann* (founded in 1957) to encourage development in these regions. The number of *Gaelscoileanna* (Irish-language immersion primary schools) outside the *Gaeltachtaí* grew from eleven in 1972 to ninety-seven in 1998 and would continue to grow. An Irish-language television station, TG4, began broadcasting in 1996 and produced stylish and successful current affairs and drama programmes watched all over the country. Irish-language colleges in the *Gaeltachtaí* remained heavily subscribed every summer.

Irish remained a core school subject for all students at primary and secondary level. However, from 1973 onwards, a failure in Irish no longer meant a failure of the entire Leaving Certificate, as it had before. Also, from 1974 it was no longer necessary to pass an Irish examination to be employed in the Civil Service. Some people believed the removal of these requirements would deal the language a death blow, but an equally compelling argument was that detaching Irish from compulsion made it more popular than before.

These decades also saw improvements in women's rights and status.

9.3.5 Women and the State

Women's membership of trade unions and other organizations (like the Irish Countrywomen's Association) had been increasing slowly by tens of thousands between 1951 and 1971, and the result of their combined lobbying was the Commission for the Status of Women, chaired by a female Departmental Secretary, Thekla Beere. Beere's report, issued in 1973, recommended an end to the marriage bar against women in the public service, equal pay, family planning information and advice, and many other reforms. The public service marriage bar was lifted immediately, and women were allowed back on juries in 1976 (they had been 'exempted' from them in 1927, having served on them since 1919). In 1973 an Unmarried Mothers' Allowance gave single mothers the choice of not giving their children up for adoption; already Cherish, a support organization for single mothers, had been set up in 1972 by Maura O'Dea. In 1974, Children's Allowance, which had been introduced in 1944 as payable in the first instance to the head of the household (usually the father), was made payable to either the father or the mother, and from then on it was usually the mother who claimed it. The Succession Act of 1965 had already protected the rights of widows, a welcome development for farmers' wives in particular, and in 1976 the Family Home Protection Act forbade a family home from being sold by either spouse without the agreement of the other. The Employment Equality Act of 1981 was EEC legislation which made paid maternity leave a statutory entitlement for women in the public and private sectors, and it brought more mothers into the workforce.

Mothers who want to perform paid work, however, must be able to control their fertility. Contraception was illegal in Ireland since a ban in 1935, and in a country so sensitive to Catholic influence, Pope Paul VI's confirmation of the Church's ban on 'artificial' family planning in *Humanae Vitae* in 1968 reinforced this. However, Irish Catholic families had been getting progressively smaller since the early 1960s, and throughout this decade birth control was discussed openly in Irish media. In December 1973 the Supreme Court ruled that the ban on the importation of contraceptives was unconstitutional, when a Dublin woman Mary McGee, imported contraceptives for her own use. In 1974 a Family Planning Bill for contraceptives to be made available (to married people only) was introduced by the Fine Gael government; the bill was defeated, with Liam Cosgrave, the Fine Gael leader and Taoiseach, voting against it. Pope John Paul II, on his hugely successful visit to Ireland in 1979, spoke out against contraception and divorce, but at this stage 64 per cent of Irish people, most of them Catholic, supported access to contraception, if only for married people. In the same year, Minister for Health Charles Haughey in his Family Planning Bill made contraceptives (including condoms) available, but by prescription only. This bill passed into law. A more liberal Family Planning Bill introduced in 1985 by Barry Desmond of Labour passed by a narrow margin. But contraception could still only be acquired by medical or clinical routes. Condoms were not in chemists' shops until the late 1980s and even then, not in all of them. Family planning clinics were only in large towns and cities and were still somewhat stigmatized. However, by 1989 even the Catholic-ethos National Maternity Hospital in Holles

Street in Dublin was giving new mothers formal lectures on all methods of family planning, Church approved or not.

This greater acceptability of contraception was partly because of a forced consensus that it was the lesser of two evils, the greater one being abortion. The Eighth Amendment to the Constitution, guaranteeing the unborn child an equal right to life with its mother, had been passed in 1983. Abortion was already illegal under the Offences against the Persons Act (1861), but the Pro-Life Amendment Campaign argued that this could be repealed as it had been in the UK. The amendment was passed in 1983 by 67 per cent to 33 per cent, and those who argued in favour of it had to concede that the stigma attached to unmarried pregnancy was one of the reasons women sought abortions. Although mother-and-baby homes ceased to operate by the end of this decade, women who had sex outside marriage were still stigmatized. When the heavy-handed behaviour of Gardai investigating the violent death of a newborn baby in Co. Kerry in 1984 came before a public tribunal in 1985–1986, much judicial attention focused negatively on the woman at the centre of the Garda inquiries – who had not killed her child – unmarried mother Joanne Hayes. Loud voices were raised in her defence, but many condemned her too.

'Illegitimacy' was abolished by the Status of Children Act of 1987, a step forward for single mothers and their children. In 1967 over 90 per cent of babies born to single mothers were adopted, but only 8.5 per cent were, in 1990, and the number continued to fall.

If the Amendment was the Catholic Church's second-last victory in Ireland (the Protestant churches opposed it) was the defeat of the divorce referendum in 1986, their last? This is debatable. When husbands were the earners, the financial implications of divorce were alarming for women, and this might be one reason why the 1986 referendum failed (63.5 per cent against, 36.5 per cent in favour). Despite the end of the public service marriage bar in 1973, in the 1980s it was still unusual for married women to work outside the home. In 1987 a quarter of mothers were in the labour force, ten years later this had increased to 50 per cent. The labour force participation of women in general increased by 100,000 between 1971 and 1991, but by 512,000 between 1991 and 1999. The second referendum on divorce, held in 1995, might have succeeded partly because more married women had money they could call their own. However, the very narrow margin of success for the pro-divorce lobby in the 1995 referendum (50.3 per cent to 49.7 per cent) in a decade when contraception, single motherhood and cohabitation were becoming acceptable and homosexual relationships unremarkable, suggests that Catholic teaching was not the only reason for opposing divorce. The constituencies where 'No' votes were around the two-third mark were the strongly agricultural Cork North West, Galway East and Longford-Roscommon, which suggests that worries about land and inheritance also played a part.

Women in the Dáil reached the unprecedented number of twenty in 1992, by which time Mary Robinson, a vigorous human rights campaigner since 1971, had been elected Ireland's first female President. (Figure 9.5) Ireland's first female head of a political party was Mary Harney, leader of the Progressive Democrats in 1993. Women's public profile had been rising since the 1970s. Feminist publishers Arlen House and Attic Press were

FIGURE 9.5 President Mary Robinson setting out for her inauguration, December 1990. Independent News and Media/Hulton Archive/Getty images. Long-time campaigner for women's rights, prisoners' rights and human rights generally, Mary Robinson was the first female elected Uachtarán na hÉireann, in 1990.

founded in 1975 and 1984, respectively, and Irish female authors were signed eagerly by publishing houses in Ireland and abroad. Maeve Binchy shot to worldwide fame with her novels, starting with *Light a Penny Candle* in 1982. Máirín de Burca, Rosita Sweetman, Mary Cummins, June Levine, and many others campaigned for women and wrote about politics, workplace discrimination, extra-marital pregnancy, prostitution, infanticide and clandestine births. However, when the very popular Derry-born, Dublin-based journalist Nell McCafferty (Figure 9.4) urged Irish feminists to support Northern Irish women in Armagh prison on the dirty protest in 1980, her plea fell on deaf ears.

Although charismatic Joyce scholar David Norris set up the Campaign for Homosexual Law Reform in 1976, gay rights did not become an issue till the 1980s. When a homosexual man, Declan Flynn, was beaten to death in Fairview Park in Dublin in 1982, all five of his murderers (self-confessed 'queer-bashers') walked from court with suspended sentences. The rise of AIDS from 1985 forced gay men into prominent public-health advocacy roles, but it also forced public recognition of the fact that many Irish heterosexuals as well as homosexuals had sex with multiple partners. Homosexuality was decriminalized in 1993.

9.4 Conclusion

The Good Friday Agreement brought the Troubles in Northern Ireland to a close, but tensions and lack of trust remained, often encompassing the whole island. For Northern Protestants/unionists, the fact that the Omagh bomb was assembled south of the border, and the plight of the 'disappeared' – people such as Belfast mother of ten Jean McConville, kidnapped and murdered by the IRA in the early 1970s and buried secretly in Co. Louth – was 'proof' that the Republic was soft on subversives. On the other side of the divide, Northern Catholics/nationalists were often hurt by the lack of support of those south of the border. Not only was Irish media muzzled by

Section 31 of the Broadcasting Act until 1994, but many in public life were afraid to protest about injustices perpetrated on the Northern Catholic/nationalist community in case this was seen as supporting 'the men of violence'. Northern Irish priests Denis Faul and Raymond Murray were drawing attention since 1977 to the unsafe convictions of six men for the Birmingham public-house bombings of 1974 (which killed twenty-one people), but it was only when British Labour MP Chris Mullin wrote a book about it in 1986 that Irish public opinion was mobilized. The 'Birmingham Six', along with eleven men and women in total convicted for the Guildford bombings (in which five people died) were released between 1989 and 1991. The IRA perpetrators of both bombings were never caught.

All the bad news in these decades meant that it did not take much to make Irish people happy. The joyful throngs which greeted the Republic of Ireland soccer team on their return from the World Cup in Italy in 1990 (having made it to the quarter-finals) caused their manager, Jack Charlton, to wonder aloud what the reception would have been like had Ireland made it to the final. Two years earlier, when Ireland beat England 1–0 in the UEFA Cup, there was such unbounded joy that popular singer-songwriter Christy Moore wrote 'Joxer Goes to Stuttgart', which brought the house down whenever he performed it live.

Three years before this, however, another song Christy Moore wrote was banned. 'They Never Came Home' mourned the forty-eight young adults who died in a conflagration in the Stardust Ballroom in Artane, Dublin, on Valentine's Night 1981, suggesting that chained fire exits on the night in question contributed to the high death toll. Although a public inquiry into the disaster which reported in 1982 condemned the closed fire exits, the highly inflammable building materials and the overall design of the building, it suggested that the fire had been started (accidentally) by the dancers themselves. The owner of the property, Eamon Butterly, claimed compensation, had his licence renewed, and got a judge to rule, in 1985, that Moore's song was in contempt of court.

This is, admittedly, an extreme example of the way successful Irish business people were rarely held to account for anything, but it is a telling one. There were strong murmurings throughout the 1980s and 1990s about payments by businessmen to politicians, adjustments and abuses of the planning system, rezoning of publicly owned land, tax evasion and other suspect ways of making money and holding on to it. There was a tribunal of inquiry into Ireland's world-famous beef industry and especially into Larry Goodman's company, in the early 1990s. The Moriarty and McCracken and Mahon Tribunals from 1997 and into the next century looked at payments to Charles Haughey, Michael Lowry, Bertie Ahern, and other politicians, and raised questions about prominent businessmen, among them telecommunications mogul Denis O'Brien and supermarket magnate Ben Dunne, and their close relationships with these and other public figures.

This culture of inquiry – and, eventually, accountability – developed alongside a growing awareness of the mistreatment of children in Ireland. Mannix Flynn's autobiographical novel *Nothing to Say*, Mavis Arnold and Heather Laskey's *Children of the Poor Clares*, and many other memoirs and works of investigative journalism described the culture of fear in state institutions up to the 1970s. The convictions in the 1990s of notorious serial sex abusers Fr Brendan Smyth and Fr Seán Fortune, among others, drew attention to the vulnerability of Catholic children in more recent times.

The full extent of the corruptions, cruelties and cover-ups perpetrated over the previous half-century would be revealed in the first two decades of the twenty-first century. The Stardust victims' relatives would have to wait until 2024, however, for verdicts of unlawful killing to be returned in respect of their loved ones.

10

Prosperity/Austerity/Prosperity?

~

1998–c. 2016

Ireland was ranked in the top five of globalized countries in the early 2000s, and many changes in Ireland between 1998 and 2018 happened all over the world: the increased use of the internet; mobile phones, then smartphones and all the changes in communications and relationships that they wrought; the rise of social media from the late 2000s; more international travelling; changes in the consumption of food and drink; an increase in online shopping, dating and gaming; and a rise in recreational drug use. There were also changes peculiar to Ireland, but the greatest of these, constantly marvelled at by Irish people, was the experience of living in what was for most of this period an economically successful country. There were other changes, too, which cannot be fully understood from a distance of under thirty years, so this chapter will be more tentative than conclusive in its observations.

10.1 Ireland

10.1.1 The Economy

Irish industrial and agricultural output increased by 350 per cent between 1995 and 2005 and Ireland's unemployment rate in 2006 was 4.3 per cent, the third lowest in the EU. Jobs in industry and in services of all kinds proliferated. Fifteen per cent of industries were multinational, but around 85 per cent were medium to small Irish businesses employing up to fifty people. The big firms (Boston Scientific was one example, Medtronic another) employed thousands, building on Ireland's existing medical devices and pharmaceutical industrial base. Dell came to Limerick in 1991 and Google to Dublin in 2003, and Amazon in 2004. The highly successful food-processing sector was led by giants like Glanbia and Kerry Foods. Smaller producers found that Ireland's comparative 'greenness' and lack of intensive farming made its cereal, livestock and especially dairy products irresistible to discerning customers. The long-established Kerrygold butter was joined by Irish cheeses from Ardrahan to Durrus to Knockanore to Wicklow Gold, as Irish dairy produce, famous for a thousand years, soared to new heights.

Irish clothes retailers Penneys/Primark, already moderately successful in Ireland and Britain, bought the UK Littlewoods in 2006 and expanded all over Europe. On a smaller scale, the Hughes Group, retailers in Co. Mayo for generations, expanded their operations and workforce worldwide as PortWest sports and workwear, from the late twentieth century. These are just two examples of the kind of economic success story that came to characterize Ireland at this time. The biggest success story of all was Ryanair, begun by Tony Ryan in the 1980s, which spread all over Europe as a low-cost airline from the late 1990s, and through its competitive pricing lowered the cost of air travel globally.

In the first decade of the millennium, one in every eight Irish jobs was in construction, and all the building trades – carpenter, plasterer, plumber, painter-decorator – flourished. When Dolores McNamara won €115 million in the Euro Lottery in 2005, she and her husband, a plumber, already owned a holiday apartment abroad, and they were by no means unusual. The building trade was so buoyant and construction so ubiquitous that some people joked that the harp should be replaced by a crane as a national symbol.

Some of this building provided houses for increasing numbers of homeowners in this decade, and banks offered more generous mortgages than ever before to first-time buyers in a market of soaring prices. As house prices rose to over eight times the average industrial wage, dual-income families became the norm, and crèches and child-minders multiplied as more young parents joined the workforce. Dublin's commuter belt extended to counties Meath, Louth, Kildare and Carlow. Motorways, which had begun in the 1980s, radiated from Dublin to Belfast, Cork and Limerick, reaching Galway and Sligo by 2010. Public transport usage soared as competition from private bus companies like CityLink forced the state service Bus Éireann into providing far more daily services throughout the country, and the number of rail services trebled. Regional airports throve on business as well as leisure customers, and the small airport outside Galway city which had hitherto served only the Aran Islands had several daily flights to Dublin and Britain and twice-weekly ones to France. The number of tourists from Europe to Ireland rose by 78 per cent in the first decade of the millennium, and many Irish people began to take two foreign holidays a year. In addition to this, the 'city break' – two or three nights in Prague or Paris, Berlin or

Budapest – became common. This phenomenon would survive the crash, unlike the three-day shopping trip to the USA, a striking feature of the early-to-mid 2000s which ceased around 2009. These passengers (usually women) brought empty suitcases with them which they filled with purchases from outlet malls on the peripheries of New York and Boston. Some estimates put the average spend per traveller at over $2,000.

This kind of spending was recognized as extreme at the time, as was the spectacle (and sound) of helicopters bringing punters on two or three-mile journeys to events like the Galway Races (at €100 a single trip). More soberly, economists warned on the eve of the crash about ever-rising debt from a banking sector only too willing to lend money. Lending institutions provided money to people not only to buy houses and cars and fund holidays but also to invest in building projects abroad, in eastern Europe and Dubai. Economists also expressed concern at the feverish level of building. Because of tax concessions to builders, house provision soon outstripped need, and by 2010, there were over 300,000 empty housing units (not counting holiday homes). Some of these were built on poor, boggy land with substandard materials. Economist David McWilliams coined the phrase 'ghost estates' for these empty, decaying, damp developments all over the country. Some were half-occupied and unfinished, without footpaths or proper roads. Tana French's haunting novel *Broken Harbour* (2012) builds a story of paranoia and fear out of a family's experience on one such (fictional) estate in Dublin.

The worldwide financial crash of 2008 was keenly felt in Ireland because of a light-touch regulatory regime towards financial institutions since the 1980s. The governor of the Central Bank of Ireland, Patrick Honohan, concluded in 2010 that the crash was worse than it might have been because of this. Six major banks, including the two biggest, Bank of Ireland and Allied Irish Banks, were in crisis, Anglo-Irish Bank failed completely, and panic drove the government's controversial decision to bail them out with €64 billion of taxpayers' money. Ireland had to borrow money to do this, and the tripartite group which administered and executed the bailout, the International Monetary Fund, the European Central Bank and the European Commission, was known as the Troika. The effects of the crisis were almost immediate. Many of the major firms had redundancies (Dell in Limerick let 1,900 employees go in 2009). Some smaller firms went out of business altogether. Unemployment rose to 14.6 per cent, almost 1980s levels, by 2012.

Ireland managed to 'exit the bailout' (pay back all its debts) by December 2013, by making severe cuts in the public sector. The public service pay bill was cut by €3.1 billion and over 7,000 employees were either redeployed or not replaced. The model of social partnership in place for decades served the governments well, as public service unions readily agreed to these cuts. Working people in both the public and private sectors paid for the banks' carelessness through wages or indirect taxes on goods and services. Demonstrations and marches against austerity took place throughout the country – one, in Dublin in 2012, filled the National Stadium to capacity, with crowds spilling out into the streets and coachloads from all over the country. When the government tried to introduce water charges over the following years, protests were so vigorous and sustained that they abandoned this plan in 2016, after spending €45 million installing water meters in private houses.

An unexpected survivor of the crash was Ireland West Airport at Knock, Co. Mayo. Built in 1985 by local priest Monsignor James Horan, who wanted to boost the numbers of pilgrims to the site of the 1879 Marian apparition, it developed far beyond pilgrim traffic, adding several holiday destinations and even transatlantic ones for a time. Its baseline, however, were flights to Britain that followed long-established west-of-Ireland migration trails which had never quite ceased since the mid nineteenth century, and which were more important than ever in the difficult years of the second decade of the twenty-first. Galway airport closed down in 2011, but Knock saw only a small decrease in passenger numbers.

Irish standards of comfort certainly rose between 1998 and 2018, but not for everybody and not in all areas of life. Food in supermarkets and shops became more varied, but it became more expensive to buy locally grown fruit and vegetables. There were more jobs, but many of these were temporary; in 2018, 200,000 Irish employees were on temporary contracts in the so-called 'gig economy'. Big teaching hospitals in large centres of population developed into centres of excellence with very good records regarding cancer and other serious diseases, but the closure of emergency departments in smaller regional hospitals led to overcrowding in the bigger centres, with delays in treatment (at best) and unnecessary deaths (at worst). Temporary employment became the norm in the public as well as the private sector, particularly in education at third and second level, and in health care. Workers' bargaining power weakened, with only 27 per cent of Irish workers in unions in 2018, compared to 62 per cent in 1980. Life got harder in other ways too. A public service early-stage employee could buy (as a first-time buyer) a two-bedroom semi-detached house in the mid 1980s. In 2018, even couples pooling two salaries found it difficult to get mortgages for ever-rising house prices. Housing standards seemed to rise; most new-build houses and apartments in the private sector from the early 2000s had ensuite toilet/showers off their master bedrooms, but these were often badly ventilated closets which trapped smells and damp, and cut space off the bedroom; a metaphor for living conditions in general, with apparent luxury masking cramped squalor. People on low incomes fared worst of all. During the building boom between 2002 and 2011, less than 4 per cent of all houses built were social or low-cost housing. Private-sector rents rose by 42 per cent between 2011 and 2016 and there were nearly 7,000 homeless people in Ireland in 2016, a rise from the 3,800 of 2011. Ireland was the eighth richest country in the world in 2018, but only 1 per cent of tax revenue was raised from houses, land or property.

Unemployment fell to 6 per cent in 2018, as jobs reappeared in hospitality, retail and manufacturing. There were some new international companies, attracted by the low corporation tax, but, from 2009 to 2014, 637,800 people left the country. Many went to Australia, and the sense of bewildered betrayal of young Irish people born into comfort and catapulted into low-paid, backbreaking work on the other side of the world is captured in E. M. Reapy's powerful 2016 novel *Red Dirt*. However, to put this very large figure into perspective, between 40 per cent and 50 per cent of those who left in these years were Irish people, the others were people who had come to Ireland before this and were leaving again. In the same years, 485,000 people came into Ireland, adding to the numbers that had been arriving over the previous fifteen years or so.

10.1.2 Immigration

From the late 1990s people all over the world were attracted to Ireland by job opportunities in construction, hospitality, and the health and caring services, and industry. Work permits were granted to people from Brazil, the Philippines, India, Pakistan, Bangladesh and many other countries. Then, the Treaty of Nice in 2001, which allowed for the accession of ten eastern European states by 2004, opened Ireland up to Polish, Latvian, Estonian, Lithuanian, Hungarian, Slovakian, Czech and Slovenian immigrants. Builders' vans met planes from eastern Europe at Shannon and Dublin to drive workers to the new-build houses they would share while working on building sites. Many of these immigrants later left the construction sector to work in retail, hospitality or white-collar work. By 2006 400,000 of Ireland's 4 million residents had been born outside Ireland, 75 per cent of these in the European Union. The accession to the EU of Bulgaria and Romania in 2007, and Croatia in 2013, added to the numbers arriving. Between 1996 and 2009 average net immigration was 37,000 per year, reaching a peak of 105,000 in 2007. This immigration slowed down a little after the crash, but, because conditions were no worse in Ireland than elsewhere, never stopped. Immigrants settled mainly in cities, but also in provincial towns, with

Longford, Portlaoise, Co. Laois, and Drogheda, Co. Louth, becoming the most ethnically diverse towns in Ireland by the middle of the second decade of the century. Making up a minority of incomers were people fleeing war and persecution who were granted asylum between 1999 and 2016, at an average of 6,500 per year.

Ireland had been an emigrant rather than an immigrant country since at least 1700, so newcomers were a great novelty, especially while the economy and infrastructure had room to spare for them. (Figure 10.1) However, some unease about the numbers coming into the country in the early years of the millennium was expressed by a referendum in 2004, which removed the right to citizenship by birth. This passed by 79 per cent, was supported by Fianna Fáil, Fine Gael and the Progressive Democrats (PDs) and the voter turnout (60 per cent) was higher than that for the 1997 referendum on the Good Friday Agreement. A Labour government in Britain also passed several laws controlling immigration around this time. Anti-immigrant sentiment was muted, however, even after the crash of 2008–2009, and anti-austerity campaigners in 2012 canvassing urban working-class areas in Dublin found little anti-immigration sentiment on the doorsteps, but plenty of criticism of bankers and businessmen, and, of course, politicians.

10.1.3 Politics

Fianna Fáil was in government from 1997 to 2011, supported by various other political parties – the PDs (who wound down in 2008) and the Greens, and Labour, who supported the bailout. Never in government were the Social Democrats, founded in 2015 as a breakaway from

FIGURE 10.1 St Patrick's Day Parade, O'Connell Bridge, Dublin, 2022. Charles McQuillan/Stringer/Getty Images News/Getty images. Since the early 2000s, St Patrick's Day parades all over the country feature people from all over the world who have made their homes in Ireland and want to take part in the national celebration.

the Labour party, but this party and the left-wing People Before Profit and Socialist Party exerted an influence out of all proportion to their size, in the anti-austerity demonstrations after 2009.

Bertie Ahern resigned as leader (and Taoiseach) in 2008 and Brian Cowen took over. Fianna Fáil took a beating because of the crash, the bailout decision and the slow drip feed of findings of the Mahon and McCracken Tribunals of inquiry into payments to politicians, many (but not all) in Fianna Fáil, and offshore accounts. In time, the revenue commissioners would recover €113 million in unpaid taxes, but very few people went to jail.

In the 2011 election Fianna Fáil was down from seventy-seven to twenty seats, its lowest showing ever, and

Fine Gael and Labour and the Greens increased their numbers, with Fine Gael forming a coalition with Labour under Enda Kenny, with Labour's Eamon Gilmore as Tánaiste. Sinn Féin under the leadership of Gerry Adams increased its number of seats from five to fourteen, and would continue to grow.

At the end of this period, the women elected to the Dáil comprised between a fifth and a quarter of all TDs, having grown from twenty in 1997 (12 per cent of all those elected) to thirty-five in the general elections of 2016 (22 per cent). Considering the number of women active in pressure groups, advocacy, professional life and journalism for nearly forty years at this stage, this was a poor showing, and gender quotas were suggested for the first time.

Nationalist feeling in Ireland had been quiet for about thirty years because of the Northern Troubles, but it re-emerged in style for the Decade of Centenaries, which began in 2013 with the 100th anniversary of the Dublin Lock-Out, and would end in 2023 with the centenary of the Civil War. These commemorations were complicated and enriched by memories and studies of Irishmen who fought and died in the Great War as well as in the revolution, and there was genuine, vigorous debate not only at historical conferences but at popular commemorative events, and on TV and radio. There was also a great market for popular history books about early twentieth-century Ireland, with well over 100 titles appearing. The headline event was the centenary of the Easter Rising in 2016, for which thousands travelled to Dublin. The identity 'Irish' as promoted in public events, whether they were government or community-sponsored, was a joyful one, in which people of all colours, creeds and ethnicities were welcome. This was the image Ireland liked to project in these years, exemplified in the joyful multi-ethnicity of annual St Patrick's Day parades. (Figure 10.1) It was accurate up to a point.

10.1.4 Social Attitudes, Religion, Women, Travellers

In the early twenty-first century, Ireland underwent dramatic changes as far as attitudes to sexual behaviour and private life were concerned. Gay marriage was legalized in 2015 with 62 per cent in favour in a referendum, and Ireland had its first openly gay Taoiseach, Leo Varadkar, in 2017.

Ireland was becoming a more globalized country and trends in private morality reflected this. The Catholic Church's authority to speak on sexual morality was damaged not only by the cover-ups of clerical sexual abuse but also by the revelations in the early 1990s that prominent media-friendly ecclesiastics Bishop Eamon Casey and Fr Michael Cleary had fathered children in the 1970s and 1980s. In 1994 one in five births were outside marriage, but by 2014, one in three were. The stigma of unmarried motherhood disappeared almost completely, in a country where it had once been (and this is no exaggeration) the worst fate that could befall a woman.

Registry office marriages became more common from the 1990s, and, in 2013, 30 per cent of all weddings were conducted without an accompanying religious ceremony. Yet Ireland remained a strongly religious country. In 2016, 90.2 per cent still professed a religion. Catholics made up the majority, at 78.3 per cent of the population.

Ireland's Muslim community almost doubled between 2006 and 2016, when it stood at 63,443 (1.3 per cent of the population), and this decade also saw rapid growth in Pentecostal and Orthodox Christians, and growth in the Church of Ireland, due to African and South American immigration. Jews experienced serious decline; there were only 2,557 in independent Ireland in 2016, compared to almost 4,000 in 1946 in a much smaller population.

Despite the decline in the proportion of Catholics, 88 per cent of state primary schools (2,760) remained under the patronage of the Catholic Church in 2016. The Church of Ireland were patrons of 5.7 per cent, 1 per cent were under other religious organizations and 5.4 per cent were non-denominational. The pioneering Dalkey School Project in the 1970s had paved the way for the setting up of Educate Together in 1984, which promoted the development of non-denominational schools around the country. By 2016 there were over 100 Educate Together schools in Ireland but many areas had none at all. This was set to change, and a promise was made in 2016 that the state would set up 400 new non-denominational schools by the year 2030.

The decline of the Catholic Church's authority continued. Six commissions or committees of inquiry in the first two decades of the twenty-first century focused on Church personnel's mistreatment of children and vulnerable adults over the previous half-century. Three of these looked at the severe, unchecked and covered-up abuse of children by secular priests in three dioceses, Ferns (Wexford), Cloyne (east Cork) and Dublin. In Dublin archdiocese alone, according to the Murphy report (presided over by Justice Yvonne Murphy) 183 priests sexually abused children between 1975 and 2004. After the publication of the Cloyne report in 2011, Taoiseach Enda Kenny excoriated the Church authorities for having covered up the rape and torture of Irish children. There were objections to his strong language, but it is hard to find fault with it. Another commission, which resulted in the Ryan Report of 2009 (called after its presiding judge, Seán Ryan) investigated religious-run residential industrial schools and reformatories, finding that rape and molestation happened routinely in some boys' institutions, and that there was severe corporal punishment and neglect in some schools for both sexes. In the worst institutions, children were kept (illegally) out of school to do housework, garden or, in one grotesquely ironic instance, to make rosary beads for sale. These state-funded institutions should have been inspected more thoroughly and criticized at an earlier stage. But state officials were afraid to criticize Catholic Church-run institutions for most of the twentieth century.

Other institutions also came under scrutiny as the Catholic Church's authority collapsed. Magdalen asylums were religious-run institutions where women inmates did impeccable laundry and mending behind firmly closed doors. Comparatively few in number (ten in the state overall), they were places for women who had either transgressed sexually or were seen to be in danger of doing so, and they wound down in the early 1980s. Some women were 'allowed' to leave them voluntarily, while others were detained for life on no legal basis whatsoever. Absconders were routinely brought back by the Gardai. The pressure group Justice for Magdalenes demanded an inquiry, which issued its report in 2013, detailing the denial of freedom and slave labour in these institutions. Taoiseach Enda Kenny issued an apology in the Dáil.

And the news kept getting worse. In 2012 an investigation by a local historian, Catherine Corless, in Tuam, Co. Galway, into extremely high levels of infant mortality in a mother-and-baby home that had operated there from 1925 to 1961, led to the unearthing of a mass grave of infant remains in a concrete vault (incorrectly described in some accounts as a septic tank) on the grounds. This focused attention on the other mother-and-baby homes (not to be confused with Magdalen asylums) in Ireland. There had been concern about these places for some years. Legal adoption had been introduced into Ireland in 1952, and many unmarried mothers and childless couples availed of this legislation in good faith, but illegal trafficking went on behind the scenes. Mike Milotte's *Banished Babies* (1997) had exposed the sale of hundreds (some estimates are of 2,000) of 'illegitimate' Irish babies for adoption abroad between the 1950s and 1970s, from mother-and-baby homes run by nuns. A commission of inquiry was set up in 2015, and it would issue its report in 2021.

The Residential Institutions Redress Board, set up in 2002 to compensate people abused in institutions, was quite busy over these years. However, former inmates of the Protestant mother-and-baby home and orphanage, Bethany Home in Dublin, were ineligible for redress from this Board, for reasons which have never been explained.

Historical injustices against women were all the more keenly felt because of a growing focus on girls' and women's reproductive rights. A series of referenda in the early 1990s, following on from some highly publicized cases (one of them involving a fourteen-year-old girl who was not allowed to travel to Britain for an abortion), modified the Eighth Amendment somewhat by allowing women the right to travel abroad for an abortion and the right to information about abortion in other countries. But the right to terminate a pregnancy if the mother's *life* (as distinct from her *health*) was in danger, won by a third referendum, embodied a fatal ambiguity which cost Savita Halappanavar her life in Galway University Hospital in 2012. She was threatening a miscarriage at seventeen weeks and developing sepsis, but medical staff would not carry out an abortion while there was still a foetal heartbeat. A movement to repeal the Eighth Amendment got under way, and a successful referendum was held in May 2018, in which 66 per cent voted for repeal and 34 per cent against (voter turnout was 64 per cent). Abortion was introduced into Ireland after this.

Ireland undoubtedly became a more tolerant and open society because of all these events and investigations, but whether it became more caring or not is debatable. Prejudice against Travelling people persisted. Public figures who would never attack immigrants could utter negative generalizations about this minority without any repercussions; writing like this in 2014 (and at several other times) did not cause one columnist for the Irish editions of the *Daily Mail* and the *Sunday Times*, to lose either her job or her audience. There were nearly 31,000 Irish (i.e. not including Roma and other non-Irish nomadic peoples) Travellers in Ireland by 2016. (Figure 10.2) This six-fold increase in numbers since 1963 is a welcome sign of Travellers' improved health and living conditions. By

FIGURE 10.2 Ballinasloe Horse Fair October 2015. Clodagh Kilcoyne/Getty Images News/Getty images. A social and commercial event dating back to the eighteenth century, this three-day horse fair is one of the traditional annual gatherings of Ireland's Travellers, and is attended by many non-Travellers too.

the second decade of the new century, 78 per cent of Travellers were settled in local authority or state-supported housing, 9 per cent were in authorized serviced halting sites, and only 5 per cent remained 'on the side of the road' in illegal encampments (the remainder had bought their own houses). Problems remained. Ten members of the Connors, Gilbert and Lynch families, five of them children, died when a fire raged through the badly serviced halting site they lived on in Carrickmines, Co. Dublin, in October 2015. Young Traveller men continued to have a much higher rate of suicide than those in the population in general, and infant mortality among Travellers was three times that of the general population. Many local authorities did not spend the portion of their budgets allocated to Traveller housing because of the fear of objections from settled people. However, in 2017, Irish Travellers gained official recognition as an ethnic minority, which gives them the same protection against discrimination and hate speech as other minorities.

The rights of the physically and intellectually disabled were defined, and improved, following the Commission on the Status of People with Disabilities in 1996. Sixty per cent of this commission's members were people with disabilities, or their parents/relatives. A series of acts followed which recognized people with disabilities as full members of society, with the same rights as everybody else, culminating in the Disability Act of 2005. Yawning, disgraceful gaps in the services would remain, but this Act was a crucial step forward for human rights. Ireland's joyful hosting of the Special Olympics in 2003 was a strong signal of the new visibility of people with special needs.

The big nineteenth-century mental hospitals had closed their doors by the early twenty-first century, having been gradually replaced, from the 1980s onwards, by outpatient care, day centres and smaller psychiatric units for acute sufferers. Both the harshness and the permanence of patient life in the old mental hospitals can be exaggerated, because there were many humane nurses and doctors, and patients were often discharged when considered cured. There are, however, credible stories of abuse: the denial in some hospitals of basic dignities like personal clothing; the overuse of physical restraint; the long-term incarceration of people who were no danger to themselves or others; and the unmarked graves. The biggest abuse of all was the overuse of the mechanism of legal committal.

Surprisingly, given the numbers incarcerated and given the thorough investigations of institutions which held far fewer people (e.g. Magdalen asylums) there has been not only no commission of inquiry into these institutions, but no demand for one.

10.2 Northern Ireland

10.2.1 Politics

Tensions continued after the Good Friday Agreement, with the IRA delaying the decommissioning of arms. This led David Trimble, the first minister of the Northern Ireland Assembly, to refuse to go into government with Sinn Féin, but there were other tensions, too, and in 2004 the IRA (though they always denied it) appear to have carried out the substantial Northern Bank robbery, the biggest bank robbery in the history of both jurisdictions. In September 2005 Canadian observer General John de Chastelain verified that the IRA had fully decommissioned its weapons. Finally, in 2007, after the St Andrews Agreement of 2006 between the Irish and British governments, the Northern Ireland Assembly was back in action. This time, the first minister was Ian Paisley and the deputy first minister, Martin McGuinness; the DUP and Sinn Féin, the two extreme, polar opposites, had emerged as the two largest parties in Northern Ireland. Working together, Paisley and McGuinness forged a friendship that would have been unthinkable a decade before.

To go into government, Sinn Féin had to agree to accept the new Police Service of Northern Ireland (PSNI). This was set up in 2001 after the Patten Report, which recommended that the old RUC be disbanded and a new, strictly impartial police force established. Overseen by the Northern Ireland Policing Board, the PSNI was to have 50:50 Protestant–Catholic membership; this happened at the senior levels but not among the rank and file. In general, though, the PSNI was far more acceptable to Northern Ireland's Catholic community than its predecessor had been.

The communities of Northern Ireland settled down into peaceful if tense co-existence. Peter Robinson succeeded Ian Paisley as first minister in 2008, with McGuinness still as deputy first minister. Robinson was succeeded by Arlene Foster in 2016, the first female premier on the island. When the vote about whether to leave, or remain within, the European Union was put to the Northern Ireland electorate, 55.78 per cent voted to remain, 44.22 per cent voted to leave, but as the United Kingdom in general voted to leave, Northern Ireland exited the EU. The economic position of Northern Ireland vis-à-vis Britain, and its closest trading partner, Ireland, would cause some fundamental disagreements in the years that followed.

An inquiry set up in 1998 to inquire into the events of 30 January 1972, (Bloody Sunday), under Lord Saville, issued its final report in 2010. It confirmed what the marchers had always claimed: paratroopers of the British Army had fired on unarmed civilians. The British government apologized.

In 2016 the Northern Ireland Assembly was hit by the 'cash for ash' scandal or Renewable Heat Incentive Scheme brought in by the DUP, whereby people could apply for grants to use renewable energy to heat their homes. Arlene Foster refused to resign, so her deputy first minister, Martin McGuinness, did so, and the Northern Ireland Assembly was dissolved in January 2017. There were also tensions about the Irish language, with the nationalist parties demanding more support for it and the DUP in particular opposing this. The Assembly would dissolve a few more times over the next few years, due to political and cultural divergences of opinion.

10.2.2 Economy and Society

Northern Ireland did not experience the Celtic Tiger, although there was some growth and investment in the development of Belfast in particular, with an entire tourist quarter devoted to the doomed Titanic. Derry also saw some important developments with a footbridge across the Foyle and heavy investment in the city's heritage areas. Aerospace, engineering and construction were the main industrial employers, but the numbers employed were nothing like those who worked in shipbuilding and textiles in their heyday. In this, however, Northern Ireland was similar to other post-industrial societies like Britain and the Rust Belt of the north-eastern United States. In Northern Ireland by the second decade of the twenty-first century, most employees (78 per cent) were in services of various kinds, including the public service. Northern Ireland was the slowest region of the United Kingdom as far as economic growth was concerned, and its per capita income in the second decade of the twenty-first century was 38 per cent less than that of Ireland. However, more people were in work in the North, whose unemployment rate in 2018 stood at 3.6 per cent, compared to 6 per cent in the Republic.

Immigration to Northern Ireland was on nothing like the same scale as to Ireland, over these years. In 2011, 4.3 per cent of the North's population had been born outside the UK and Ireland, (compared to 10 per cent in Ireland in 2004) and this number only rose slightly over the following decade.

There are no longer any army or police checkpoints at border crossings into and out of Northern Ireland, and the only indication of having passed into another jurisdiction are the different speed limit signs (the North follows the British habit of using miles rather than kilometres), the red pillar boxes and the white-lined hard-shoulder markings on roads. Money must be changed into sterling for any cash transactions, but there is no customs border. When Brexit became hard reality and Britain definitively exited the EU under Prime Minister Boris Johnson, the question of whether there should be a customs border in the Irish Sea or on the island of Ireland became a controversial one, which has not been solved at the time of writing. There is still a Common Travel Area between Ireland and Britain in general, so a land border in Ireland does not make sense.

Regardless of Brexit, some kinds of co-operation between the two states remain strong. Several north–south consultative bodies were set up by the Good Friday Agreement. Accident victims in east Donegal or in other border areas of the Republic are often brought to Altnagelvin hospital in Derry or the Royal Victoria hospital in Belfast if those are nearer than Irish hospitals and/or have spare capacity in their emergency departments, and there is a non-emergency reciprocal arrangement for many kinds of elective medical treatment between the two jurisdictions. The Dublin–Belfast railway line is operated jointly by Iarnród Éireann and Northern Ireland Railways. People from the North have been coming south on holidays for decades, but the traffic has become two-way since 1997, with many more people from Ireland venturing north of the border for concerts and other cultural and sporting events, holidays and shopping.

10.3 Conclusion

Anyone travelling through small towns anywhere on the island towards the end of this twenty-year period would be struck by the number of empty, boarded-up shops and business premises. The decline in the number of rural and village public houses can be explained not only by more stringent drink-driving laws in both jurisdictions, but also by falling alcohol consumption due to dwindling tolerance for prolonged male absence from domestic responsibilities. The decline in rural shops however, especially apparel and other specialized retailing, other than food, is due to the opening-up of bigger, cheaper shops on the edges of bigger towns, and their easier accessibility due to almost universal car-ownership. This decline can also be seen in other European countries, England and France, in particular, and has long been a feature of North America. On the other hand, in Ireland (and possibly in other countries) the roll-out of broadband internet made small-town residence a possibility for people working in cities but priced out of the urban housing market, long before the Covid-19 pandemic made working from home a necessity that turned into a long-term accommodation to workers' needs. So there is some rural revitalization.

The children of 'blow-ins' boost the numbers in local schools and sports clubs, local labour is employed for house renovations, and local libraries and post offices are also supported. The cafés and gift shops which characterize towns and villages in the commuter belts of Belfast, Dublin, Cork, Limerick, Galway and Waterford might be a poor economic substitute for the hardware and drapery shops of yesteryear, but they keep some semblance of commercial life going and provide communal spaces for sociability, attracting people of all ages into the towns.

Government and local authority investment in public space over thirty or so years has also made many places more pleasant to linger in. Northern Ireland was ahead of the Republic in this regard, with the Ulster Way and Giant's Causeway walks developed in the 1970s and 1980s. All over the island from the late 1990s canals were cleared of weeds and rubbish and riverside amenities developed in towns as far apart as Belmullet, Co. Mayo, and Banagher, Co. Offaly. The Westport Greenway for cyclists and walkers, on the route of the old railway, opened in 2010, the Waterford Greenway in 2017, and walkways and footbridges were laid out along the Barrow and the Blackwater, the Shannon and the Suir, the Liffey and the Lee and many other places. (Figure 10.3) In the midlands, bog tours on special bog trains, which caused incredulous derision when first mooted, were heavily subscribed from about 2005 onwards and are growing in popularity as bogs return to their natural state. Local museums – some private, some public – and heritage centres flourish. The Atlantic coast of Ireland was 'rebranded' the Wild Atlantic Way in 2014, a hugely successful tourist initiative which also attracts Irish people. Emphasis on the conservation of

FIGURE 10.3 Great Western Greenway, viaduct at Newport, Co. Mayo. Trish Punch/Lonely Planet RF/Getty images. One of the many positive environmental developments in Ireland in these decades, greenways, of which there are several throughout the country, are reserved for walkers and cyclists. This greenway from Westport to Achill Island was opened in 2011.

green spaces and river ways also raises environmental awareness among people in general.

From the early 1990s one of Ireland's key resources, wind, was harnessed, and by 2016 there were almost 300 wind farms in the Republic, mostly on land, but some offshore on the east coast. (Figure 10.4) Peat-burning power stations in the midlands were gradually closed, and sadly, although for good environmental reasons, the peat bricquette produced by Bord na Móna which heated Irish homes efficiently and aromatically for over seventy years would be gradually phased out in the early 2020s. Smaller changes improved public spaces; from 2001 consumers in the Republic had to pay for their plastic bags in

FIGURE 10.4 Wind turbines in Inis Mór, Oileáin Árainn, Co. Galway. Sean De Burca/The Image Bank/Getty images. These elegant or clumsy structures (depending on one's point of view) which generate electrical power from an abundant source, became a familiar sight in Ireland in the first two decades of the twenty-first century.

shops, which dramatically reduced the amount of public rubbish, and from this year also, several local authorities introduced the separated 'three-bin' rubbish disposal system. From 2004 smoking was outlawed in all workplaces in Ireland, including public houses and restaurants, and there was almost universal compliance with this ruling. In Dublin, the Luas light rail line which began in 2004 reduced urban traffic significantly and made travelling around the city much quicker, linking Heuston and Connolly, the two mainline railway stations. Cycleways were introduced in many towns and cities from early in the second decade, and bike-rental schemes for short trips were set up. Local bus services in towns and cities multiplied and all parts of the country became more accessible.

The popularity of Irish-language broadcast media and the promotion of Irish by charismatic figures like Des Bishop, Hector Ó hEochagáin and Manchán Magan, among others, were welcome developments for the language. Alongside all this positivity, and the growth of *Gaelscoileanna* throughout the country, the language, according to the census of 2016, would appear to be in crisis. A majority of Irish people love the language for its own sake – 62 per cent of the population believed it was worth preserving, in 2010 – but they do not use it as a means of everyday communication. In the population as a whole in 2016, less than 0.5 per cent of the population claimed to speak Irish daily (outside of education), and even in the *Gaeltachtaí*, only 66.3 per cent of the population could speak Irish, and only 21.4 per cent spoke it every day. These figures all represented a decline since the previous census of 2011. A more cheerful way of looking at this, however, is that the Irish language has been under attack since the Statutes of Kilkenny in 1366, and has managed to survive somehow, outside scholarship, in the shadow of one of the most powerful languages on the globe, while many other minority languages in Europe have died. Most Irish people understand some Irish, and broadcasters even on English-language media channels regularly use Irish phrases for greeting or signing-off. Irish-language publishers Coiscéim and Cló-IarChonnacht (among others) continue to sell books. Irish is still a very popular subject at third-level colleges and *Gaelscoileanna* continue to increase in number.

There are several well-supported *Gaelscoileanna* in Northern Ireland, too, supported by the nationalist communities. But Irish is also part of the heritage of Ulster unionists. The embarrassing derision of the language by some members of the DUP should not be taken as typical of all unionist attitudes. Linda Ervine, whose brother David was a founder of the Progressive Unionist Party, set up the Turas Irish Language Project in 2011 and is only one of many unionists eager to reclaim part of their history. *Naíscoil na Seolta* (Nursery School of the Sails), an integrated Irish-language pre-school was set up in Protestant east Belfast in 2021 and hopes to develop into a primary school. Irish must have been understood by some of the Ulster settlers of the seventeenth century in order to enable them to do business with Catholic neighbours. Place names and surnames all over Northern Ireland are steeped in the language. If *Gaeilge* can give Unionist/loyalist and nationalists all over the country a culture in common despite diverging political outlooks, this is as good a use for it as any other.

Conclusion

Down through the centuries, the Irish have been innovators, quickly learning the universal language of Christendom, Latin, in the first millennium so as to communicate with people in Britain and on the European continent. They were also adaptors, using Latinised script to write their own language, and in the twelfth century, they were quick to set up dioceses and parishes, and to welcome new styles of monastic dwelling. And if they did not exactly welcome either the Scandinavians or the Anglo-Normans from the eighth to the twelfth centuries, they accustomed themselves deftly and rapidly to the new kinds of settlement, architecture, commerce and often, costume, brought by these incomers. Later, when reforming monks arrived in the thirteenth century, they put down roots in urban and rural communities that have lasted until the twenty-first century. It could be said that this habit of innovation failed when most Irish people (of both Gaelic and Anglo-Norman background) refused to convert to Protestantism, but, as has been explained, no strenuous conversion efforts were made, and in any case, Irish Catholics of both Gaelic-Irish and Anglo-Norman origin took on board the challengingly different Counter-Reformation Catholicism, with its new Tridentine regulations, devotions and clerical celibacy. In the ensuing centuries, Irish people would enthusiastically adopt potato-growing and print culture, inoculation and education, transport, technology and tea.

The Irish also adopted the English language, but even when English became the common vernacular of most of the island in the twentieth century, not only did some Irish speakers *ó dhúchais* (from birth and rearing) survive but the language itself remained just below the surface of spoken English and anglicized names.

C.1 Places and Names

When somebody speaking Irish wants to say, 'I am going home [i.e. to my dwelling-place]' he or she says, '*Tá mé ag dul abhaile*' which literally translates as 'I am going to the *baile* [i.e. settlement/town/townland]'. Though there are words for house (*teach*), hearth (*tinteán*) and household (*teaghlach*), the common term for the domestic space as destination is identical to the term for the social space. A *baile* is any settlement from a large town to a tiny townland.

Townlands are small rural units of territory, some only the size of a field, and even the smallest has a name preserved in oral usage and set down for posterity by the Ordnance Survey of the early nineteenth century. This mapping of Ireland, carried out by English military personnel and administrators between the 1820s and 1840s, has been criticized for formalizing the anglicization of Irish place names, and the results were sometimes clumsy; two examples are *Gort an Uisce* (the watery field), in Lusmagh, Co. Offaly, which became Gortaniskey, and *Tóin na Broice* (the badger's sett), Co. Galway, which became Thonabrucky. However, the Irish names were preserved in the name-books kept by scholars John O'Donovan, Eugene O'Curry and George Petrie, so this survey did priceless preservation work. Armed with a little glossary, the visitor to Ireland can decipher place names by common prefixes and occasionally, suffixes; Bally is *baile*, but Bal or Bel is usually *béal*, a river-mouth or estuary. Ath (as mentioned in Chapter 1) is *áth*, a ford, one of the oldest place names, dating to prehistoric times; Dun, *dún*, or fortress; Clon, *cluain*, a watery meadow; Cappa, *ceapach*, usually a tilled field; Gort is *gort*, a small field; Rath is *ráth*, a ring fort (the early medieval settlements described in Chapter 1), and so is Lis, *lios*; Knock is *cnoc*, a small hill, as is Tulla (*tullach*); Derry is *doire*, an oak tree or wood; Moy is *maigh*, a plain; Kil is *cill*, a church; Inish or Ennis is *inis*, an island. Carrow is *ceathrú* or quarter, referring to a division of land; Lecarrow, a village in Roscommon, is *Leath-Ceathrú*, half a quarter. *Tiobrad* or *Tobar* is a spring or a well; Tipperary is *Tiobrad Árainn*, the spring of *Ára*, a local sept. The suffix 'beg' is *beag*, little, and 'more' is *mór*, big; -een comes from *ín* and means small or little; Crusheen, Co. Clare, is *Croisín*, little cross. The multiple Lisheens and Raheens around the country show how old some place names are, as the *lios/rath* as a settlement type died out in the eleventh century.

Not all place names are from the Irish, and not all are old. Waterford, Wicklow, Arklow, Wexford and Carlingford are Norse names, although Dublin, settled by the Vikings, is from the Irish *Dubh Linn* (Black pool). The 'official' Irish for Dublin is *Baile Átha Cliath* (The town of the ford of the hurdles), which was the name of another settlement on the Liffey. Some argue that Limerick is from Old Norse (Hlymryk) while others claim it as from the Irish *Luimneach*, the bare spot (or the bare spot of the horses), neither of which makes descriptive sense for a settlement on good fertile land, well watered by the Shannon. The provincial titles of Mumha, Laighin and Ulaidh were (like many English places) supplied by the Scandinavians with the suffix – ster and became Munster, Leinster and Ulster. Connacht's name remained unchanged, though it was often anglicized as Connaught. The Anglo-Normans used Irish names (with anglicized spelling) for their new towns – Ballinrobe, Kilmallock, Athenry, Askeaton, Kilkenny, Clonmel, and many more. Bettystown in Co. Meath is an example of a hybrid, a combination of *biatach* – a tenant who owes food rent to his landlord – and town. Most sixteenth- and seventeenth-century planters also used Irish names for the new towns they built (or developed on the sites of older settlements): Tallow, Lismore, Youghal, Bandon, Belfast, Bangor, Coleraine, to name just a few in Munster and Ulster. However, Westport in Co. Mayo was built and named in English by the Marquess of Sligo in 1780. Inistioge in Co. Kilkenny is a new Irish-language name given to an eighteenth-century landlord-built village – *inis*, the island, of *Tíog*, the well-respected Tighe landlord family of Woodstock House. Maryborough and Philipstown, established by Mary Tudor in the sixteenth century, were successfully renamed Port Laoise and Dangan after 1922, and the counties in which they were located were renamed as Leix or more commonly Laois (Queen's county) and Offaly (King's). However, attempts to replace the name of Charleville in Co. Cork (called after Charles II in 1661) with Ráth Luirc failed, as did the attempt to revert to the older name of

Muine Bheag for Bagenalstown in Co. Carlow. And Castlecoote, Cootehall and Cootehill, in Roscommon and Cavan, although called after the hated seventeenth-century Lord President of Connacht, have never been renamed. Convenience rather than sentiment more often than not dictates popular usage.

The changing of people's surnames from Irish to anglicized forms was also a long process, in train since the twelfth century, when surnames began to be used on these islands. Irish had been a written language since the sixth century, and in the fourteenth and fifteenth centuries the educated Gaelic-Irish and some Anglo-Normans had books in Irish in their libraries, wrote in Irish, spoke Irish with one another and had legal contracts in Irish drawn up by brehon lawyers, with their names in Irish. The political and religious changes of the sixteenth century, however, forced all of those who engaged with the Crown in any capacity, especially the leaders, to become familiar with the language of the conquerors. English was the language of O'Neill's officers and generals during the Nine Years' War (1594–1603) and it was also the lingua franca of the Confederate Catholic officers of the 1640s, although they all had to speak and understand Irish to communicate with the other ranks. At this stage all the leaders, Gaelic-Irish as well as Anglo-Norman/Old English, commonly used the anglicized forms of their names, although the Earl of Tyrone, Hugh O'Neill, was defiantly invested as The O'Neill in a ceremony in Ulster in 1595 which was conducted mostly in Irish.

Norman names also changed since the twelfth century, some dropping 'de' – *de Burgo* became Burke; *de Paor*, Power; *de hÓra*, Dore or Hoare; *de Barra*, Barry; *de*

Clare, Clear, to take just a few examples. All the eighteenth-century Irish-language poets mentioned earlier were known by their anglicized as well as their Irish names; the Maigue poet Seán Ó Tuama was John Toomey when he worked as a tutor for a local gentry family. Eibhlín Dhubh Ní Chonaill exemplified living in two languages. She wrote her *caoineadh*/lament for her dearly loved husband Art in fluent Irish and identified herself authorially by her Irish-language maiden name. To her twin Mary (Mrs Baldwin), and to her predominantly English-speaking social circle, however, and on all legal documents, she was first Nelly O'Connell and, on her first marriage, Mrs O'Conor, then, at the time she wrote her famous poem, Mrs O'Leary. Her nephew, Daniel, the architect of Catholic Emancipation and father of modern Irish constitutional nationalism, also spoke Irish fluently and even gave speeches in it, but expressed no regret at what he saw as its inevitable decline.

The censuses and birth, marriage and death registrations of the nineteenth century, therefore, universalized an anglicizing process which had been going on for centuries. As with place names, most anglicized Irish surnames bear a strong resemblance to their original – O'Flaherty is *Ó Flaithearta*, Kelly is *Ó Ceallaigh*, Ryan is *Ó Riain*, Lenihan *Ó Luineacháin*, Larkin *Ó Lorcáin*, and so on. Some anglicizations were translations of what the name meant; *MacGabhann* became Smith (when it wasn't McGowan), and *Mac an Rí* became King (when it wasn't McEnery or Conry). There were some strange 'pseudo-translations': the Donegal name *Ó Duibhne* (also anglicized as Deeny), because it sounded like the Irish word for people (*daoine*), was sometimes translated as Peoples; *Ó Cuirc* (also anglicized as Quirke) became Oates, because it sounded like the Irish word for this crop (*coirce*). *Ó Cadhain* (which is usually Coyne, or Kyne) was sometimes anglicized as Barnacle – a *cadhan* is a wild or Barnacle goose. Wanting to avoid calling somebody 'Goose' was obviously the motivation here, but the same scruple did not apply to the name of another wild creature trapped for food, and *Ó Coinín*, also anglicized as Cuneen, Cunnane and Kineen, became Rabbitte in some parts of the country. There are also many English surnames in Ireland, many dating from those who came in with the Anglo-Normans (Synnott, for example, common in Wexford and Kilkenny), and some of more recent origin – the English name Smith, Jones, Little, Wilson, Johnson, Mathews, Herbert, and so on. In Ulster, as might be imagined, Scottish and English surnames are more common among Protestants, and Gaelic-Irish and Norman ones among Catholics, but this is by no means a hard-and-fast rule. There are Protestant McGuinnesses, Peopleses, Maguires, O'Neills and McNeills, and Catholic Humes, Adamses, Morrisons, Fitts (to name but a few). The traditional term 'Taigs', used by some Protestants to describe Catholics, comes from the huge popularity of the first name *Tadhg* (pronounced Taig in Ulster, Tygue everywhere else on the island, often anglicized as Timothy) among seventeenth- and eighteenth-century Catholic boys and men.

Even in parts of the country where Irish remained the first language, the English forms of surnames were used for official purposes well into the twentieth century, and it is unusual, even in Gaeltacht areas, to find a gravestone bearing a name in its Irish form dating from before independence. In independent Ireland all children's names were Gaelicized as a matter of course on the rolls of National schools up to the 1960s. All names of Defence Forces personnel are still Gaelicized for ceremonial purposes. From the late nineteenth century, names of English origin were sometimes Gaelicized for political and cultural reasons. Cathal Brugha, who died on the Republican side in the Civil War of 1922–1923, was originally Charles Burgess. Theatrical impresario and founder of Dublin's Gate Theatre (in 1928) Micheál MacLiammóir, was originally Michael Wilmore from Willesden, London, with no Irish connections whatsoever. The Methodist lay preacher Risteard Ó Glaisne, born Richard Giles in Co. Cork in 1927 into a family descended from seventeenth-century planters, changed his name to an Irish form and published many books in Irish, including an influential history of Irish Methodists.

Today, most people, including many native speakers of Irish, use the anglicized forms of their surnames.

C.2 The Changing Landscape

The appearance of much of Ireland changed over these 1,600 years. Early medieval Ireland, though mainly characterized by clusters of small settlements, saw the growth of monastic cities, and conurbations also evolved around the forts of kings, and mills from the ninth century. Some monastic settlements like Tuam, Armagh and Kildare, developed into towns, but Clonard, Clonmacnoise and Glendalough, which were every bit as populous in their heyday and as convenient to rivers (especially Clonmacnoise) and land routes, did not, and no historian has explained why. In early medieval Ireland the built landscape was low to the ground except for the dramatic round-towers built between the ninth and twelfth centuries. The Scandinavian longhouses, market squares and meeting-halls were permanent contributions to the urban landscape. The Anglo-Normans' large castles, and the new monasteries pioneered by the Cistercians in the same century, were multi-storied, stone, solid and impregnable, efficiently drained and chimneyed; they must have provoked the same awe from people as skyscrapers did in the twentieth-century city.

Ireland in the thirteenth century and again in the seventeenth was shired into the counties we know today. Every territorial unit had administrators, which led to a multiplicity of civic buildings – tholsels and town halls, and the designation of some towns as county capitals. All this necessitated more efficient communications, and the planters of the sixteenth, seventeenth and eighteenth centuries, in particular, built more roads and bridges. Roads usually followed older, well-established routes. Tracks had been laid through bogs from time immemorial (these were called *'tóchair'* or toghers) on raised planks and rushes; the pre-motorway Athlone to Dublin road runs through a number of these 'passes': Tyrellspass, Rochfortbridge and Milltownpass. The names are all English ones – Tyrell was an Anglo-Norman lord – but the *slighe* or way dates back to the early medieval period. Canals changed the landscape, cutting through fields in straight lines. By the time they were open to heavy and constant traffic (the early nineteenth century), fast coaches were also spreading everywhere. Many roads were built in the eighteenth and nineteenth centuries, for militia and police access, for surveying and as public works, and Ireland has one of the most extensive road networks of any European country.

Forests and woodlands were destroyed in the seventeenth and eighteenth centuries so as to build roads, extend pasture lands, build houses and (not least) provide ships for the British navy. '*Cad a dhéanfaimid feasta gan adhmaid? Tá deireadh na coillte ar lár*' (What will we do without wood? The end of the forests is at hand) was the opening lament in the anonymous eighteenth-century poem *Cill Cais* (Kilcash) about a denuded estate in south Tipperary. Ireland had always been well wooded, although never to the extent described by the New English of the early modern period, who dressed up their relentless plunder of the natural environment as the bringing of civilisation to wood-dwelling primitives. Irish wolves and wild boar disappeared with the forests, but any settlers who hoped that the Irish people would become extinct, too, were disappointed. Whether of Gaelic-Irish, Anglo-Norman or Scandinavian stock, or hybrids of all three, the Irish were better off than their luckless counterparts in North America, which was being settled around the same time, and although thousands (in Ireland) were massacred, evicted and exiled during the terrible sixteenth and seventeenth centuries in particular, they were never wiped out. Some were protected by political leaders (both Gaelic-Irish and Anglo-Norman) who converted early to Protestantism but retained strong ties with the Catholics under their authority – the Butlers of Ormond, for example. Ireland, moreover, was a small country, and (unlike in North America) there were no limitless tracts of unsettled land to which the natives could be exiled and forgotten about. Connacht and

Clare, the destinations of the landowners banished in the 1650s, were not that far from much of Leinster and Munster even at that time, and had plenty of good land on their eastern edges. Ulster saw the most complete plantation of all, but even here, a minority of the original population hung on, although others were dispersed to Connacht, their scattering evident in the Ulster surnames which crop up in Mayo and Galway – Gallagher, O'Donnell, O'Boyle. Workers were at a premium because of the big changes happening in the countryside from the early eighteenth century onwards. Ireland's abundant hedgerows, which bloom dramatically white in May, and the distinctive drystone walls west of the Shannon, date from this century, as the open-field system of agriculture gave way to enclosure.

The frost famine of 1740–1741 was devastating and noted as such by contemporaries, but recovery was fairly swift. The disappearance of nearly 2 million of the poorest Irish people over the decade 1841 to 1851 through death and emigration must have caused the levelling of thousands of cabins and other small dwellings, and a considerable thinning out of the populace. Yet there is little sense of yawning absence either in the official sources or in the memoirs of the period, or even in the extensive folklore collections. Ireland in the 1850s and 1860s still gave the impression of being crowded with the impoverished, probably because the catastrophe of the Famine had brought heightened sensitivity to the precarity of their existence. Visitors to the west of Ireland in the 1870s were amazed by the multitudes making a living on such bad land, and the poorest regions of Ireland were still considered 'congested' – inhabited by more people than they could support – in the 1890s. Population loss happened unevenly and gradually all over the island, and the flood of outward movement from the 1880s to 1914 was masked by the rapid developments in transport, working lives, schooling, politics and associational culture, which brought Irish people into more daily contact with each other than ever before.

The railways and the cuttings and embankments which accompanied them, in their first vigorous building phase in the 1850s and 1860s and the second in the 1880s and 1890s, also changed the look of the land. Trains delivered Dublin newspapers all over the country on the day they were printed, hastened postal deliveries, stimulated the retail trade and allowed people, especially in the thickly networked hinterlands of Belfast, Derry, Dublin and Cork, and, to a lesser extent, Galway, Limerick, Waterford and Wexford, to travel longer daily distances to work than before. Ireland's first commuters were in the 1890s. (Map 7.1) The passage of trains through many parts of rural Ireland several times a day intensified the observance of clock-time, already creeping into everyday life due to schooling and more regular religious observance. If the smoky, noisy railway disrupted the tranquillity of Irish rural life, there is no record of Irish people complaining about it. Their commitment to novelty was, then as later, unwavering.

C.3 *Ar Scáth A Chéile A Mhaireann Na Daoine*: Irish People, Good People, People

Facing the future firmly was also seen in the almost universal welcome given to two big changes to the landscape of independent Ireland in the first half of the twentieth century. The first of these was the flooding of part of east Co. Clare (near Limerick city) around Ardnacrusha for the Shannon hydro-electric scheme between 1926 and 1928, and the second, the flooding near Blessington, Co. Wickow of Poulaphouca in 1940 for a similar scheme to improve electricity delivery to the east of the country. In both places some livelihoods were lost forever, with only minimal compensation, but any complaints were drowned along with the fields, lanes, houses, farms, shops and smithies. These two place names which became synonymous with modernity, Ardnacrusha and Poulaphouca, refer to the supernatural world; *Ard na Croise* means 'the high place of the Cross', and *Poll a'Phúca* means 'the pooka's hole/lair'. The *púca* – the kind of mischievous shapeshifter who features in a lot of folktales all over the world – was one of the many beings like the *leipracán* and the *Bean Sí*/Banshee and the *Sidhe*/Good People or Fairies who lived alongside the Irish for millennia. Belief in these supernatural entities by no means annulled adherence to formal religion, nor was it confined to Catholics. Some people who were old in the 1970s used to say that rural electrification and the motorcar had driven the 'fairies' away forever. A sod falling out of the fire onto the hearth or a door that blew open would be greeted with 'Come in, sit down, you're welcome' (often accompanied by a self-conscious laugh, but uttered nonetheless), and no child or calf would ever be admired without God's protection being invoked quickly, so as to deter the covetous otherworldly beings who might be hovering, ready to exchange it for a sickly creature of their own.

Conclusion

If cars on country roads frightened the fairies away from human habitation then the motorways of the late twentieth and early twenty-first centuries routed them altogether. Clare folklorist Eddie Lenihan campaigned to have the path of the Limerick–Ennis motorway diverted slightly in 1999 so as to avoid disturbing a tree which marked one of the many crossing-places of the Good People. (The tree was spared, in the end, though some say that the plans never involved going through it in the first place.) Motorways in Ireland, as in all other countries, speed up travelling distances, avoid traffic bottlenecks and (most importantly of all) reduce road fatalities, but they come, in Ireland as elsewhere, at a cost. With their often broad panoramas over vast areas of landscape, they give the traveller what is almost an aerial view, and taking the exits to specific destinations can be like descending from the air, with about as much sense of the changing landscape of the journey. This, however, has the advantage of attracting mass tourism, and tourism is one of Ireland's most important industries.

Ever since the lakes of Killarney became a visitor attraction in the mid eighteenth century, people have been coming to Ireland on their holidays, and the Irish have been remarked upon for their hospitality. In the Republic, the Irish tourist board was called Bord Fáilte in 1955 (Fáilte Ireland since 2003) embodying the Irish word for welcome. Visitors to Ireland in the nineteenth and twentieth centuries always noted Irish people's friendliness. Even Honor Tracy, whose ridicule of Ireland after a visit in the early 1950s aroused much indignation, noticed this universal warmth towards the stranger. Some decades earlier, 'Alpha of the Plough', Alfred George Gardiner, an English journalist, described the cups of milk which he and his bicycling friend enjoyed (offers to pay were indignantly refused) while sitting in the cool shade of a cabin somewhere between Sneem and Derrynane, Co. Kerry, conversing with the grandmother of the house. He compared this experience with a similar drink for which he and his friend were charged 3d each, standing outside a much more prosperous house in the Highlands of Scotland, observed by the unsmiling owner. Gardiner and his friend were probably the umpteenth in a daily line of work-interrupting visitors to that strategically placed house in the Highlands, which had far more walkers in the early twentieth century than Kerry. Still, it cannot be denied that Irish people go out of their way to be charming to strangers not only from abroad, but from other parts of Ireland. This is not necessarily a 'historically subordinate' mainly Catholic class ingratiating itself with its 'betters'; Irish Protestants of all backgrounds, north and south, are also hospitably inclined and prodigious talkers and listeners. And even though rural people have (or had, historically) more time to down tools and talk, Dublin city people are the friendliest in Ireland, with Belfast people running them a close second or, some would argue, surpassing them.

Maybe this famous hospitality is nothing more virtuous than curiosity and a love of novelty. Whatever it is, does it extend to all those who want to make their homes in independent Ireland permanently in the early twenty-first century? At the time of writing (2024) over a fifth of all people living in the state were not born in Ireland. Anti-immigrant sentiment, a muted grumble in the first two decades of the century, is gaining ground, especially as run-down public services fail to keep up with the housing and medical demands of a greatly expanded population. In the summer of 2024, when English anti-immigration riots spilled over into Northern Ireland, for the first time ever the Union Jack and the Tricolour were hoisted aloft side-by-side as agitators from both sides of the border joined forces in a Belfast demonstration against immigrants. This kind of action is rare, and there was a much larger counter-demonstration in which people from both jurisdictions also participated, but overall, the highly visible presence of immigrants has prompted a new exploration of what it means to be both Irish and Northern Irish.

The 'New Irish', as they are sometimes called, are mainly from Asia, Africa, South America and eastern Europe. Unlike the 'New English' of the sixteenth and seventeenth centuries or the earlier invaders, they do not rob and evict the country's existing inhabitants, nor do they plunder the natural environment or impose their religious beliefs on the population. Like the Europeans who flocked to the New World after 1850, most are 'instant adults', arriving unencumbered by dependents, ready to roll up their sleeves and work straightaway in a country which did not have the expense of rearing or educating them. They stripe the entire occupational sector, and though the stripe might grow a little broader towards the lower end of the pay scale, this is not strikingly so; immigrants are doctors, nurses, paramedics of various kinds, administrators, public servants, bank employees, factory workers, business owners, taxi drivers, builders, hospitality workers, shop assistants, fast-food deliverers, cleaners and fruit-and-vegetable pickers. They live in the same localities as the 'Old Irish' and though they tend, because few if any are farmers, to live in urban areas, these are as often small towns as big cities. Those who learn Irish – and many do – would claim proudly that they are *'abhaile'* in Ireland – at home, in the *'baile'*, the social space they share with others.

Ireland has been changing, adapting, innovating and absorbing for the best part of two millennia now. The complications of Irish history from the fifth century onwards have led many who were of Scandinavian, English, French, Scottish, Welsh, Flemish origin not only to call Ireland home but also to claim an Irish identity of one kind of another. Young Irelander Thomas Davis was of 'New English' settler stock. In 1844, the year before his untimely death at the age of thirty-one, he made a plea in his poem 'Celts and Saxons' for anyone who wanted to be Irish, regardless of origin, to be accepted as such:

> What matter that at different shrines
> We pray unto one God?
> What matter that at different times
> Your fathers won this sod?
> In fortune and in name we're bound
> By stronger links than steel:
> And neither can be safe nor sound
> But in the other's weal.

Or, as the Irish *seanfhocal* (proverb) puts it: *'Ar scáth a chéile a mhaireann na daoine'*. The people survive in the shelter of one another.

APPENDIX:

~

Irish Population, 1821–2016

A.1 From 1821 to 1911

A.1.1 Ireland

YEAR	POPULATION
1821	6,801,827
1841	8,175,124
1851	6,552,385
1861	5,798,967
1871	5,412,377
1881	5,174,836
1891	4,704,750
1901	4,458,775
1911	4,390,219

A.2 From 1926 to 2016

A.2.1 Ireland (Twenty Six Counties)

YEAR	POPULATION
1926	2,971,992
1936	2,968,420
1946	2,955,107

(cont.)

YEAR	POPULATION
1951	2,960,593
1956	2,898,264
1961	2,818,341
1966	2,884,002
1971	2,978,248
1981	3,443,405
1991	3,525,719
2002	3,917,203
2011	4,588,252
2016	4,761,865

A.2.2 Northern Ireland

YEAR	POPULATION
1926	1,256,561
1937	1,279,745
1951	1,370,921
1961	1,425,042
1966	1,484,775
1971	1,536,065
1981	1,543,000
1991	1,607,300
2001	1,685,267
2011	1,810,863
2016	1,862,000

FURTHER READING

General Works Covering Most or All of the Entire Period

Aalen, F. H., Matthew Stout and Kevin Whelan (eds.), *Atlas of the Irish Rural Landscape* (Toronto: University of Toronto Press 2010).

Bartlett, Thomas, Brendan Smith, Jane Ohlmeyer and James Kelly (eds.), *The Cambridge History of Ireland*, vols. 1–4 (Cambridge: Cambridge University Press 2018).

Clarke, Howard B. (ed.), *Irish Cities* (Cork: Mercier 1995).

Curtayne, Alice, *The Irish Story: A Survey of Irish History and Culture* (Dublin: Clonmore & Reynolds 1962).

Dargan, Pat, *Exploring Ireland's Historic Towns* (Dublin: The History Press 2010).

Day, Peter, *Dictionary of Religious Orders* (London: Burns & Oates 2001).

Killeen, Richard, *A Timeline of Irish History* (Dublin: Gill & Macmillan 2003).

MacLysaght, Edward, *The Surnames of Ireland: Origins, Locations, Variants* (Dublin: Irish University Press 1973).

Moody, T. W. and F. X. Martin (eds.), *The Course of Irish History* (Cork: Mercier [1967] 1984).

Ó Cróinín, Dáibhí, Art Cosgrove, F. X. Martin, J. F. Byrne, W. E. Vaughan and J. R. Hill (eds.), *A New History of Ireland*, vols. 1–8 (Oxford: Oxford University Press 2008–2011).

Introduction

Brown, Frances, 'Songs of Our Land', in A. A. Kelly (ed.), *Pillars of the House: An Anthology of Verse by Irish Women* (Dublin: Wolfhound 1998).

Eliot, George, *Middlemarch* (London: Pan Classics 1977).
Kavanagh, Patrick, 'Memory of Brother Michael', in Antoinette Quinn (ed.), *Patrick Kavanagh: Selected Poems* (London: Penguin 1996).
Samuel, Raphael, *Theatres of Memory* (London: Verso 1994).
Wilson, Ann, *The Picture Postcard: A New Window into Edwardian Ireland: Reimagining Ireland*, vol. 103 (Oxford: Peter Lang 2021).

Transformation: Early Medieval Ireland, c. 430–1169

Relevant Sections of General Works Cited Previously

Surveys

Charles-Edwards, Thomas, *Early Christian Ireland* (Cambridge: Cambridge University Press 2000).
Cooney, Gabriel and Eoin Grogan, *Ireland in Pre-history* (Dublin: Worldwell 1994).
Harbison, Peter, *Pre-Christian Ireland: From the First Settlers to the Early Celts* (London: Guild 1989).
Jaski, Bart, *Early Irish Kingship and Succession* (Dublin: Four Courts 2000).
Ó Cróinín, Dáibhí, *Early Medieval Ireland 400–1200* (London: Longmans [1995] 2017).

Other Sources

Bhreathnach, Edel, 'Communities and Their Landscapes', in Brendan Smith (ed.), *The Cambridge History of Ireland* (Cambridge: Cambridge University Press 2018), pp. 15–46.
Bhreathnach, Edel, *Monasticism in Ireland AD 900–1250* (Dublin: Four Courts 2024).
Bitel, Lisa, *Isle of the Saints: Monastic Settlements and Christian Communities in Early Ireland* (Ithaca: Cornell University Press 1990).

Brown, Michelle P., *How Christianity Came to Britain and Ireland* (Oxford: Oxford University Press 2006).

Byrne, J., 'Early Irish Society', in T. W. Moody and F. X. Martin (eds.), *The Course of Irish History* (Cork: Mercier [1967] 1984), pp. 43–60.

Carey, John, 'Learning, Imagination and Belief', in Brendan Smith (ed.), *The Cambridge History of Ireland* (Cambridge: Cambridge University Press 2018), pp. 47–75.

Collins, Tracy, *Female Monasticism in Medieval Ireland* (Cork: Cork University Press 2021).

Comber, Michelle, 'Square Ringforts? A Contribution to the Identification of "Ringfort" Types', *Medieval Archaeology* 63 (2019), pp. 128–53.

Curtayne, Alice, *Irish Saints for Boys and Girls* (Dublin: Talbot 1955).

Dillon, Myles (ed.), *Irish Sagas* (Cork: Mercier 1959).

Gilligan, Nikolah, 'Dishing Up the Past: A Review of Plant Foods, Food Products and Agriculture in Early Medieval Ireland', in Dorothy Cashman and Máirtín MacConIomaire (eds.), *Irish Food History: A Companion* (Dublin: Royal Irish Academy 2024), pp. 106–132.

Hughes, Kathleen, 'The Golden Age of Early Christian Ireland', in T. W. Moody and F. X. Martin (eds.), *The Course of Irish History* (Cork: Mercier [1967] 1984), pp. 76–90.

Killen, John, *The St Patrick Treasury* (Belfast: Blackstaff 2018).

Lacey, Brian, *St Columba: His Life and Legacy* (Dublin: Columba 2013).

Lehane, Shane, 'Beekeeping and Honey in Ancient Ireland', in Dorothy Cashman and Máirtín MacConIomaire (eds.), *Irish Food History: A Companion* (Dublin: Royal Irish Academy 2024), pp. 166–193.

Mallory, J. P., 'Food in Irish Prehistory: Archaeological, Linguistic and Early Literary Evidence', in Dorothy Cashman and Máirtín MacConIomaire (eds.), *Irish Food History: A Companion* (Dublin: Royal Irish Academy 2024), pp. 30–61.

McCormick, Finbar, 'Lovely Bones: Osteo-Archaeological Evidence of Animal Produce in Ireland', in Dorothy Cashman and Máirtin MacConIomaire (eds.), *Irish Food History: A Companion* (Dublin: Royal Irish Academy 2024), pp. 62–81.

Mitchell, Frank, 'Early Settlement and Society before 500 AD', in William Nolan (ed.), *The Shaping of Ireland: The Geographical Perspective* (Cork: Mercier 1986), pp. 28–43

Nolan, William, 'Some Civil and Ecclesiastical Territorial Divisions', in William Nolan (ed.), *The Shaping of Ireland: The Geographical Perspective* (Cork: Mercier 1986), pp. 67–83.

Ó Cuiv, Brian, 'Ireland in the 11th and 12th Centuries', in T. W. Moody and F. X. Martin (eds.), *The Course of Irish History* (Cork: Mercier [1967] 1984), pp. 107–22.

Ó Fiaich, Tomás, 'The Beginnings of Christianity', in T. W. Moody and F. X. Martin (eds.), *The Course of Irish History* (Cork: Mercier [1967] 1984), pp. 61–75.

O'Riordan, John J., *Brigid of Ireland* (Limerick: Redemptorist Publications, 2015).

O'Riordan, John J., *Clonmacnoise of Ciarán* (Limerick: Redemptorist Publications, 2014).

O'Riordan, John J., *St Columban: Missionary Extraordinary* (Limerick: Redemptorist Publications, [2014, 2015] 2017).

Pochin-Mould, Daphne, *Irish Pilgrimage* (Dublin: Gill 1955).

Proinsias Mac a'Bhaird, *Flaitheas:úrscéal ar bheatha Cholm Cille* (Baile Atha Cliath: Leabhar Breac 2023).

Paor, Liam de, 'The Age of the Viking Wars', in T. W. Moody and F. X. Martin (eds.), *The Course of Irish History* (Cork: Mercier [1967] 1984), pp. 91–106.

Sayers, William, 'Irish Diet in the 11th Century', in Dorothy Cashman and Máirtin MacConIomaire (eds.), *Irish Food History: A Companion* (Dublin: Royal Irish Academy 2024), pp. 212–32.

Sikora, Maeve and Isabella Mulhall, 'A History of Bog Butter in Ireland', in Dorothy Cashman and Máirtin MacConIomaire (eds.), *Irish Food History: A Companion* (Dublin: Royal Irish Academy 2024), pp. 136–65.

Further Reading

Simms, Anngret, 'Continuity and Change: Settlement and Society in Medieval Ireland c.500–1500', in William Nolan (ed.), *The Shaping of Ireland: The Geographical Perspective* (Cork: Mercier 1986), pp. 44–65.

Waddell, Helen, *The Wandering Scholars* (London: Constable 1927).

Woolf, Alex, 'The Scandinavian Intervention', in Brendan Smith (ed.), *The Cambridge History of Ireland*, vol. 1 (Cambridge: Cambridge University Press 2018), pp. 107–30.

Invasions: Late Medieval Ireland, 1169–1520

Relevant Sections of Surveys and Other Sources Cited Previously

Surveys

Ellis, Steven G., *Ireland in the Age of the Tudors 1447–1603: English Expansion and the End of Gaelic Rule* (London: Longmans 1998).

Lydon, James, *Ireland in the Later Middle Ages* (Dublin: Gill 1973).

Nicholls, Kenneth, *Gaelic and Gaelicised Ireland in the Middle Ages* (Dublin: Gill 1972).

Other Sources

Cosgrove, Art, 'The Gaelic Resurgence and the Geraldine Supremacy', in T. W. Moody and F. X. Martin (eds.), *The Course of Irish History* (Cork: Mercier [1967] 1984), pp158–173

Crooks, Peter, 'Politics in Theory and Practice 1210–1541', in Brendan Smith (ed.), *The Cambridge History of Ireland* (Cambridge: Cambridge University Press 2018), pp. 441–68.

Frame, Robin, 'Contexts, Divisions and Unities: Perspectives in the Later Middle Ages', in Brendan Smith (ed.), *The Cambridge History of Ireland* (Cambridge: Cambridge University Press 2018), vol. 1, pp. 523–50.

Hartland, Beth, 'The Height of English Power', in Brendan Smith (ed.), *The Cambridge History of Ireland* (Cambridge: Cambridge University Press 2018), pp. 222–43.

Lydon, J. F., 'The Medieval English Colony', in T. W. Moody and F. X. Martin (eds.), *The Course of Irish History* (Cork: Mercier [1967] 1984), pp. 144–57.

Lyons, Mary Ann, 'The Onset of Religious Reform 1460–1550', in Brendan Smith (ed.), *The Cambridge History of Ireland* (Cambridge: Cambridge University Press 2018), pp. 498–522.

Martin, F. X., 'The Normans: Arrival and Settlement', in T. W. Moody and F. X. Martin (eds.), *The Course of Irish History* (Cork: Mercier [1967] 1984), pp. 123–43.

McAlister, Victoria L., *The Irish Tower House: Society, Economy and Environment c.1300–1650* (Manchester: Manchester University Press 2019).

Murphy, Margaret, 'The Economy', in Brendan Smith (ed.), *The Cambridge History of Ireland* (Cambridge: Cambridge University Press 2018), pp. 385–414.

O Clabaigh, Colman, 'The Church 1050–1460', in Brendan Smith (ed.), *The Cambridge History of Ireland* (Cambridge: Cambridge University Press 2018), pp. 355–84.

Ó Clabaigh, Colman, *The Friars in Ireland 1224–1540* (Dublin: Four Courts 2012).

Ó Héideáin, Eustás, *The Dominicans in Galway 1241–1991* (Claddagh 1991).

Ó Murchadha, Ciarán, *The Diocese of Killaloe: An Illustrated History* (Ireland: Booklink 2008).

Simms, Katharine, "The Political Recovery of Gaelic Ireland', in Brendan Smith (ed.), *The Cambridge History of Ireland* (Cambridge: Cambridge University Press 2018), pp. 272–99.

Simms, Katharine, 'Gaelic Culture and Society' in Brendan Smith (ed.), *The Cambridge History of Ireland* (Cambridge: Cambridge University Press 2018), pp. 415–40.

Smith, Brendan, 'Disaster and Opportunity', in Brendan Smith (ed.), *The Cambridge History of Ireland* (Cambridge: Cambridge University Press 2018), pp. 244–71.

Wars: From Silken Thomas's Rebellion to the Penal Laws, 1534–1704

Relevant Sections of Surveys and Other Sources Cited Previously

Surveys

Beckett, J. C., *The Making of Modern Ireland 1603–1923* (London: Faber 1966).
Canny, Nicholas, *From Reformation to Restoration: Ireland 1534–1660* (Dublin: Helicon 1987).
Cullen, L. M., *Economic History of Ireland since 1660* (London: Batsford 1972).
Foster, R. F., *Modern Ireland 1600–1972* (London: Allen Lane 1988).
Lenihan, Pádraig, *Consolidating Conquest: Ireland 1603–1727* (London: Longmans 2008).
MacCurtain, Margaret, *Tudor and Stuart Ireland* (Dublin: Gill 1972).

Other Sources

Armstrong, Robert, 'Establishing a Confessional Ireland 1641–1691', in Jane Ohlmeyer (ed.), *Cambridge History of Ireland*, vol. 2 (Cambridge: Cambridge University Press 2018), pp. 220–45.
Clarkson, L. A. and E. M. Crawford, *Feast and Famine: A History of Food and Nutrition in Ireland 1500–1920* (Oxford: Oxford University Press 2001).
Corish, Patrick J., *The Catholic Community in the Seventeenth and Eighteenth Centuries* (Dublin: Helicon 1981).
Flavin, Susan, 'Domestic Materiality in Ireland', in Jane Ohlmeyer (ed.), *Cambridge History of Ireland*, vol. 2 (Cambridge: Cambridge University Press 2018), pp. 321–45.
Gillespie, Raymond, 'Economic Life 1550–1730', in Jane Ohlmeyer (ed.), *Cambridge History of Ireland*, vol. 2 (Cambridge: Cambridge University Press 2018), pp. 171–345.

Gillespie, Raymond, *The Transformation of the Irish Economy 1550–1700* (Dundalk: Dundalgan Press 1991).
Lennon, Colm, 'Protestant Reformations 1550–1641', in Jane Ohlmeyer (ed.), *Cambridge History of Ireland*, vol. 2 (Cambridge: Cambridge University Press 2018), pp. 196–219.
MacLysaght, Edward, *Irish Life in the Seventeenth Century* (Dublin: Irish Academic Press [1939] 1979).
Margey, Annaleigh, 'Plantations 1550–1641', in Jane Ohlmeyer (ed.), *Cambridge History of Ireland*, vol. 2 (Cambridge: Cambridge University Press 2018), pp. 555–83.
Murphy, D., *Our Martyrs* (Dublin: Fallon [1896], 2011).
Ó hAnnracháin, Tadhg, 'Counter-Reformation in Ireland: The Catholic Church 1550–1641', in Jane Ohlmeyer (ed.), *Cambridge History of Ireland*, vol. 2 (Cambridge: Cambridge University Press 2018), pp. 171–95.
Ó Tuama, Seán and Thomas Kinsella (eds.), *An Duanaire 1600–1900: Poems of the Dispossessed* (Mountrath: Dolmen 1981).
O'Dowd, Mary, 'Men, Women and Family 1550–1730', in Jane Ohlmeyer (ed.), *Cambridge History of Ireland*, vol. 2 (Cambridge: Cambridge University Press 2018), pp. 298–320.

Peace? Ireland's Short Eighteenth Century, 1704–1791

Relevant Sections of Surveys and Other Sources Cited Previously

Surveys

Johnston, Edith, *Ireland in the Eighteenth Century* (Dublin: Gill 1974).
McBride, Ian, *Eighteenth-Century Ireland: The Isle of Slaves* (Dublin: Gill & Macmillan 2009).

Other Sources

Barnard, Toby, *Making the Grand Figure: Lives and Possessions in Ireland 1641–1770* (New Haven: Yale University Press 2004).

Bartlett, Thomas and David Hayton, *Penal Era and Golden Age* (Ulster: Ulster Historical Foundation 1979).

Beckett, J. C., 'Literature in English 1691–1800', in T. W. Moody and W. E. Vaughan (eds.), *A New History of Ireland*, vol. 4 (Oxford: Oxford University Press 2008–2011), pp. 424–70.

Cahill, Katherine, *Mrs Delany's Menus, Medicines and Manners* (Dublin: New Island 2005).

Corkery, Daniel, *The Hidden Ireland: A Study of Gaelic Munster in the 18th Century* (Dublin: Gill 1925).

Cullen, L. M., 'Economic Development 1691–1750', in T. W. Moody and W. E. Vaughan (eds.), *A New History of Ireland*, vol. 4 (Oxford: Oxford University Press 2008–2011), pp. 123–57.

Dickson, David, *Arctic Ireland: The Extraordinary Story of the Great Frost and Forgotten Famine of 1740–41.* (Belfast: White Row 1997).

Dickson, David, 'Society and Economy in the long 18th Century', in James Kelly (ed.), *Cambridge History of Ireland*, vol. 3 (Cambridge: Cambridge University Press 2018), pp. 153–78.

Finnegan, Frances, *Introspections: The Poetry and Private World of Dorothea Herbert* (Waterford: Congrave 2011).

Gurrin, Brian, 'Population and Emigration 1730–1845', in James Kelly (ed.), *Cambridge History of Ireland*, vol. 3 (Cambridge: Cambridge University Press 2018), pp. 204–30.

Geary, Laurence, *Medicine and Charity in Ireland 1718–1851* (Dublin: UCD Press 2004).

Keogh, Daire, *Edmund Rice 1762–1844* (Dublin: Four Courts 1996).

Morley, Vincent, *The Popular Mind in Eighteenth-Century Ireland* (Cork: Cork University Press 2017).

Ó Cuiv, Brian, 'Irish Language and Literature 1691–1845', in T. W. Moody and W. E. Vaughan (eds.), *A New History of Ireland*, vol. 4 (Oxford: Oxford University Press 2008–2011), pp. 374–423.

Ó Ciosain, Niall, *Print and Popular Culture in Ireland 1750–1850* (London: Palgrave 1997).

Ó Sé, Seán, 'Iníon an Phailitínigh', *Ó Riada Sa Gaiety* (Baile Átha Cliath: Gael Linn 1970).

Sheridan, Geraldine, 'Irish Periodicals and the Dissemination of French Enlightenment Writings in the 18th Century', in T. Bartlett, D. Dickson, D. Keogh and K. Whelan (eds.), *1798: A Bicentenary Perspective* (Dublin: Four Courts 2003), pp. 28–51.

Sweeney, Paschal, '756 Christmases in Multy', *St Anthony Brief*, Jan. 2025.

Tillyard, Stella, *Aristocrats: Caroline, Emily, Louisa and Sarah Lennox* (London: Chatto & Windus 1994).

Walsh, T. J., *Nano Nagle and the Presentation Sisters* (Dublin: Gill 1959).

Construction and Destruction: War, Peace and Famine, 1791–1851

Relevant Sections of Surveys and Other Sources Cited Previously

Surveys

Jackson, Alvin, *Ireland 1798–1998: War, Peace and Beyond* (London: Wiley Blackwell 2010).

Ó Tuathaigh, Gearóid, *Ireland before the Famine 1798–1848* (Dublin: Gill 1972).

Vaughan, W. E. and A. J. Fitzpatrick, *Irish Historical Statistics: Population 1821–1971* (Dublin: Royal Irish Academy 1978).

Other Sources

Aalen, F. H., Matthew Stout and Kevin Whelan (eds.), *Atlas of the Irish Rural Landscape* (Toronto: University of Toronto Press 2010).

Akenson, Donald, *The Irish Diaspora: A Primer* (Toronto: University of Toronto 1993).
Bielenberg, Andy, *Cork's Industrial Revolution 1780–1870: Development or Decline?* (Cork: Cork University Press 1991).
Chambers, Liam, 'The 1798 Rebellion in North Leinster', in T. Bartlett, D. Dickson, D. Keogh and K. Whelan (eds.), *1798: A Bicentenary Perspective* (Dublin: Four Courts 2003), pp. 122–35.
Connell, K. H., *The Population of Ireland 1750–1845* (Oxford: Oxford University Press 1950).
Crossman, Virginia, *The Poor Law in Ireland 1838–1948* (Dundalk: Dundalgan Press 2006).
Curtin, Nancy, 'The Transformation of the United Irishmen into a Mass-Based Revolutionary Organization' *Irish Historical Studies* 24 (1985), pp. 463–72.
Dickson, David, 'Smoke without Fire? Munster and the 1798 Rebellion', in T. Bartlett, D. Dickson, D. Keogh and K. Whelan (eds.), *1798: A Bicentenary Perspective* (Dublin: Four Courts 2003), pp. 147–73.
Edwards, R. Dudley and T. Desmond Williams (eds.), *The Great Famine: Studies in Irish History 1845–52* (Dublin: Browne & Nolan 1956).
Elliott, Marianne, 'Religious Polarisation and Sectarianism in the Ulster Rebellion', in T. Bartlett, D. Dickson, D. Keogh and K. Whelan (eds.), *1798: A Bicentenary Perspective* (Dublin: Four Courts 2003), pp. 279–98.
Fitzpatrick, David, *Irish Emigration 1801–1921* (Dundalk: Dundalgan Press 1985).
Flynn, Kathleen and Stan McCormack (eds.), *Westmeath 1798: A Kilbeggan Rebellion* (Kilbeggan: Flynn & McCormack 1998).
Gacquin, William, *Roscommon before the Famine 1749–1845* (Dublin: Irish Academic Press 1996).
Gahan, Daniel, 'The Rebellion of 1798 in south Leinster', in T. Bartlett, D. Dickson, D. Keogh and K. Whelan (eds.), *1798: A Bicentenary Perspective* (Dublin: Four Courts 2003), pp. 104–21.

Geoghegan, Patrick, *King Dan: The Rise of Daniel O'Connell 1775–1829* (Dublin: Gill & Macmillan 2010).

Grell, O. P., A. Cunningham and R. Jutte (eds.), *Healthcare and Poor Relief in 18th and 19th-century Northern Europe* (London: Routledge 2002).

Hufton, Olwen, *The Poor of Eighteenth-Century France* (Oxford: Clarendon Press 1974).

Leadbeater, Mary, *Cottage Dialogues among the Irish Peasantry* (London: J. Johnson 1811).

MacDonald, Brian, 'South Ulster in the Age of the United Irishmen', in T. Bartlett, D. Dickson, D. Keogh and K. Whelan (eds.), *1798: A Bicentenary Perspective* (Dublin: Four Courts 2003), pp. 226–42.

MacSuibhne, Breandán, 'Politicisation and Paramilitarism: North-West and South-West Ulster 1772–1798', in T. Bartlett, D. Dickson, D. Keogh and K. Whelan (eds.), *1798: A Bicentenary Perspective* (Dublin: Four Courts 2003), pp. 243–78.

MacCavery, Trevor, 'As the Plague of Locusts Came Down on Egypt: Rebel Motivation in North Down', in T. Bartlett, D. Dickson, D. Keogh and K. Whelan (eds.), *1798: A Bicentenary Perspective* (Dublin: Four Courts 2003), pp. 212–25.

McDowell, R. B. (ed.), *Social Life in Ireland 1800–45* (Dublin: Sign of the Three Candles 1957).

Moran, Gerard, *Sending Out Ireland's Poor: Assisted Emigration to North America in the Nineteenth Century* (Dublin: Four Courts 2004).

Ó Ciosáin, Niall, *Ireland in Official Print Culture 1800–1850: A New Reading of the Poor Inquiry* (Oxford: Oxford University Press 2014).

Ó Gráda, Cormac, *Ireland: A New Economic History 1780–1939* (Oxford: Clarendon Press 1994).

Ó Murchadha, Ciarán, *The Great Famine: Ireland's Agony 1845–1852* (London: Continuum 2011).

O'Ferrall, Fergus, *Catholic Emancipation: Daniel O'Connell and the Birth of Irish Democracy* (Dublin: Gill & Macmillan 1985).

Ollerenshaw, Peter and Liam Kennedy (eds.), *Ulster since 1600: Economy, Politics and Society* (Oxford: Oxford University Press 2012).

Snell, K. D. M., *Annals of the Labouring Poor: Social Change in Agrarian England 1660–1900* (Cambridge: Cambridge University Press 1985).

Woodham-Smith, Cecil, *The Great Hunger* (London: Hamish Hamilton 1962).

Modernization: From the Famine to the Farmers' Victory, 1850–1903

Relevant Sections of Surveys and Other Sources Cited Previously

Surveys

Boyce, D. G., *Nineteenth-Century Ireland* (Dublin: Gill & Macmillan 1990).

Clear, C., *Social Change and Everyday Life in Ireland 1850–1922* (Manchester: Manchester University Press 2007).

Lee, J. J., *The Modernisation of Irish society* (Dublin: Gill 1972).

Other Sources

Barr, Colin, 'The Re-energising of Catholicism 1790–1880', in J. Kelly (ed.), *Cambridge History of Ireland*, vol. 3 (Cambridge: Cambridge University Press 2018), pp. 280–304.

Bartlett, Thomas, *Ireland: A History* (Cambridge: Cambridge University Press 2010).

Bielenberg, Andy, *Cork's Industrial Revolution* (Cork 1991).

Boyce, D. G. (ed.), *The Revolution in Ireland 1870–1923* (London: Longmans 1987).

Callanan, Frank, *The Parnell Split 1890–91* (Cork: Cork University Press 1992).

Carbery, Mary, *The Farm by Lough Gur* (Cork: Mercier [1933] 1995).
Clark, Samuel and James Donnelly (eds.), *Irish Peasants: Violence and Political Unrest* (Madison: University of Wisconsin 2003).
Clear, Caitriona, 'Social Conditions 1880–1914', in T. Bartlett (ed.), *Cambridge History of Ireland*, vol. 4 (Cambridge: Cambridge University Press 2018), pp. 145–67.
Clear, Caitriona, *Nuns in Nineteenth-Century Ireland* (Dublin: Gill & Macmillan 1987).
Comerford, R. V., *The Fenians in Context: Irish Politics and Society 1848–1882* (London: Merlin [1985] 1998).
Conley, Carolyn, *Melancholy Accidents: The Meaning of Violence in 19th-Century Ireland* (Lenham: Lexington Books 1999).
Connell, K. H., *Irish Peasant Society* (Oxford: Oxford University Press 1967).
Cronin, Maura, *Country, Class or Craft? The Politicisation of the Skilled Artisan in 19th-Century Cork* (Cork: Cork University Press 1994).
Fitzpatrick, David, *Oceans of Consolation: Personal Accounts of Irish Migration to Australia* (Ithaca: Cornell University Press 1994).
French, Percy, *Prose, Poems and Parodies* (Dublin: Talbot 1939).
Gailey, Andrew, *Ireland and the Death of Kindness: The Experience of Constructive Unionism 1885–1903* (Cork: Cork University Press 1987).
Geary, Laurence, *The Plan of Campaign* (Cork: Cork University Press 1988).
Griffin, Brian, 'The Irish Police: Love, Sex and Marriage in the 19th and Early 20th Centuries', in Margaret Kelleher and James Murphy (eds.), *Gender Perspectives in Nineteenth-Century Ireland* (Dublin: Irish Academic Press 1997), pp. 168–78.
Guinnane, Timothy, *The Vanishing Irish: Households, Migration and the Rural Economy in Ireland 1850–1914* (Princeton: Princeton University Press 1997).
Harkness, David and Mary O'Dowd (ed.), *The Town in Ireland: Historical Studies*, vol. 13 (Belfast: Appletree 1981).
Hearn, Mona, *Below Stairs: Domestic Service Remembered in Dublin and Beyond 1880–1922* (Dublin: Lilliput 1993).

Hearne, Dana (ed.), *Anna Parnell's Tale of a Great Sham* (Dublin: Arlen House 1986).

Hegarty, Susan and James Kelly (eds.), *Schools and Schooling 1650–2000: New Perspectives on the History of Education* (Dublin: Four Courts 2017).

Holmes, Andrew, 'Protestantism in the 19th Century: Revival and Crisis', in J. Kelly (ed.), *Cambridge History of Ireland*, vol. 3 (Cambridge: Cambridge University Press 2018), pp. 331–52.

Hoppen, K. T., *Elections, Politics and Society in Ireland 1832–1885* (Oxford: Oxford University Press 1984).

Jackson, Alvin, 'The Origins, Politics and Culture of Irish Unionism c.1880–1916', in T. Bartlett (ed.), *Cambridge History of Ireland*, vol. 4 (Cambridge: Cambridge University Press 2018), pp. 89–116.

Jackson, Alvin, *The Ulster Party: Irish Unionists in the House of Commons 1884–1911* (Oxford: Oxford University Press 1989).

Kelly, Matthew, 'Radical Nationalisms 1882–1916', in T. Bartlett (ed.), *Cambridge History of Ireland*, vol. 4 (Cambridge: Cambridge University Press 2018), pp. 33–61.

Lee, David and Debbie Jacobs (eds.), *Made in Limerick: History of Industries, Trade and Commerce*, vol. 1 (Limerick: Limerick Civic Trust 2003).

Logan, John, 'The Dimensions of Gender in 19th-Century Schooling', in Margaret Kelleher and James Murphy (eds.), *Gender Perspectives in Nineteenth-Century Ireland* (Dublin: Irish Academic Press 1997), pp. 36–49.

Magray, Mary Peckham, *The Transforming Power of the Nuns: Women, Religion and Cultural Change in Ireland 1750–1900* (Oxford: Oxford University Press 1998).

Marley, Laurence, *Michael Davitt: Freelance Radical and Frondeur* (Dublin 2007).

Maume, Patrick, 'Parnell and the IRB Oath', *Irish Hsitorical Studies* 24, 115, May 1995, pp. 363–70.

Mulvagh, Conor, 'Home Rulers at Westminster 1880–1914', in T. Bartlett (ed.), *Cambridge History of Ireland*, vol. 4 (Cambridge: Cambridge University Press 2018), pp. 62–88.

Ó Glaisne, Risteard, *Na Modhaigh: scéal pobail, scéal eaglaise* (Corcaigh 1998).
O'Connor, Emmet, *A Labour History of Ireland 1824–1960* (Dublin: Gill & Macmillan 1992).
O'Dowd, Anne, *Spalpeens and Tattie Hokers: The History and Folklore of the Irish Agricultural Worker in Ireland and Britain* (Dublin: Irish Academic Press 1990).
O'Neill, Berrie, *Tones That Are Tender: Percy French 1854–1920* (Dublin: Lilliput 2016).
Raftery, Deirdre, *Irish Nuns and Education in the Anglophone World: A Transnational History* (London: Palgrave Macmillan 2023).
Rynne, Stephen, *Green Fields: A Journal of Irish Country Life* (London: Jonathan Cape 1938, Dingle: Brandon Press 1995).
The authoritative version of 'The Coleraine Regatta' is by The Johnstons from the album *The Barleycorn* (London: Transatlantic 1968). The most popular version of the 1880s song 'Courting in the Kitchen' is by Irish singer Delia Murphy, recorded in the 1940s and collected on the album *The Queen of Connemara* (N. Y. Irish Prestige Records 1962)
Turner, Michael, *After the Famine: Irish agriculture 1850–1914* (Cambridge: Cambridge University Press 1996).
Ward, Margaret, *Unmanageable Revolutionaries: Women and Irish Nationalism* (Dingle: Brandon 1989).
Whelehan, Niall, *The Dynamiters: Irish Nationalists and Political Violence in the Wider World 1867–1900* (Cambridge: Cambridge University Press 2012).

Revolution: Twenty Decisive Years, 1903–1923

Relevant Sections of Surveys and Other Sources Cited Previously

Surveys
Ferriter, Diarmuid, *The Transformation of Ireland 1900–2000* (London: Profile 2005).

Hill, Myrtle, *Women in Ireland: A Century of Change* (Belfast: Blackstaff 2003).
Keogh, Dermot, *Twentieth-Century Ireland* (Dublin: Gill & Macmillan 1994).
Lee, J. J., *Ireland 1912–1985* (Cambridge: Cambridge University Press 1989).

Other Sources

Barnes, Jane, *Irish Industrial Schools 1868–1908* (Dublin: Irish Academic Press 1989).
Bourke, Joanna, *Husbandry to Housewifery: Women, Economic Change and Housework in Ireland 1890–1914* (Oxford: Clarendon 1993).
Bradley, Dan, *Farm Labourers: Irish Struggle 1900–1976* (Belfast: Athol 1998).
Chinnéide, Máiréad Ní, *Máire de Buitléir: bean athbheochana* (Baile Átha Cliath: Comhar 1993).
Clancy, Mary, 'The Western Outpost: Local Government and Women's Suffrage in Co. Galway 1898–1918' in Raymond Gillespie and Gerard Moran (eds.), *Galway: History and Society* (Dublin: Geography Publications 1995), pp. 557–88.
Clear, Caitriona, 'The *Lady of the House*' in L. Scholl (ed.), *The Palgrave Encyclopaedia of Victorian Women's Writing* (Switzerland 2020).
Crossman, Virginia, *Poverty and the Poor Law in Ireland 1850–1914* (Liverpool University Press 2013).
Cunningham, John, *Labour in the West of Ireland: Working Life and Struggle 1890–1914* (Belfast; Athol 1995).
Curtayne, Alice, *Francis Ledwidge: A Life of the Poet* (London: Martin Brian and O'Keeffe 1972).
Davis, Richard, *Arthur Griffith and Non-violent Sinn Fein* (Tralee: Anvil 1974).
Dolan, Anne and William Murphy, *Michael Collins: The Man and the Revolution* (Cork: Collins 2018).
Finnane, Mark, *Insanity and the Insane in Post-Famine Ireland* (New York: Barnes & Noble 1981).
Fitzpatrick, David, *Politics and Irish Life 1913–1921* (Cork: Cork University Press 1998).

Foster, R. F., *Vivid Faces: The Revolutionary Generation in Ireland 1890–1923* (London: Allen Lane 2014).

Fraser, Murray, *John Bull's Other Homes: State Housing and British Policy in Ireland 1883–1922* (Liverpool University Press 1996).

Hart, Peter, *The IRA and Its Enemies: Violence and Community in Cork 1916–1923* (Oxford: Oxford University Press 1998).

Hopkinson, Michael, *Green Against Green: The Irish Civil War* (Dublin: Gill & Macmillan 2004).

Horne, John (ed.), *Our War: Ireland and the Great War* (Dublin: Royal Irish Academy 2009).

Jones, Greta and Elizabeth Malcolm (eds.), *Medicine, Disease and the State in Ireland 1650–1930* (Cork: Cork University Press 1999).

Jones, Mary, *The Other Ireland: Changing Times 1870–1920* (Dublin: Gill & Macmillan 2011).

Kearns, Kevin C., *Dublin Tenement Life: An Oral History* (Dublin 1996).

Kelly, Brendan, *Hearing Voices: The History of Psychiatry in Ireland* (Dublin: Irish Academic Press 2016).

Kettle, Thomas, 'To My Daughter Betty' in Fiona Biggs (ed.), *Pocket Irish Poetry* (Dublin: Gill 2015).

Laffan, Michael, *The Resurrection of Ireland: The Sinn Fein Party 1916–1923* (Cambridge: Cambridge University Press 2005).

Lee, J. J., 'The railways in the Irish economy' in L. M. Cullen (ed.), *The Formation of the Irish Economy* (Cork: Mercier 1976), pp. 77–88.

Matthews, Ann, *Renegades: Irish Republican Women 1900–1922* (Cork 2010).

McAuliffe, Mary and Liz Gillis, *Richmond Barracks 1916: We Were There: 77 Women of the Easter Rising* (Dublin: Dublin City Council 2016).

McCarthy, Cal, *Cumann na mBan and the Irish Revolution* (Cork: Mercier 2014).

McCoole, Sinead, *Easter Widows: Seven Irish Women Who Lived In the Shadow of the 1916 Rising* (Dublin: Doubleday Ireland 2014).

McCullough, David, *De Valera: Rise 1882–1932* (Dublin: Royal Irish Academy 2017).

McGarry, Fearghal, *The Rising: Ireland, Easter 1916* (Oxford: Oxford University Press 2010).

Murphy, Cliona, *The Women's Suffrage Movement and Irish Society in the Early Twentieth Century* (Brighton: Harvester 1989).

Ó Comhraí, Cormac, *Ireland and the First World War: A Photographic History* (Cork: Mercier 2014).

Ó Murchadha, Ciaran, 'Paphian nymphs and worshippers of the Idalian goddess: prostitution in Ennis in the mid-19th century' *The Other Clare* 27 (2000), pp. 32–6.

Owens, Rosemary Cullen, *Smashing Times: A History of the Irish Women's Suffrage Movement 1882–1924* (Dublin 1984).

Paseta, Senia, *Irish Nationalist Women 1900–1918* (Cambridge: Cambridge University Press 2013).

Smithson, Annie M. P., *Her Irish Heritage* (Dublin: Talbot 1917).

Smithson, Annie M. P., *Carmen Cavanagh* (Dublin: Talbot 1921).

Smithson, Annie M. P., *Myself – and Others* (Dublin: Talbot 1944).

Townshend, Charles, *The Republic: The Fight for Irish Independence* (London: Penguin 2014).

Urquhart, Diane, *Women in Ulster Politics 1890–1940* (Dublin: Irish Academic Press 2000).

Stability, 1922–1969

Relevant Sections of Surveys and Other Sources Cited Previously

Surveys

Bew, Paul, Peter Gibbon and Henry Patterson, *Northern Ireland 1921–2001: Political Forces and Social Classes* (London: Serif 2002).

Buckland, Patrick, *A History of Northern Ireland* (Dublin: Irish Books and Media 1981).

Hennessy, Thomas, *A History of Northern Ireland 1920–96* (Dublin: Gill & Macmillan 1997).

Mitchison, Rosalind and Peter Roebuck (eds.), *Economy and Society in Scotland and Ireland 1500–1939* (Edinburgh University Press 1988).

Tonge, Jonathan, *Northern Ireland: Conflict and Change* (London: Longmans 1998).

Other Sources

Augusteijn, Joost, *Ireland in the 1930s: New Perspectives* (Dublin: Four Courts 1999).

Ayiotis, Daniel, *Moral Formations: Discipline and Religion in the Irish Army 1922–32* (Dublin: Eastwood/Wordwell 2024).

Barrington, Ruth, *Health, Medicine and Politics in Ireland 1900–1970* (Dublin: Institute of Public Administration 1987).

Bhreathnach, Aoife, *Becoming Conspicuous: Irish Travellers, Society and the State 1922–70* (Dublin: UCD Press 2006).

Brady, Deirdre, *Literary Coteries and the Irish Women Writers' Club 1933–1958* (Liverpool University Press 2021).

Central Statistics Office, *That Was Then, This Is Now: Change in Ireland 1949–1999* (Dublin: Stationery Office 2000).

Clear, Caitriona *Women's Voices in Ireland: Women's Magazines in the 1950s and 60s* (London: Bloomsbury 2016).

Clear, Caitriona, *Women of the House: Women's Household Work in Ireland 1922–1961* (Dublin: Irish Academic Press 2000).

Crone, Anne, *My Heart and I* (London: Heinemann 1955).

Cronin, Michael G., *Impure Thoughts: Sexuality, Catholicism and Literature in Twentieth-Century Ireland* (Manchester: Manchester University Press 2012).

D'Alton, Ian and Ida Milne, *Protestant and Irish: The Minority's Search for Place in Independent Ireland* (Cork: Cork University Press 2019).

Daly, Mary E., *Sixties Ireland: Reshaping the Economy, State and Society 1957–1973* (Cambridge: Cambridge University Press 2016).

de Cléir, Síle, *Popular Catholicism in 20th-Century Ireland* (London: Bloomsbury 2017).

Further Reading

Deeney, Ciarán and David Clarke, *Man on the Bridge: The Photos of Arthur Fields* (Cork: Collins 2014).

Delaney, Enda, *Demography, State and Society: Irish Migration to Britain 1921–1971* (Liverpool University Press 2000).

Delay, Cara, *Irish Women and the Creation of Modern Catholicism 1850–1950* (Manchester: Manchester University Press 2019).

Doherty, Gabriel and Dermot Keogh (eds.), *De Valera's Irelands* (Cork: Mercier 2003).

Dolan, Anne, 'Politics, Economy and Society in the Irish Free State', in T. Bartlett (ed.), *Cambridge History of Ireland*, vol. 4 (Cambridge: Cambridge University Press 2018), pp. 323–48.

Doyle, David M. and Liam O'Callaghan, *Capital Punishment in Independent Ireland: A Social, Legal and Political History* (Liverpool University Press 2019).

Farmar, Tony (ed.), *James Deeny: The End of an Epidemic – Essays in Irish Public Health 1935–65* (Dublin: A & A Farmar 1995).

Farmar, Tony, *The History of Irish Book Publishing* (Stroud: History Press 2018).

Finn, Tomas and Tony Varley (eds.), *Inside Rural Ireland: Power and Change since Independence* (Dublin: UCD Press 2024).

Gilmore, Tom, *Big Tom: The King of Irish Country* (Dublin: O'Brien 2018.)

Greally, Hanna, *Bird's Nest Soup* (Dublin: Allen Figgis 1971).

Hanley, Brian and Scott Millar, *The Lost Revolution: The Story of the Official IRA and the Workers' Party* (London: Penguin 2008).

Harris, Mary, *The Catholic Church and the Foundation of the Northern Irish State* (Cork: Cork University Press 1993).

Hayes, Alan (ed.), *Hilda Tweedy and the Irish Housewives Association: Links in the Chain* (Dublin: Arlen House 2012).

Holohan, Carole, *Reframing Irish Youth in the Sixties* (Liverpool University Press 2018).

Kearney, Joe and P. J. Cunningham (eds.), *From the Candy Store to the Galtymore: Stories from Ireland's Showband Era of the 1950s–70s* (Bray: Ballpoint 2017).

Kearns, Kevin C., *A Year of Glory and Gold: 1932 Ireland's Jazz Age* (Dublin: Gill 2023).

Keogh, Dermot, Finbarr O'Shea and Carmel Quinlan (eds.), *The Lost Decade: Ireland in the 1950s* (Cork: Mericer 2004).

Keogh, Dermot, *Jews in 20th-Century Ireland* (Cork: Cork University Press 1998).

Kilgannon, David, *Intellectual Disability and Ireland 1947–1996: Towards a Full Life?* (Liverpool University Press 2023).

Lane, Temple, *Friday's Well* (Dublin: Talbot 1943).

Laverty, Maura, *Lift Up Your Gates* (London: Longmans, Green 1946).

Livingston, Jim, *Bridie Gallagher: The Girl from Donegal* (Cork: Collins 2015).

The Ludlows, 'Sea Around Us' (D. Behan) (Dublin: Sanctuary Records 1966).

MacDermott, Eithne, *Clann na Poblachta* (Cork: Cork University Press 1998).

MacGowan, Brendan, *Taking the Boat: The Irish in Leeds 1931–1981* (Killala: Arts Council 2009).

MacManus, Francis (ed.), *The Years of the Great Test 1926–1939* (Cork: Mercier 1978).

Maguire, Moira J., *Precarious Childhood in Post-Independence Ireland* (Manchester: Manchester University Press 2009).

McKenna, Yvonne, *Made Holy: Irish Women Religious at Home and Abroad* (Dublin: Irish Academic Press 2006).

McNamara, Meadhbh and Paschal Mooney, *Women in Parliament: Ireland 1918–2000* (Dublin: Wolfhound 2000).

McNeill, Janet, *The Other Side of the Wall* (London: Hodder & Stoughton 1956).

Moylan, Therese, 'Women entrepreneurs and self-employed business owners in Ireland 1922–1972' unpublished PhD thesis, National University of Ireland 2015.

O'Donnell, Ian and Eoin O'Sullivan, *Coercive Confinement in Ireland: Patients, Prisoners and Penitents* (Manchester: Manchester University Press 2014).

O'Hara, Aidan, *I'll Live Till I Die: The Delia Murphy Story* (Manorhamilton: Drumlin Books 1997).

O'Leary, Eleanor, *Youth and Popular Culture in 1950s Ireland* (London: Bloomsbury 2018).
Pim, Sheila, *The Flowering Shamrock* (London: Hodder & Stoughton 1947).
Plunkett, James, *Strumpet City* (London: Hutchinson 1969).
Purcell, Patrick, *Hanrahan's Daughter* (Dublin: Talbot 1940).
Robertson, Olivia, *Field of the Stranger* (London: Peter Davies 1948).
Robertson, Olivia, *The Golden Eye* (London: Peter Davies 1952).
Sheridan, John D., *Joe's No Saint and Other Poems* (Dublin: Talbot 1949).
Stack, Sr de Lourdes *As We Lived It* (Tralee: Kerryman n.d., c. 1980).
Suenens, Leon-Joseph, *Edel Quinn (1907–1944): Envoy of the Legion of Mary to Africa* (Dublin: C.J. Fallon 1954).
Tobin, Fergal, *The Best of Decades? Ireland in the 1960s* (Dublin: Gill & Macmillan 1984).
Walsh, Dermot, *Beneath Cannock's Clock: The Last Man Hanged in Ireland* (Cork: Mercier 2009).

The Thirty Year 'Troubles', 1969–1998

Relevant Sections of Surveys and Other Sources Cited Previously

Surveys
Finnegan, R. B. and E. T. McCarron, *Ireland: Historical Echoes, Contemporary Politics* (Boulder: Westview 2000).
Sweeney, Eamonn, *Down, Down, Deeper and Down: Ireland in the 70s and 80s* (Dublin: Gill & Macmillan 2010).

Other Sources
Arnold, Mavis and Heather Laskey, *Children of the Poor Clares* (Belfast: Appletree 1985).

Coulter, Colin, *Contemporary Northern Irish Society: An Introduction* (London: Pluto 1999).

Daly, Mary E., *The Battle to Control Female Fertility in Modern Ireland* (Cambridge: Cambridge University Press 2023).

Farmar, Anna (ed.), *Traveller: An Autobiography by Nan Joyce* (Dublin: Gill & Macmillan 1985).

Fetherstonhaugh, Neil and Tony McCullagh, *They Never Came Home: The Stardust Story* (London: Merlin 2001).

Flynn, Mannix, *Nothing to Say* (Dublin: Ward River 1983).

Foster, R. F., *Luck and the Irish: A Brief History of Change from 1970* (Oxford: Oxford University Press 2008).

Glassie, Henry, *Passing the Time in Ballymenone: Culture and History of an Ulster Community* (Bloomington: University of Indiana Press 1995).

Heaney, Seamus, 'Casualty', in *Field Work* (London: Faber 1979).

Jackson, Pauline, 'Outside the Jurisdiction: Irish Women Seeking Abortion' in C. Curtin, P. Jackson and B. O'Connor (eds.), *Gender in Irish Society* (Galway: Officina Typographica 1987), pp. 203–23.

Kennedy, Stanislaus, *But Where Can I Go? Homeless Women in Dublin* (Dublin: Arlen House 1985).

Maher, Sean, *The Road to God Knows Where: A Memoir of a Travelling Boyhood* (Dublin: Talbot 1972).

McCafferty, Nell, *Peggy Deery: An Irish Family at War* (Dublin: Attic 1989).

McCafferty, Nell, *A Woman to Blame: The Kerry Babies Case* (Dublin: Attic 1985).

Moore, Christy, *One Voice: My Life in Song* (London: Hodder & Stoughton 2003).

Mullin, Chris, *Error of Judgment: The Birmingham Bombings* (London: Chatto & Windus 1986).

Murray, Sean, Christine Bohan and Nicky Ryan, *The Last Disco: The Story of the Stardust Tragedy* (London: Eriu 2024).

Ní Dhuibhne, Éilís, *Fáinne Geal an Lae* (Gaillimh: Cló Iar-Chonnacht 2023).

O'Malley, Pádraig, *Biting at the Grave: The Irish Hunger Strikes and the Politics of Despair* (Belfast: Beacon 1990).
Riain, Seán Ó, *Seal le Siomóin* (Baile Átha Cliath: An Clóchomhar Teo 1984).
Rose, Catherine, *The Female Experience: The Story of the Woman Movement in Ireland* (Galway: Arlen House 1975).
Smyth, Sam, *Thanks a Million, Big Fella* (Dublin: Blackwater 1997) (about the relationship between Charles Haughey and supermarket magnate Ben Dunne).
Sweetman, Rosita, *'On Our Knees': Ireland 1972* (London: Pan 1972).
Whelan, Diarmuid (ed.), Peter Tyrrell, *Founded on Fear* (Dublin 2006).
Women's Committee of the National Union of Public Employees, *Women's Voices: an oral history of Northern Irish Women's Health 1900–1990* (Dublin: Attic Press 1992).

Prosperity/Austerity/Prosperity? 1998–c. 2016

Relevant Sections of Surveys and Other Sources Cited Previously

Corless, Catherine, *Belonging: One Woman's Search for Truth and Justice for the Tuam Babies* (Dublin: Hachette 2022).
Deleuze, Marjorie, 'A New Craze for Food: Why Is Ireland Turning into a Foodie Nation?' in M. Mac Con Iomaire and E. Maher (eds.), *'Tickling the Palate': Gastronomy in Irish Literature and Culture*, vol. 57, *Reimagining Ireland* (Bern: Peter Lang 2014), pp. 143–58.
The Ferns Report: an inquiry into the responses to allegations of child abuse in the Catholic diocese of Ferns (2005).
French, Tana, *Broken Harbour* (London: Hodder 2012).
Lucey, Brian, Eamon Maher and Eugene O'Brien (eds.), *Recalling the Celtic Tiger*, vol. 93, *Reimagining Ireland* (Bern: Peter Lang 2019).

McCabe, Conor, *Sins of the Father: The Decisions That Shaped the Irish Economy* (Stroud: History Press 2011, 2013).

McWilliams, David, *Renaissance Nation: How the Pope's Children Rewrote the Rules for Ireland* (Dublin: Gill 2018).

Milotte, Mike, *Banished Babies: The True Story of Ireland's Baby Export Business* (Dublin: New Island 1998, 2012).

Reapy, E.M. *Red Dirt* (London: Head of Zeus 2016).

Report by Commission of Investigation into the Catholic Diocese of Cloyne (2011).

Report of the Commission of Investigation into the Catholic Archdiocese of Dublin (2009). [under Justice Yvonne Murphy, hence 'the Murphy report'].

Report of the Commission to Inquire into Child Abuse (of children in institutions) vols. 1–5 (2009) [under Justice Sean Ryan, hence 'the Ryan report'].

Report of the Interdepartmental Committee to establish the facts of State involvement with Magdalen laundries (2013). [under Martin McAleese, hence the 'McAleese report'].

Figures in this chapter which relate to immigration, people seeking refugee status, Travellers, the Irish language and religious affiliation are taken from the *Censuses of Ireland* 2011 and 2016.

Conclusion

Relevant Sections of All Sources Cited Previously

Corlett, Christiaan, *Beneath the Poulaphouca Reservoir* (Dublin: Stationery Office 2008).

Davis, Thomas, 'Celts and Saxons', in T. W. Rolleston (ed.), *Thomas Davis: Selections from his Prose and Poetry* (London: Gresham Publishing Company n.d., c. 1928).

Gardiner, Alfred George, 'Two Drinks of Milk' in *Alpha of the Plough: Third Series, Chosen By the Author* (London: Dent 1932).

Lenihan, Eddie, *Meeting the Other Crowd: The Fairy Stories of Hidden Ireland* (Dublin: Gill & Macmillan 2003).

McCarthy, Michael, *High Tension: Life on the Shannon Scheme* (Dublin: Lilliput 2005).

Mulligan, Paul, *Irish Ordnance Survey Maps: A User's Guide* (Dublin: Wordwell 2024).

Ó Cionnaith, Finnian, *The Origin of Ireland's Ordnance Survey: Taxation, Townlands, and Topography* (Dublin: Four Courts 2024).

Tracy, Honor, *Mind You I've Said Nothing! Forays in the Irish Republic* (London: Methuen 1953).

INDEX

à Kempis, Thomas, 60
Abbey Theatre, 174
Abduction of heiresses, 111
Abernethy, John, 108
abortion, 244, 278–9
Act of Settlement (1652), 75
Act of Union, 125
Action for the Homeless, 252
Acts of Supremacy and Uniformity, 69
Adam and Eve's, 92
Adams, Gerry, 241, 274
administration, 44, 82
adoption, 278
adoption abroad, 278
Aer Lingus, 211
Agnew, Paddy, 247
agrarianism, 117
Agricultural Wages Board, 183
agriculture, 7, 11, 53, 54, 83, 84, 99, 137, 183, 212, 217, 229
Ahern, Bertie, 241, 262, 273
Aidan, 24
AIDS, 260
Ailbe, 21
Airgialla, 8
airports, 212–13, 266
Aldershot, 234
Alliance Party, 234
Alpha of the Plough', (Alfred George Gardiner), 305
amateur dramatics, 215
Amazon, 265
An Claidheamh Soluis, 173
Anglo-Normans, 30, 36

Annals of the Four Masters, 86
anti-immigration, 307
Anti-Partition League, 227
Antrim, 70
Antwerp, 79
Anúna, 254
Aran islands, 24
Archbishop King of Dublin, 101
Ard Macha/Armagh, 21
Ardagh, 49
Ardnacrusha, 304
Ards Peninsula, 70
Arigna, 99
Arlen House, 258
Armagh, 8, 32, 52, 81, 82, 99, 122, 260
Arnold, Mavis, 262
Article 44 of 1937 Constitution, 220
Ashe, Thomas, 195
Asicus, 21
Askeaton, 66
Asmal, Kader, 249
asses, mules and jennets, 151
Association of Parents and Friends of Mentally Backward Children, 215
associational culture, 172
asylum attendants, 154, 182
Athboy (*Áth Buí*), 10
Athenry, 54, 55, 109
Athlone (*Áth Luain*), 10
Atlantic Ocean, 10
Atracta of Sligo, 22
atrocities, 237

Index

Augustinian canons, 32, 48
Augustinian nuns, 51
Augustinians, mendicant, 48
austerity, 268
Auxiliaries, 197

Bachelors Walk, 190
Bagenal, Lord, 68
Baghdad, 14
Baile Bhúirne (Ballyvourney) in, 24
bailout, 268
'B' Specials, 228
'B' and 'C' Specials, 225
Bairéad, Riocaird, 106
Ballinasloe Horse Fair, 280
Ballingarry, 145
Ballinrobe, 48, 54
Ballymahon, 109
Ballynacally, 51
Ballyneety, 77
Ballyshannon, 68
Baltics, 14
Bandon, 82
Bank of Ireland, 102
banking sector, 267
Bann, 10
Banna Strand, 192
Bantry Bay, 123
Baptist church, 82, 90, 219
Barbados, 75
Barleycorn, 245
Barrow, 10
Barry, Garret, 73
Barry, Tom, 196
Battle of Aughrim, 77
Battle of Benburb, 74
Battle of Clontarf, 28, 29
Battle of Kinsale, 68
Battle of Knockdoe, 44
Battle of O'Brien's Bridge, 44
Battle of the Boyne, 77
Battle of the Diamond, 122

Battle of the Yellow Ford, 68
Bean na hEireann, 187
Beatles, 231
Bede, 60
Bedell, Bishop of Down and Connor, 80
beehive huts, 13
Beere, Thekla, 255
Begley, Philomena, 253
Belfast (*Béal Feirste*), 10, 82, 113, 119
Belfast blitz, 226
Belmullet, 143
Bennet, Richard, 49
Bennett, Louie, 187
Beresford, John, 98
Beresford, Thomas, 129
Berkeley, George, bishop of Cloyne, 95, 108
Bernard of Clairvaux, 32
Betha Colaim Cille, 52
Beveridge report, 229
Bianconi, Charles, 145
Big Tom, 231
Big Wind, 139
Biggar, Joseph, 162
Binchy, Maeve, 259
Birch, Peter, bishop of Ossory, 222
Birmingham public-house bombings, 261
Bishop, Des, 290
Black and Tans, 197
Black Death, 39, 56
Blackwater, 10
Blackwater valley, 83
Blair, Tony, 241
Blakes, 94
Blaney, Neil, 245
Bloody Sunday, 235, 246, 283
Blueshirts, 206, 210
Bobbio, 23
Bogside, 235

Index

Boleyn, Anne, 63
Bologna, 51
Book of Ballymote, 8, 61
Book of Fermoy, 61
Book of Kells, 25
Book of Lismore, 61
booleying, 84
Boomtown Rats, 253
Bord Fáilte, 305
Bord Iascaigh Mhara, 211
Bordeaux, 79
border campaign, 208
Boston Scientific, 265
Bothy Band, 253
Boundary Commission, 224
Bowen-Colthurst, Captain John, 193
Bowyer, Brendan, 231
Boycott, Charles, 164
Boyle, Henry earl of Shannon, 50, 96
Boyne, 10, 27
Brega, 20, 27
Brehon law, 26, 45
Breifne, 29
Brendan, 21, 33
Brewing, 101
Brexit, 285
Brian Boru, 28, 29
Brigid, 21, 24, 25, 34
Brigidines, 171
Bristol, 53
Britain, 9
British army, 233, 283
British Embassy, 246
Brooke, Charlotte, 110
Brooke, Henry, 110
Brooke, Peter, 242
Brown, Frances, 1
Browne, Dr Noel, 214
Bruce invasion, 56, 59
Bruce, Edward, 38
Brugha, Cathal, 197, 200, 299

bubonic plague, 86
building trades, 266
Bunratty, 39
Burke, Honoria, 80
Burke, John, 74
Burke, Thomas, 166
Burntollet, 228
Burrishoole, 80
Butler Education Act, 229
Butler, Edmund, 108
Butler, James, 45, 69
Butler, James duke of Ormond, 96
Butler, Mary, 185
Butler, Piers of Ormond, 63
Butler, Richard, 60
Butler, Jean, 45, 254
Butlers, 38, 42
Butlers of Ormond, 39
Butt, Isaac, 159
Butterly, Eamon, 262
Byrne, Edward, 119

Caibidil Críostaí, 86
Caisil Mumhan, 10
Cambridge, 51
camogie, 173
Campaign for Homosexual Law Reform, 260
Campaign for Social Justice, 227
Canice, 54
Canterbury, 30, 46
capital punishment, 231
Captain Rock, 128
Carew, Peter, 66
Carlingford, 54
Carlow, 8, 45, 48, 144
Carmelites, 48, 49
Carnsore Point, 251
Carrickfergus, 54, 116
Carrickmines, 280
Carrickshock, 131
Carson, Edward, 185

Index

Carton House, 103
Casement, Roger, 191, 194
Casey, Bishop Eamo, 275
Cashel, 10, 18, 32, 37, 60
cashels/ring forts, 12
Castlebar, 124
Castlecomer, 99, 145
Castledermot, 37
castles, 57
Catherine of Aragon, 63
Catholic Association, 127, 128
Catholic Committee, 98, 119, 122
Catholic Confederation, 74
Catholic Convention, 119
Catholic Emancipation, 126
Catholic or Counter-Reformation, 79
Catholic rent, 128
Catholics, 70, 90–3
cathracha, 15
Cattle Acts of 1663 and 1667, 83
Cavan, 10, 82, 122
Cavendish, Frederick, 166
Ceannt, Eamonn, 193
Céli Dé, 31
Cell Íte (Killeedy), 24
Celtic Tiger, 251
Celts, 7
censorship, 231
charitable institutions, 113
Charleville, 82
Charlton, Jack, 261
Chartists, 145
Cherish, 255
Chichester-Clark, James, 228
Chieftains, 253
children, 263
Children's Allowance, 255
chocolate, 102
Christchurch, 43
Christian Brothers, 133
Christianity, coming of, 8, 20
Church of England, 81

Church of Ireland, 72, 76, 78, 79, 81, 95, 96, 120, 161, 169, 219, 276
Ciarán of Clonmacnoise, 21, 25
Ciarán of Ossory, 21
Cill Cais (Kilcash), 301
Cill Dara, Kildare, 10
cinema, 231
Cistercian order, 32, 47, 53
CityLink, 266
Civil Constitution of the Clergy, 119
Civil War, English, 72
Civil War, Irish, 202
civil unrest, 228
Clann na Poblachta, 209, 210
Clann na Talmhan, 209, 210
Clannad, 253
Clanrickard Burkes, 42, 44
Clare, 8, 10, 42, 75, 82, 129
Clarke, Kathleen, 200
Clarke, Thomas, 193
Cleary, Fr Michael, 275
clerical sexual abuse, 275
clerks, 154
Cliffs of Moher, 139
climate, 10
Clinton, President Bill, 240
Clogher, 50
Clogher valley, 70
Cló-IarChonnacht, 290
Clonard, 15, 21, 50, 57
Clonbroney, 24
Clonfert, 50
Clonmacnoise, 21
Clonmel (*Cluain Meala*), 12, 15, 21, 24, 31, 37, 74, 116, 145
Clontarf, 130
clothes, 15, 56, 85, 104, 155
Cloyne report, 277
Coade, Jame, 193
cobblers, 155
coffee, 102

coins, 55
Coiscéim, 290
Cole, Paddy, 231
Coleraine, 82
College Green, 96
Collins, Michael, 196, 199
Colman, 23
Columbanus, 23, 25
Columcille/Columba, 21, 25, 34
Combat Poverty, 251
Comhlucht Siúcra Éireann, 211
Commission for the Status of Women, 255
Commission of Inquiry into the Relief of the Poor in Ireland, 135
Commission on Emigration, 216
Commission on the Status of People with Disabilities, 281
communications, 119, 145, 250, 254
compensation (*éiric*), 26
Compostella, 79
Concern, 252
Condell, Frances, 223
Confederate Catholics, 73
Congested Districts Board, 169
Connacht, 8, 18, 29, 32, 42, 45, 72, 75, 106
Connaught Telegraph, 163
Connolly, James, 186, 189, 193
Connolly, Sybil, 217
Conolly, Katherine, 110
Conolly, William, 96
conscription, 196, 226
Constructive Unionism, 324
contraception, 244, 256–7
Coolgreaney, 124
Cooper, Bob, 234
Cooper, Catherine, 230
Cooper, Ivan, 234
Coote, Charles, 74, 83
Coras Iompair Éireann, 211

Corca Dhuibhne (the Dingle peninsula), 24, 33
Corcomru, 32
Cork, 7, 8, 27, 37, 42, 45, 53, 54, 79, 83, 92, 99, 106, 113
Corless, Catherine, 278
corporal punishment, 230
Corrigan, Mairéad, 238
corruption, 262
Cosgrave, W. T., 206
Cosgrave, Liam, 256
Costello, John A, 206, 209
Coughlan, Anthony, 228
Council of Trent, 79
Coventry, 208
Cowen, Brian, 273
coyne and livery, 41
Craig, James, 187, 199, 225
crash of 2008, 267
Crawford, William, 110
cricket, 173
Croke Park, 198
Cromwell, Oliver, 74
Cronan of Roscrea, 22
Crone, Anne, 230
Croom, 107
croppies, 122
cross-community activity, 238
Crummey, Frank, 230
Cualu, 10
Cumann na mBan, 189, 190, 191, 198, 200
Cumann na nGaedheal, 185, 206
Cummins, Mary, 259
Cunningham, Larry, 232
Curragh 'mutiny', 190
Currie, Austin, 234
Cusack, Michael, 172
Customs House, 113
cycling, 172
Cyprus, 211

Dáil, 197, 205

Index

dairy produce, 83, 265
Dal gCais, 29
Dal Riata, 18, 38
Dalton, Emmet, 196
Daly, Bishop Cahal, 239
Daly, Cyril, 230
Daly, James, 163
Damer House, 101
Dana (Rosemary Brown), 102, 253
Dances, 215
David Trimble, 23
Davies, John, 86
Davis, Thomas, 130, 145, 308
Davitt, 164
Davitt, Michael, 158, 162, 158
de Burca, Máirín, 259
de Burgos/Burkes, 38, 39
de Chastelain, General John, 282
de Clare, Elizabeth, 48
de Clare, Richard, 30, 36
de Clares, 38, 39, 42
de Courcys, 37
de Lacys, 38
de Valera, Eamon, 193, 197, 199, 206, 207
De Valera's Constitution (Bunreacht na hÉireann), 207
Deasy's Land Act of 1860, 161
Decade of Centenaries, 274
Declan, 21
Declaration of Indulgence, 76
Declaratory Act of 1720, 95, 98
Deeny, Dr James, 228
Defence Forces, 211
Defenders, 122, 124
Delahunty, Mick, 215
Delany, Mary, 111
Dell, 265
Delvin, Lord, 65
Democratic Left, 248
Democratic Socialist Party, 248
Democratic Unionist Party (DUP), 235

Denmark, 27
Department of Agriculture and Technical Instruction, 169
Department of Health, 213
depression, 138, 163, 244
Derry, 21, 82, 99, 120
Desmond, earls of 48, 38, 40, 42, 49, 63, 64, 65, 68
Desmond Rebellion, 66
Desmond, Barry, 256
Devlin, Bernadette, 228, 236
Devlin, Joseph, 226
devotions, 221
Devoy, John, 162
Dickson, Thomas, 193
diet, 11, 12, 16, 56, 84, 138, 175, 178, 180
Dillon, John, 165, 193
Dingle, 53, 59
dioceses, 32–3, 47
Direct rule, 237
dirty protest, 239
Disabled Person's Maintenance Allowance, 214
discrimination, 227
Disraeli, Benjamin, 162
dissolution of the monasteries, 78
divorce, 257–8
Doherty, Kieran, 247
Dolan, Joe, 231
domestic servants, 112
domestic service, 155
Dominican nuns, 79, 113
Dominican Third Order, 80
Dominicans, 48, 52, 78, 171
Don Juan del Aguila, 68
Donatus, 24
Donegal, 1, 25, 51, 69, 70, 82, 99
Donegan, Paddy, 246
Donlevy, Fr, 106
Douai, 79
Down and Connor, 69
Dr Bartholomew Mosse, 114

Dr Steeven's, 113
Drapier's Letters, 95
Drennan, William, 119
dressmaking, 155
Drogheda, 37, 43, 48, 49, 51, 74
Drumcree, 240
Drummond, Thomas, 132
Dublin, 32, 42, 45, 48, 51, 54, 86, 106, 119, 123, 125, 246, passim.
Dublin Castle, 96, 125
Dublin Lock-Out, 189
Dublin Metropolitan Police, 132, 190
Dublin tenements, 27, 36, 37, 177
Duelling, 116
Duffy, Charles Gavan, 130, 161
Dungannon, 82
Dungannon Clubs, 185
Dunne, Ben, 262
Dunnes Stores, 252
Durrow, 21
dwellings, 12, 14, 53–4, 55, 58, 84, 104, 176, 213, 280
Dympna, 24

Earl Grey's scheme, 143
Earl of Essex, 68
East Anglia, 24
Easter Monday, 191
Ecgfrith, 20
economy, 53, 99, 284
Edgeworth, Maria, 110
Eighth Amendment to the Constitution, 257
electoral boundaries, 225
Electricity Supply Board, 211
Eliot, George, 2
Emain Macha, 8, 10, 18
Emergency, 208
Emergency Powers Act, 247
emigration, 104, 138, 144, 216, 229, 249, 251, 271

Emmet, Robert, 125
Emmet, Thomas Addis, 125
Employment Equality Act of 1981, 255
Enda/*Éanna*, 21
English, Ada, 201
Ennis, 130
Enniskillen, 82
entertainment, 231
environmentalism, 288–9
Eogánacht, 18
Ervine, Linda, 291
Eucharistic Congress, 219, 226
European Economic Community (EEC), 249
European Union, 283
Eurovision Song Contest, 253
evictions, 143
Ewart-Biggs, Christopher, 239
exports, 53, 83, 99

faction-fighting, 116
Fáilte Ireland, 305
Fairs and markets, 55
falconry, 53
Fallon, Garda Richard, 245
Family Home Protection Act, 255
famine, 56, 138, 140–4
Famine, Great, 140
Faroe Islands, 28
Farrell, M.J., 223
fashion and cosmetic firms, 217
fashions, 215
Faul, Fr Denis, 239, 261
Faulkner, Brian, 234, 237
Fay, William, 174
Feilimid macCrimthainn, 29
Female hairdressers, 217
female trades, 112
Fenians, 157–59, 162 (*see also* Irish Republican Brotherhood IRB).
Fermanagh, 52, 82

Index

Fiacra, 24
Fianna Fáil, 207, 209, 210, 248, 249, 272, 273
Fiesole, 24
filidhe/poets, 15, 18, 26, 60
Finbar of Cork, 25
Fine Gael, 206, 209, 248, 249, 274
Fingal, 94
Finnian, 21, 23, 34
First Home Rule Bill, 166
fisheries, 55
Fitt, Gerry, 237
Fitzgerald, Garret, 239, 248
Fitzgerald, Lord Edward, 120
Fitzgerald, Vesey, 129
Fitzgeralds, 38, 39, 42, 49
Fitzgibbon, John, Lord Clare, 98
FitzStephens, 38
Fitzwilliam, Lord, 121
Flanders, 53, 69
Flatley, Michael, 253
Flight of the Earls, 69
Flood, Henry, 97
flying columns, 198
Flynn, Declan, 260
Flynn, Mannix, 262
football, 173
Foras Feasa ar Eirinn, 86
forests, 301
Fort Erie, 158
Fortune, Fr Seán, 263
Foster, Arlene, 283, 284
Foster, Vere, 147
Fottrell, Fr. John, 92
Four Courts, 113
Four Masters, 2
Fox, Billy, 246
Foyle, 10
France, 9, 53, 62, 63, 65, 89, 119, 121
Franciscans, 48, 49, 78, 94
Free State Constitution, 204

French Sisters of Charity, 171
French, Tana, 267
frost famine 1740–1, 105
Furey Brothers, 253
Fursey, 24

Gaelic Athletic Association, 173
Gaelic League, 173, 185, 187, 215
Gaelic-Irish, 36
Gaelscoileanna, 254
Gallagher, Bridie, 231
Gallagher, Rory, 253
gallowglasses, 39
Galway, 53, 54, 59, 79, 82, 113, 144
Garda Síochána, 206
Garland, Roger, 248
garrison towns, 97
Gascony, 53
gay marriage, 275
Gearóid Iarla (Earl Garrett), 60
Gearóid Mór (Great Gerald), of Kildare, 43
Gearóid Óg, 44, 63
General Post Office, 192
Gerald of Wales, 60
gerrymandering, 225–6
Gheel, 24
ghost estates, 267
gig economy, 269
Gilbert, Irene, 217
Gilmore, Eamon, 274
Gladstone William, 159, 161–5
Glanbia, 265
Glasgow, 51
Glassie, Henry, 238
Glendalough, 15, 24, 31
Gobnait, 24
Goldsmith, Oliver, 109
Gonne, Maud, 185, 191
Good Friday Agreement, 242, 243, 247
Goodbodys, 104

345

Goodman, Larry, 262
Google, 265
Gore-Booth, Eva, 189
Government of Ireland Act, 199
government posts, 154
Graces, 72
Grand Canal, 103
Grattan, Henry, 126
Grattan, Henry, 97, 98, 125
Grattan's Parliament, 98, 119
Greally, Hanna, 219
Great Schism, 52
Greece, 52
Green Alliance/*Comhaontas Glas*, 248
Greens, 274
greenways, 288
Gregory, Augusta, 5
Gregory, Robert, 4
Griffith, Arthur, 184, 194, 199
Guildford bombings, 261
Gwynn, Stephen, 187

Haicéad, Pádraigín, 87
Halappanavar, Savita, 279
Hamburg, 107
handball, 173
Harney, Mary, 258
Harvey, Bagenal, 124
Haughey, Charles, 245, 247, 248, 256, 262
Hayes, Joanne, 257
H-Block /Maze prison, 239
health, 228–9
Healy, T. M., 187
Heaney, Seamus, 238
Hearts of Oak, 116
Hearts of Steel, 116
Heath, Edward, 235
Herbert, Dorothea, 111
Herberts, 94
Herman's Hermits, 231
hides, 53

Highways Act of 1614, 82
Hillsborough Agreement, 240, 247
Hoche, ship, 124
Hoche, General Lazare, 123
Hollies, 231
Home Government Association, 162
Home Rule Party, 162, 164, 165, 166, 167, 184, 186, 187, 197
Homosexuality, 260
Honohan, Patrick, 268
Horan, Monsignor James, 269
horse-racing, 115
Horslips, 253
hospitality, 306
hospitals, 113, 133, 214, 269, 285
hotels, 217
Housing Executive, 244
Howth, 190
Humbert, General, 124
Hume, John, 234, 241, 242
Hundred Years' War, 39
Hungarian Hussars, 108
Hungary, 52
hunger strikers, 239
hunger strikes, 247
hurling, 173
Hutcheson, Francis, 108
Hutchinson, Billy, 235
Hyde, Douglas, 173, 206

Ibar, 21
Imleach/Emly, 18
immigration, 285, 307–8
industrial action, 218
industrial schools, 182, 219, 277
industry, 7, 83, 101, 137, 182, 212, 218, 229, 284
infant mortality, 112, 180, 213, 229, 278, 280
influenza (1918), 179

Inghinidhe na hEireann/
    Daughters of Ireland, 185
Iníon an Phailitínigh/'The
    Palatine's Daughter', 115
Inis Cathaig or Scattery, 21
Inisbofin, 62
INLA, 237, 239
institutions, 277
Intermediate Education Act,
    156
internment, 235, 239, 246
Inter-Party Government, 209
Iona, 21, 25
Ireland West Airport, 269
Ireland, Bishop, 148
Ireton, Henry, 75
Irish Agriculture Organization
    Society, 169
Irish Church Missions, 170
Irish Church Temporalities Act
    of 1835, 131
Irish Citizen Army, 189, 191
Irish Constabulary, 132
Irish Countrywomen's
    Association, 255
Irish Housewives
    Association, 230
Irish Independent., 209
Irish Land and Labour
    Association, 185
Irish language *see* language
Irish National Liberation Army
    (INLA), 234
Irish Press, 209
Irish Republican Army (IRA),
    197, 208, 227, 234, 237, 239,
    240, 245, 246, 282
Irish Republican Brotherhood
    (IRB), 157, 191, 192 *See also*
    Fenians
Irish scholarship, 86
Irish Sea, 8, 10
Irish Sisters of Charity, 171

Irish Socialist Republican
    Party, 186
Irish Trade Union Congress and
    Labour Party, 186
Irish Trade Union Council, 185
Irish Transport and General
    Workers Union, 183, 186, 188
Irish Travellers, 87, 218, 253, 279
Irish Volunteers, 189, 190, 191
Irish Women Workers'
    Union, 187
Irish Women's Franchise
    League, 187
Irish Women's Suffrage
    Federation, 187
Irishwomen's Reform
    League, 187
Ironworks, 101
Italy, 53
Íte, 24, 34

Jadotville, 211
James Joyce's *Ulysses*, 172
Jehovah's Witnesses, 223
Jervis St, 113
Jesuits, 79
Jews, 126, 172, 219, 276
Johannes Scotus Eriugena, 8, 26
Johnson, Thomas, 200
Johnston, Roy, 228
Johnstons, 219
Joyce, Nan, 253
Justice for Magdalenes, 277

Kavanagh, Patrick, 2
Kearney, Peadar, 159
Keating, Geoffrey, 86
Kells, 21, 60
Kelly, Hugh, 103
Kelly, Sandy, 253
Kemmy, Jim, 248
Kenmare, Lord, 94, 98
Kenny, Enda, 274, 277, 278

Keogh, John, 119
Kerry, 7, 8, 27, 42, 45, 127
Kerry Foods, 265
Kettle, Thomas, 196
Kickham, Charles, 157
Kilbeggan, 123
Kilcreevanty, 50
Kilculiheen, 51
Kildare, 8, 10, 21, 25, 30, 42, 45, 106, 123
Kilfenora, 32
Kilkenny, 10, 32, 37, 38, 42, 45, 49, 54, 73, 74, 79, 92, 106, 144
Killala, 49, 124
Killaloe, 33, 52
Killarney, 82
Killian, 24
Kilmacduagh, 23, 31
Kilmainham Treaty, 164
Kilmallock, 54, 66
Kiltartan, 4
King Charles I, 71
King Charles II, 76
King Charles V, 63
King Edward III, 40
King Edward IV, 55
King Francis I, 63
King George III, 126
King Haakon of Norway, 38
King Henry II, 30, 36
King Henry IV, 49
King Henry VI, 57
King Henry VII, 43
King Henry VIII, 44, 63
King James II, 76, 77
King James I, 76
King John, 36, 44
King John's Castle, 37, 57
King Louis XIV, 77
King Philip III, 68
King Richard II, 41
King's County, 65, 82

kingship, 16, 17, 18, 29
Kingsmill, 237
Kinks, the, 231
kinship, 16, 17, 20

Labour Party, 186, 200, 206, 208, 248, 273
labourers, 150-1, 183
Ladies' Land League, 164, 189
Laigin, 18
Lalor, James Fintan, 161
land, 161
Land Act 1870, 161
Land Act 1881, 164
Land League, 163
landscape, 299-303
Lane, Temple, 223
language, 15, 40, 42, 59, 80, 86, 87, 106, 115, 173, 254, 284, 293
Laois, 8, 33, 65
Larkin, Delia, 187
Larkin, James, 186, 209
Larne, 190
Laskey, Heather, 262
Latin, 23, 25
Lauzun, General, 77
Laverty, Maura, 231, 232
law, 26, 27, 44, 45
Law, 132
Leadbeater, Mary, 137
Lebar Brecc, 61
Lecan, 8
Ledwidge, Francis, 192, 196
Legion of Mary, 215
Leinster, 8, 42
Leinster House, 103
Leitrim, 82, 83
Lemass, Noel, 202
Lemass, Seán, 209, 210, 227
Levine, June, 259
Liberal Alliance, 167
Liffey, 10, 27

Lille, 79
Limerick, 8, 10, 24, 27, 37, 42, 45, 51, 54, 79
Lindisfarne, 24
linen, 53, 99
Lisbon, 53, 79
Lismullen, 51
Lissoy, 109
livestock fairs, 101
local government franchise, 225
Locke, John, 5
Lombardy, 52
Londonderry (county), 82
Longford, 8, 45, 82, 109, 110, 124
Loreto nuns, 171
Lough Swilly, 124
Louth, 8, 10, 42, 45, 106
Louvain, 79, 86, 87
Lowry, Michael, 262
loyalist bombs, 246
loyalists, 233
Luby, Thomas Clarke, 157
Lucan, Lord (George Bingham), 143
Ludlows, 232
lunatic asylums, 133
Luxeuil, 23
luxury, 102
Lynam, Ray, 253
Lynch, Jack, 209, 245
Lynn, Kathleen, 189

Maastricht Treaty, 248
Mac Aingil, Aodh, 87
MacCann, Eamon, 228
MacCárthaigh, Cormac, 14
MacCarthaig/McCarthys, 29
MacColl, Ewan, 219
MacConmara, Donncha Rua, 107
MacCraith, Aindrias, 107
MacCubhthaigh, Art, 106
MacDavid, Cormac, 50
MacDermotts, 39

MacDiarmada, Sean, 193
MacDonagh, Bishop Michael, 92
MacDonagh, Thomas, 193
MacDonaghs, 39
MacGearailt, Piaras, 106
MacGiolla Pádraig, Brian, 84
MacKeown, Ciarán, 238
MacLiammóir, Micheál, 299
MacLochlainns, 29
MacMahons, 39
MacManus, Frank, 236
MacManus, Terence Bellew, 157
MacMurchadas/MacMorroghs, 29, 39, 64
MacMurrough, Aoife, 36
MacMurrough, Diarmait, 29
Macnamaras, 49
MacNeill, Eoin, 173, 189, 192
Macra na Feirme, 215
Macra na Tuaithe, 215
MacSwiney, Mary, 187, 200, 201
Mael Ruain, 31
Mael Seachnaill, 29
Magan, Manchán, 290
Magean, Honoria, 80
Maguire, Hugh, 68
Maguire, Tomas Og, 52
Maguires, 39
Maher, Sean, 253
Mahon and McCracken Tribunals, 273
Major, John, 240
Malachy, 32
Mallow, 82
Manchester Martyrs, 159
Manfred Mann, 231
Manning, Mary, 252
Manning, Michael, 230
Marco Polo, 60
markets, 101
Markievicz, Constance, 189, 193, 197
marriage, 154–5, 216

marriage bars, 216, 255
Martins, 94
Martyn, Edward, 174
Mary Queen of Scots, 69
Mass Rocks, 81
massacres, 72
maternal mortality, 179, 214
maternity leave, 255
Mathew, Fr Theobald, 140
Mathews, 94
Maynooth, 64, 121
Mayo, 27, 82, 85, 124, 144
McAteer, Eddie, 227
McBride, John, 193
McCafferty, Nell, 252, 260
McCarthys, 39, 40, 42, 44
McCluskey, Conn and Patricia, 227
McConville, Jean, 260
McCormick, Richard, 119
McCourtney, Sr Una, 252
McCracken, Henry Joy, 124
McDonnell, Joe, 247
McDonnells, 39
McGee, Mary, 256
McGuinnes, Martin, 282, 284
McIntyre, Patrick, 193
McMorrogh-Kavanaghs, 42
McNamara, Dolores, 266
McNeill, Janet, 230
McVerry, Peter, 252
McWilliam Burkes, 68
McWilliams, David, 267
McWilliams, Monica, 243
Meath, 8, 10, 15, 32, 42, 45, 106, 123
Meath hospital, 113
Medtronic, 265
Meelick, 49
Mellifont, 32, 48, 68
Mellows, Liam, 201
mendicant friars, 48, 49, 78, 79
mental hospitals, 219, 281

Mercer's hospital, 113
Merchants' Quay, 78
Merriman, Brian, 107
Methodists, 90, 170, 219
Miami Showband, 253
Míde, 8, 18
Milotte, Mike, 278
Mitchel, John, 145
Mitchell, George, 240
Molua of Sligo, 34
Molyneux, William, 95
Monaghan, 82, 104, 122, 246
Monasterboice, 60
monasteries, 31, 47, 48
Money Bill Dispute 1751–1753, 97
Monteagle, Lord, 143
Moone, 60
Moore, Christy, 261
Morison, Fynes, 86
Morrison, Van, 253
mother-and-baby homes, 278
motte and bailey, 57
Mount Brandon, 33
Mountbatten, Louis, 239
Mountjoy, Lord, 68
Mountmellick, 82
Mowlam, Marjorie('Mo'), 241
Muintir na Tíre, 215, 223
Mulally, Teresa, 112
Mulgrave, Lord, 132
Mullin, Chris, 261
Multyfarnham, 94
Mumu/Mumha, 8
Municipal Corporation Act of 1840, 131
Munro, Henry, 124
Munster, 8, 18, 68, 106, 116
Munster Plantation, 66
Munster Women's Franchise League, 186
Munster, 29
Murphy report, 276

Murphy, Delia, 231
Murphy, Fr John, 123
Murray, Dr Daniel, 135
Murray, Fr Raymond, 261
Múscraighe, 18
music, 215, 253–4
musical bands, 172
Muslim community, 276

Naas, 37
Nagle, Joseph, 93
Nagle, Nano, 92, 112, 113
Nanetti, J. P., 186
Napier, Oliver, 234
Napper Tandy, James, 119
National Board of Education, 132
National Labour Party, 208
National Maternity Hospital, 256
National Pay Agreements, 249
National teachers, 154
National Union of Dock Labourers, 186
National Union of Public Employees, 238
National Volunteers, 190
Ne Temere, 223
Neave, Airey, 239
Neilson, Samuel, 119
neutrality, 208
New English, 62
New Ireland Forum, 239
Newfoundland, 99, 107, 138
Newry, 54
Newtownbarry, 131
Ní Chonaill, Eibhlín Dhubh, 104, 107, 297
Ní Mháille, Grainne/ O'Malley, Grace, 85
Niall of the Nine Hostages, 16
Niemba, 211
Nine Years' War, 67, 70
Nore, 10

normalisation, Ulsterization and criminalization, 238
Norman invasion, 35
Norris, David, 260
North Cork Militia, 123
North Infirmary, 113
North King St, 192
North Strand bombing, 208
Northern Bank robbery, 282
Northern Ireland, 199, 203, 223, 228, 230, 233, 237, 238, 239, 241, 243, 244, 245, 247, 282, 283, 284, 290
Northern Ireland Assembly, 235, 282, 283
Northern Ireland Civil Rights Association, 228
Northern Ireland Labour Party (NILP), 234
Northern Ireland Policing Board, 283
Northern Ireland Women's Coalition (NIWC), 243
Northern Ireland's industries, 228
Northern Irish nationalists, 226, 227
Northern Star, 121
north-south consultative bodies, 285
Norton, William, 209
Norway, 27
Nova Scotia, 138
nunneries, 25
nuns, 51, 79, 80, 85, 151, 171, 221–2
nurses, 154, 169, 220

Ó Bruadair, Dáibhí, 87
Ó Ceallaigh, Seán T., 206
O Cléirigh, Micheal, 87
Ó Conchúir, Tadhg Rua, 87

Index

O'Conor, Ruairi, 36
Ó Corcráin, Johannes, 50
Ó Dalaigh President
  Cearbhall, 246
Ó Dálaigh, Gofraid, 60
Ó Domhnaill, Manus, 52
O Fiaich, Cardinal Tomás, 239
Ó Glaisne, Risteard, 299
Ó hEochagáin, Hector, 290
Ó Mealláin, Feardorcha, 75
Ó Méalseachlainn,
  Murchadha, 50
Ó Rathaille, Aodhagán, 106
Ó Riada, Seán, 210
Ó Súilleabháin, Eoghan
  Ruadh, 106
Ó Tuama, Seán, 107, 297
O'Brien, Denis, 262
O'Brien, Morrough, 74
O'Brien, Tadhg, 38
O'Brien, William, 165, 187, 208
O'Briens, 39, 42, 44
O'Byrnes, 39, 64
O'Carroll, Margaret, 52
O'Carrolls, 63
O'Connell, Daniel, 127–30, 297
O'Connells, 94
O'Connors, 63, 64, 65
O'Conor, Charles, 108
O'Conor, Felim, 38
O'Conor, Ruairi, 30, 36
O'Conors, 39, 50
O'Curry, Eugene, 294
O'Dea, Maura, 255
O'Devany, Bishop Conor, 69
O'Doherty, Cahir, 69
O'Donnel, Bridget, 141
O'Donnell, Daniel, 253
O'Donnell, Peadar, 201
O'Donnell, Red Hugh earl of
  Tyrconnell, 68
O'Donnells, 39, 40, 42, 141
O'Donovan Rossa, Jeremiah, 157
O'Donovan, John, 294
O'Farrel, William, 49
O'Farrelly, Agnes, 189
O'Flahertys, 39
O'Haras, 39
O'Hussey, Bonaventure, 86
O'Kelly, Murtough, 50
O'Kellys, 39
O'Leary, Art, 104
O'Leary, John, 157
O'Maddens, 39, 49
O'Mahony, John, 157
O'Malley, Des, 248
O'More, Rory, 72
O'Mores, 63, 64, 65
O'Neill, Phelim, 72
O'Neill, Brian, 38
O'Neill, Conn, 44
O'Neill, Eoghan Rua/Red
  Hugh, 73
O'Neill, Hugh, earl of Tyrone,
  67, 68, 296
O'Neill, Terence, 210, 225,
  227, 234
O'Neills, 39, 40, 42, 64, 69, 78
O'Reilly, William, 49
O'Rourke, Dervorgilla, 29
O'Rourke, Tiernan, 29
O'Rourkes, 39
O'Shea, Katherine, 167
O'Sullivan, Seumas, 192
O'Tooles, 39
Oath of Supremacy, 72, 78
Odlums, 104
Offaly, 8, 15, 65
Official Sinn Féin/IRA, 234
Ogham, 7
oireacht, 41
Old Age Pension, 180
Old English, 62
Old Irish, 15, 25
Omagh, 243
one man (sic) one vote, 228

Orange Order, 122, 128, 233
Ordnance Survey, 293
Ormond, 38, 43, 49, 60, 74
Ormonds, 40, 42
Osraighe (Ossory), 10
Ossory, 32, 84
Oxford, 51

Paine's *The Rights of Man*, 119
Paisley, Reverend Ian, 227, 235, 282
Pale, 42, 62
Palladius, 20
Pallas, Tynagh, 58
Pankhurst, Christabel, 187
paper mills, 101
Paris, 51, 79, 266
parishes, 32
parliament, 36, 64, 71, 76, 95, 96, 125
Parnell, Anna, 164, 167
Parnell, Charles Stewart, 162–8
partition, 199, 200, 224
Pastorini prophecies, 128
Pasture farming, 84
Patrick, 6, 20, 24, 34, 81
Patten Report, 282
Pavee Point, 253
PAYE workers, 249
Peace People, 238
peace process, 240
Pearse, Patrick, 189, 193
Pearse, Willie, 193
Peel, Robert, 1, 126, 129, 140
Penal Laws, 89, 90, 91–4, 95, 112, 119, 120, 121
Penneys/Primark, 265
Pentecostal church, 276
People Before Profit, 273
people on the move, 88
People's Democracy, 228
Percy French, William, 173
Peronne, 24

Peter's Cell, 51
Petrie, George, 294
Phoenix Park murders, 166
Pim, Sheila, 223
Pioneer Total Abstinence Association, 215
Pitt, William, 124, 126
placenames, 293–6
plantation, 65, 70, 75, 88
Planxty, 253
Plunket, William, 126
Plunkett, James, 218
Plunkett, Bishop Oliver, 76
Plunkett, Joseph, 193
police, 154, 159
Police Service of Northern Ireland (PSNI), 282
political parties, 248
Poor Clares, 78, 113, 171
Poor Law, 169, 171
Poor Law of 1838, 134
Pope Adrian IV, 30
Pope Celestine, 20
Pope Clement VII, 52
Pope John Paul II, 256
Pope John XXII, 59
Pope Pius V, 67
Pope Urban VII, 52
population, 8, 57, 75, 86, 105, 111, 135, 136, 138, 146, 271, 302–3
Portadown, 240
PortWest, 265
potato, 83, 84, 105, 138, 140
Poulaphouca, 304
poverty, 105, 139, 176, 211
Power, John O'Connor, 162
power-sharing, 236
Poynings, Edward, 42
Poynings' Law, 43, 98
Presbyterianism, 108
Presbyterians, 72, 82, 90, 104, 120, 170, 219

Presentation Nuns, 112, 113
Preston, Thomas, 73
priest-hunters, 92
printers, 101
Prior, James, 239
prison wardens, 154
prisons, 182
Programme for Economic Recovery, 217
Progressive Democrats, 248, 272
Progressive Unionist Party, 235, 291
proportional representation, 204, 225, 236
prostitution, 178
Protestant-Catholic conflict, 225
Protestants, 70, 95, 222–3
Provisional Sinn Féin/IRA, 234
Public Health Act of 1874, 179
public servants, 217

Quakers *see also* Society of Friends, 82, 90
Quebec, 144
Queen Elizabeth, 65, 69
Queen Mary, 65
Queen Victoria, 173
Queen's County, 65, 82
Queen's University Belfast, 229
Quin, 49

Raidio na Gaeltachta, 254
Railways, 181, 303
Rathgurreen, 13
Raymond le Gros, 36
Real IRA, 243
Reapy, E. M., 270
rebellion, 123–4
Red Hand Commando, 233
Redmond, John, 168, 184, 188, 190
Redmond, Willie, 187
Reformation, 78

reformatories, 182
reforms, 131–2
refugees, 245
regattas, 172
religion, 30, 46, 77, 275–6 passim.
Renewable Heat Incentive Scheme, 283
renewal, 287
Repeal, 129–30
Report of the Commission on Itineracy, 218
republican and loyalist violence, 240
Republican Socialist Party (IRSP), 234, 235
Residential Institutions Redress Board, 278
revenue commission, 96
Reynolds, Albert, 240
rí thar chaladh/the king across the water, 88
Ribbonmen, 128
Rice, Edmund Ignatius, 104
Richard, duke of York, 43
ring forts, 12
Rinuccini, Giovanni Battista, 74
Rising, 1916, 194–5
roads, 103, 145, 301, 305
Robinson, Mary, 258
Robinson, Peter, 283
Rock of Cashel, 19
Rock, Dickie, 232
Romans, 8
Rome, 30, 32, 33, 46, 52, 62, 69, 79
Rooney, Willie, 174
Roscommon, 45, 83, 144, 173
Rotunda Lying-in Hospital, 113
round tower, 31
Royal Black Preceptory, 234
Royal Canal, 103
Royal Ulster Constabulary, 225

Index

Royal Ulster Constabulary (RUC), 235
Royal Victoria hospital, 113
rugby, 172
Russell, George (AE), 192
Russell, Lord John, 140
Russell, Thomas, 119
Ryan Report, 277
Ryan, Brendan, 253
Ryanair, 265

sacramental test, 90
Sacred Heart nuns, 171
Sagar, Pearl, 243
Salamanca, 79
Salisbury, Lord, 166
Salzburg, 24
Samthann, 24
Sands, Bobby, 239
Saor Eire, 245
Saorstát Éireann, the Irish Free State, 202
Sarsfield, Patrick, 77
Saunderson, Colonel Edward, 168
Saville Inquiry, 283
Sawdoctors, 251
Scandinavians, 27–8, 31
Sceilg Mhichíl, 21
schools, 133, 140, 156, 254, 276, 290–1
scológ, 84
Scotland, 18, 38, 63, 65
Scullabogue, 124
Scullion, 253
Seanad of 1922, 204
Second Home Rule Bill, 168
Second World War, 226
Section 31 of the Broadcasting Act, 247, 261
Sedulius Scotus, 26
Senan, 21

Shackletons, 104
Shankill Butchers, 237
Shannon, 8, 10, 83
Shannon Scheme, 211
Sheehy Skeffington, Francis, 192
Sheehy, Fr Nicholas, 93, 116
Sheridan, John D., 220
Sheridans, 108–9
Shiel, Richard Lalor, 127
shiring, 45, 82
shops, 103, 137, 153
Sidhe/Good People or Fairies, 304
Silken Thomas, 64
Silken Thomas's rebellion, 64
Simnel, Lambert, 43
Simon Community, 252
singleness, 149
Sinn Féin, 185, 187, 197, 240, 274, 282,
Sinn Féin the Workers Party, 248
Sir Patrick Dun's, 113
Sisters of Mercy, 171
Sitric, 28
Skeffington, Sir William, 64
Slaney, 10
slavery, 16
Sliabh Liag (Donegal, 21
Sligo, 54, 55, 82, 144
Smerwick, 66
Smith O'Brien, William, 145
Smithson, Annie M. P., 180
Smithwick, John, 103
Smyth, Fr Brendan, 263
Soccer, 172
Social Democratic Labour Party (SDLP), 234, 240, 241, 242
Social Democrats, 272
Socialist Party, 273
socialists, 186
Society of Friends, 81, 82, 85, 142, 219

Index

soldiers, 88
Solemn League and Covenant, 188
Somerville and Ross, 186
soup kitchens, 142
soviets, 198
spa towns, 116
Spain, 9, 52, 53, 62, 69, 75, 89, 113
Spanish, 59
Special Criminal Court, 246
Special Olympics, 281
Spenser, Edmund, 66, 86
sport, 232
St Andrews Agreement of 2006, 282
St John, Elizabeth, 44
St Louis Sisters, 171
St Patrick's College, Carlow, 121
St Patrick's Purgatory, 52
St Ruth, General, 77
Stack, Áine, 221
Stanihurst, Richard, 86
Stardust Ballroom, 261
Statutes of Kilkenny, 40, 55
Status of Children Act 1987, 257
Stays, 102
Steelboys, 116
Stephens, James (Fenian), 192
Stephens, James (writer), 157
Stoke, 43
Stormont, 224
Strongbow, *see also* de Clare, Richard, 30, 36, 40
Stuart, Villiers, 129
Succession Act of 1965, 255
suffrage movement, 186
sugar production, 101
Suir, 10
Sunningdale, 237
surnames, 49, 87, 297–8, 299
Surrender and Regrant, 65

Swarbriggs, 253
Sweetman, Rosita, 259
Swift, Jonathan, 95, 108
Synge, Edward bishop of Elphin, 95
Synod of Rath Bressail, 32
Synod of Kells, 32
Synod of Whitby, 23

Talbot, Peter, 76
Talbot, Richard, 76
Tallaght, 31
taoiseach, 41
Tara, 130
tea, 102
teachers, 217
Teamhrach/ Tara, 10, 18, 29
technology, colleges of, 250
Teilifís Éireann, 222
TG4, 254
Thatcher, Margaret, 239
The Bucks of Oranmore, 116
The Case of Ireland ... Stated, 95
the Disability Act of 2005, 281
The Irish People, 157
'The Mountains of Mourne', 202
The Nation, 130
The Programme for National Recovery, 249
The Rakes of Mallow, 115
The Times, 166
The Word, 222
the Wyndham Act, 165
theatres, 108
Thin Lizzy, 253
Third Home Rule bill, 188
Third Order of St Francis, 52
Third Reform Act of 1884, 166
Thomond, 38, 39, 42
timber, 53
Tintern Abbey, 48
Tipperary, 8, 18, 42, 45, 49, 116, 144

tithe, 116, 128, 131
Tithe Rent Charge Act of 1838, 131
tobacco, 84
Tory Island, 124
tourism, 266
tower houses, 57
towns, 28, 54, 82, 99, 137, 153
Townshend, George, 97
trade unionism, 183, 186
trades, 15, 55, 101, 157
Tralee, 82
transport, 103, 144, 153, 169, 286, 289
Travellers *see* Irish Travellers
Treaty (Anglo-Irish), 199–200, 207
Treaty debates, 200
Treaty of Limerick, 77, 89
Trim, 37, 54, 57
Trimble, David, 241, 242, 282
Trinity College, 80, 81, 110
Trócaire, 252
Tuam, 32, 52, 81
tuatha, 17
tuberculosis, 179, 213
Tuke, James Hack, 148
Turas Irish Language Project, 291
Tyrone, 82, 110, 144

U 2, 253
Ua Conchobhair, 18
Údarás na Gaeltachta (the Gaeltacht Authority), 254
Uí Briain/O'Briens., 28, 29, 33
Uí Brúin, 18
Uí Cennsalaig, 18
Ui Chonchobair/O'Conors, 29
Uí Dunchadha, 18
Uí Néill, 16, 18, 29
Uí Ruairc/O'Rourke, 29
Ulaidh, 8, 18

Ulster, 8, 16, 18, 42, 45, 62, 106, 116, 168
Ulster Constitution Defence Committee, 227
Ulster custom, 161
Ulster Defence Association, 233
Ulster Defence Regiment (UDR), 235
Ulster Plantation, 69
Ulster Says No, 240
Ulster Television, 229
Ulster Unionist Party (UUP), 234
Ulster Volunteer Force, 233
Ulster Volunteers, 188, 190
Ulster Workers' Counci, 237
Ulster, 8
Ulysses, 194
undertakers, 96
Undertones, the, 253
unemployment, 216, 244, 249, 264, 268, 270, 284
Unemployment, 228
unionism, 188, 202
United Irish League, 165
United Irishmen, 119, 122, 123, 124
United Nations, 211
universities, 51, 156, 250
Unmarried Mothers' Allowance, 255
Ursulines, 113
Ussher, James, 81
UUP, 241

Vandaleur, Crofton, 143
Varadkar, Leo, 275
Vatican II, 222
Venice, 14
viceroy, 125
Vinegar Hill, 124
Virgilius, 24
Volunteers, 97

Wages Standstill Order, 208
Wales, 36
Walsh, 38
War for Independence, 197, 198–9
Warbeck, Perkin, 43
Wars of the Roses, 42
Waterford, 8, 27, 36, 37, 45, 53, 54, 55, 83, 99, 129
welfare, 213, 214
Wellesley, Arthur, Duke of Wellington, 129
Wentworth, Thomas, 72
Westmeath, 8, 42, 45, 82
Westport, 124
Wexford, 8, 10, 36, 45, 48, 74, 123, 144
Whately, Dr Richard, 135
Whelan, Bill, 253
White, Jack, 189
Whiteboys, 116
Whitelaw, William, 236
Wicklow, 8, 10, 15, 42, 82
Wicklow Militia, 123
wigs, 103
Wild Geese, 89

William of Orange, 76
Williamite wars, 76
Williams, Betty, 238
Wilson Hartnell, 195
wind farms, 288
wine, 56
Wolfe Tone, Theobald, 119, 121–4
Wolfe Tones, 247
women, 85, 111, 169, 206, 210, 216, 217, 244, 255–60, 274
women religious *see* nuns
women's work, 85, 150
Wood's Halfpence, 95
wool, 53, 99
workhouses, 135, 142, 171, 180
writing, 25
Wurzburg, 24, 50
Wyse-Power, Jennie, 189, 201

Yeats, W.B., 174, 192
Yola, 38
Youghal, 48, 51, 66, 79
Young Ireland, or the Irish Confederation, 145

For EU product safety concerns, contact us at Calle de José Abascal, 56–1°, 28003 Madrid, Spain or eugpsr@cambridge.org.

www.ingramcontent.com/pod-product-compliance
Lightning Source LLC
LaVergne TN
LVHW011757060526
838200LV00053B/3619